GREAT INTERRUPTION

Books by Laurence Irving:
Henry Irving — His Life and Times
The Successors
The Precarious Crust

Edited and Illustrated:
A Selection of Hakluyt's Traffics and Discoveries
Bligh's Journal of the Voyage of the Bounty
The Wreck of The Maid of Athens: the journal of Emily
Wooldridge

Illustrated:
Philip the King. John Masefield
The Mirror of the Sea. Joseph Conrad
A Theatre of Natures. John Aubrey and others
Flight to Arras. Antoine de St. Exupery

GREAT INTERRUPTION

Laurence Irving

We should realise that the war is only the Great
Interruption and that your career *must* continue.

Sir Osbert Sitwell
Letter to my Son

Airlife
England

©

1983
LAURENCE IRVING

First Published in 1983
by Airlife Publishing Ltd.

ISBN 0 906393 29 9

Airlife Publishing Ltd.

7 St. John's Hill, Shrewsbury, England.

Printed by Livesey Limited, Shrewsbury, England.

To Pete and Andy
and to
all the companions
of
35 WING
committed to their charge.

Acknowledgements

It is to Mr Frank Wootton that I am most deeply indebted for his intuition and initiative that led to the publishing of this book. We met in the beach head in Normandy shortly before the defeat of the German forces containing it. He had been commissioned to portray the Royal Air Force in action by Air Chief Marshal Leigh Mallory, C-in-C of the 2nd Tactical Air Force, during their operation in close support of 21 Army Group on the left flank of the American Army in the landings on D-day and in the subsequent liberation of the countries in Western Europe occupied by the Germans.

He had been a young draughtsman serving in a technical department of the R.A.F., when the historian Hilary St. George Saunders recognised his remarkable talent as a painter whose eyes beheld beauty in mechanical contrivances. He told the Air Chief Marshal of his discovery of this gifted painter perfectly equipped and informed to record the decisive actions to be fought and won in gaining air superiority throughout the coming campaign. Wootton's first attachment was to 35 Photographic Reconnaissance Wing in which I was serving. Our young pilots welcomed him to their tented camps as we advanced from airstrip to airstrip in pursuit of the retreating enemy. Naturally as a fellow painter, I shared their delight in the revelation of his keen observation and precocious skill as he set to work on what proved to be an incomparable record of the achievements of the Royal Air Force and his unique distinction as an airscape painter.

Thirty years later he read the manuscript of what were to have been my last volumes reviewing the progress of the English stage from 1850 to 1950 through the eyes of one theatrical family. I had felt it obligatory to record events that had obscured my vision of it for six years. My father H. B. Irving and his brother Laurence had died in their forties at the peak of their careers. Had they been ten years younger they might have lost their lives in the first German war and thus invalidated the continuity of my theme. Frank urged me to allow him to ask his friend, Air Chief Marshal Neil Wheeler, G.C.B., K.C.B., D.S.O., D.F.C., to read the chapters relevant to my own war service in the R.A.F. Together they persuaded me to extract them from the, as yet unpublished, sequel to my theatrical trilogy and Mr. Robert Pooley to add it to the publications of his firm Airlife, that specialises in what Sir Winston Churchill would have called "the air affair".

To Air Chief Marshal Neil Wheeler I am most grateful for

vii

his generous approval of my recollections of the war in the air in which he fought as one of "the first of the few" who, against formidable odds, made the liberation of Europe a possible eventuality, and for his invaluable revision of my references to his contemporaries.

To the late Air Marshal Douglas Colyer, C.B., C.M.G., D.F.C., who was the Air Attaché in our Embassy in Paris before and during the débâcle in 1940, I owe more than I can express to his help and understanding at that time and to our lasting friendship that enabled him to read and to approve my record of events to which he had been a witness of impartial integrity.

Readers of this book will gauge the depth of my gratitude to Mr. William Dring, R.A., for his kindness in allowing his portraits of some of my companions in 35 Wing to illustrate the variety of their response to their exacting commitment that called for their individual exercise of keen observation and tactical judgement on which the value of low level visual and photographic reconnaissance was determined. Earlier Eric Kennington, using the same chalk medium with sculptural force, portrayed the victors of the Battle of Britain as almost superhuman Lacedemonians endowed with the self-sacrificial courage by which the survival of their country would be assured. Dring, I think, more subtly discerned the natural characteristics and humour of his sitters, often with an emotive sympathy such as he expressed in his drawing of Squadron Leader K. K. Majumdar, D.F.C.

Above all I wish to affirm that my inspiration to presume to play the historian, that is not my métier, has been my abiding admiration for the young pilots I was privileged to serve throughout the rehearsals and production of an heroic drama such as only the theatre of war can contain. Heedless of applause, immune to the lure of stardom, when death or disablement ended their performance they confidently surrendered their roles to understudies of their own calibre perfectly instructed in the demanding parts they had to play.

My gratitude to Mr. Laurence Whistler for his permission to quote a verse of his poem *A Portrait in the Guards* can be measured by the emotion it evokes that no words of mine could express.

Finally, if I have committed any breach of copyright, personal or official, in apology I must plead inadvertency and the difficulty of identifying ownership of it.

Contents

Foreword

On the morning of Sunday September 3rd 1939, Gabriel Pascal and I were conferring with Nicholas Davenport at his house near Farringdon. His advice and help had been indispensable to the spasmodic and at times critical financing of our film of Shaw's *Pygmalion.* Now Pascal, flushed with its success phenomenal here and in the United States, was planning to produce *Major Barbara.* Together he and I had written a treatment for the film and I had begun my work for it as production designer. Instead of seeking piecemeal financial contributions with a begging bowl, Davenport's present task was to choose the most dependable of the many applicants eager to invest in this apparently gilt-edged enterprise.

At 11.15 we paused to hear Mr. Chamberlain's fateful broadcast to the nation. My heart sank as I listened to what must have been the most half-hearted declaration of a crusade in Christian memory. The Prime Minister's tone was sorrowful, the intrusion of his personal feeling of reluctance emasculating him as a leader and the sombre pessimism of his call to action as dispiriting as could be. The nation, though at present divided as to where its duty lay, was ready to accept whatever hardships and sacrifices the ultimate defeat of the Nazis might entail. The hearts of the people could not have been raised by that gloomy commitment to war. At the same time Hitler and his vulgar entourage must have rubbed their hands together as they heard the feeble challenge of the only enemy champion they feared who evidently had no stomach for a fight to the death.

For the rest of the month I worked with diminishing belief in the relevance of what I was doing to the prospect before us, and became increasingly impatient with the cynical epigrams of Undershaft and the equivocations of his dependents. I hoped that if it was not too late the Undershafts of Great Britain were as capable as the Krupps of Germany of arming us for the fray.

I was depressed by the atmosphere of optimistic make-believe that persisted among well-intentioned liberals whose convictions, hitherto, I had shared. There would be no war on any scale; a civilised compromise would resolve our differences with Hitler, whom the Germans, their patriotic ardour cooled by our declaration of intent, would put under restraint. In *The Times* the sentiments and reflections of Mrs. Miniver seemed designed to enervate rather than encourage a martial spirit in the Establishment. From many friends mobilised as territorials or officers on the Supplementary Reserve, I gathered that they were chafing at the sluggish flow to their units of arms and equipment which, when they were issued, suggested that the coming war would begin where the previous one had ended tactically if not strategically. To my surprise, for purposes of research I was given the run of several large armament factories. Together Gaby (now in the nick of time a British citizen) and I watched the leisurely production of anti-aircraft guns and unimpressive looking armoured vehicles. I welcomed the refusal of the Air Ministry to put the aircraft industry at our disposal. Perhaps, after all, we had a secret weapon up our otherwise empty sleeves.

These excursions only aggravated my personal unease. I knew that painters and scenic artists were being recruited by the War Office to revive the totally forgotten craft of camouflage; others were being commissioned as 'war artists' under the leadership of the veteran Sir Muirhead Bone who had made an incomparable graphic record of our earlier war effort. But, perversely no doubt, I preferred, if I could not evade the issue, to abandon altogether the art I loved rather than to practice it in a kind of purgatory where the pliant beholder could discern beauty in the ugliness of war. Camouflage, I felt, like the gas-masks and trench digging of the Munich crisis, was a defeatist if necessary precaution fostering the illusion that the hellish forces unleashed in Europe could be overcome by anything but superior force backed by moral conviction in the justice of opposing them. I knew I was too old for service that would be more active than many British and French politicans and commercial opportunists were leading us to expect. Nor could I abandon my Shavian post to sit at some para-military desk wearing a uniform to cloak my conscience. In my heart I think I was desperate to do something without delay that might save my son and the sons of my friends from having to pay the price of the failure of their elders to prevent the resurgence of German militarists cynically flirting with any ideology that served their sinister purpose. Recently, while working in Hollywood I had witnessed the rough handling of a friend of mine, George Putnam, by the bully boys of the Nazi *bund* operating as far afield as California.

So daily my despondency deepened as feverish indecision found no relief in the usually analgesic concentration on my drawing board.

My beloved wife, Rosalind, was well aware of my unease. Together we had braced ourselves to face the prospect of our daughter, Pamela, and of our son, John, becoming embroiled in the approaching conflict. Pamela had joined the A.T.S. after her flight from Berlin during the Munich crisis and was now a teleprinter operator at the War Office. John had two more years to spend at Winchester College before he could fulfil his intention of becoming a pilot in the Royal Air Force. Nevertheless Rosalind, with her usual courageous and realistic approach to crises of any kind, agreed that if, thanks to my youthful experience in the R.A.F. I could be of service by rejoining it, I must do so. The interruption of the happiness we had shared for twenty years in such a variety of enterprises would be hard to bear, but she in turn was to find distraction from her anxieties by joining the Oxford Constabulary in which, throughout the war, she served as a typist and driver at the Henley Police Station.

Once again a chance encounter at the Garrick Club changed the course of my life. One day, arriving early for lunch, I found myself alone in the cockpit below the stairs with a young barrister whose frank enjoyment of our society and friendly disposition had for some time past endeared him to me. He was Lionel Heald, K.C. the most sought after 'silk' at the patent bar with a thriving practice that he had now abandoned to do what he conceived to be his duty in a task not only unremunerative but, as he well knew, one that was likely to be controversial. He was wearing the uniform of a Flight Lieutenant in the Royal Air Force Volunteer Reserve. We lunched together and in the course of it he invited me to join him in the delicate but, he believed, very necessary commission he had undertaken at the request of the Air Council. He had been charged to form a security section of the Department of Intelligence that would be responsible for the relations between the Royal Air Force and the media of communication, including the establishment of a system of censorship that would be acceptable to both parties. He knew of my flying service in the first war and judged that my instinctive and sympathetic understanding of problems peculiar to air warfare would be of help to him. He did not know that the shade of my godfather, Sir Edward Tyas Cook[1], who had been the progenitor of the censorship of the press in 1917, was hovering over us and inspiring my acceptance of Lionel's proposal subject to the honourable discharge of my obligations to G.B.S. and Gaby.

It did not take me long to make up my mind. My work, as production designer for *Major Barbara* was done. My assistant, John Bryan, whose physical disability made it unlikely that he would be called up for active service from a reserved occupation, was capable of seeing our plans realised on the studio floor. When I asked Gaby to release me from my contract he was at first hurt by the prospect of my desertion. But I knew that, in his heart, the old cavalry officer understood my discontent and had he not been ex-patriate with only tenuous allegiances to the opponents of Hitler, he too would have made the same dutiful choice. No doubt G.B.S. declared that Irving had once again been drunk (he had made a similar diagnosis of my condition when he read my treatment of *Major Barbara* aimed to animate his static disputations with lively action) and easy prey to a recruiting sergeant. Nevertheless, we parted on friendly terms. A few days later I presented myself at the Air Ministry and together with men of various ages volunteering for active service as air crew, I was commissioned as a Pilot Officer. So, cheerfully, I put the responsibility for my immediate future in Lionels' hands, not realising, perhaps, that I had committed myself to serve wherever and in whatever capacity the Air Ministry might think fit.

Lionel had no difficulty in adding me to his establishment. For the Director of Intelligence at the Air Ministry was Kenneth Buss, now an Air Commodore but twenty years ago the Engineer Lieutenant R.N.R. upon whose skills the lives of the instructors and their pupils at the R.N.A.S. training station

[1] *See The Successors.*

at Chingford depended.[1] Buss's *alter ego* was a civil servant, Archie Boyle, who handled the less orthodox and shadier aspects of intelligence: he in turn, had appointed as his aide Evelyn Baring, an urbane banker, congenial companion and an experienced man of the world of commerce. Between them Heald and Baring brought to the Air Ministry a broad-minded *savoir-faire* which, exercised with fearless discretion and uncompromising integrity, gave the Royal Air Force in matters of Intelligence, a perspicacity that, for the time being, the other services lacked.

Soon I discovered that since my Uncle Teddie had laid aside his blue pencil as the first and Chief Censor of the press at the end of the last war, his precepts and practices had been forgotten and no steps had been taken to promote mutual trust or a *modus operandi* for a necessary and reasonable degree of censorship between the services and the press. The newly created Ministry of Information was still a nebula of whirling amateur bureaucrats and publicists, and remained so until it became coherent under the steadying hand of Brendan Bracken. Lionel conceived his duties as being of negative and positive significance. The sole purpose of censorship was to deny the enemy information that could be to his strategical or tactical advantage; the higher aim of 'security' as he saw it, was to establish such confidence between the press and those fighting the war that the latter, trusting that 'off-the-record' information was respected as such, could, when occasion arose, count upon the press and B.B.C. to play its part in operational planning and to invigorate our embattled people in spirit and in truth.

Before the year ended three incidents had justified our existence and proved the efficacy of our method and epitomised the variety of problems that almost hourly had to be resolved.

One morning we received a telephone call from an R.A.F. Intelligence Officer in Yorkshire reporting that a Heinkel bomber and its crew had been forced to land intact on the moors near Scarborough. On inspecting the aircraft he discovered that the pilot had been posted from the Polish front to a Luftwaffe airfield in Northern Germany whence he had taken off soon after his arrival on a sortie across the North Sea. Consequently he carried with him operational maps covering the whole field of German operations including a gridded

[1] See *The Precarious Crust*

chart of the North Sea. The latter, for purposes of radio interception, was a prize beyond price to those operating our defence system. The young officer, realising it was vital that the enemy should be unaware that all this information had fallen into our hands, had kept curious sightseers at bay and with commendable courage but without authority had confiscated several cameras in their possession.

One of the major hazards of the 'twilight war', as Chamberlain had called it, was the ease with which enemy agents or sympathisers could pass information to German intelligence organisations. All they had to do was to ring up the German Legation in Dublin for their message to be relayed by wireless to Berlin. In this case Lionel instantly appreciated the situation; his counter move was imaginative. The vigilant officer was authorised to continue his surveillance and, if necessary, punitive action against snap-shooters. Meanwhile, Lionel suborned a friend of his in the House of Commons to spread, under oaths of secrecy, the news that a German bomber had been brought down on the north east coast and that the crew had been rescued from the burning wreckage. Within two hours this confidential report had spread through both Houses and our telephone was kept busy with requests for further information. To our deep satisfaction, in the evening the D.N.B.[1] in its news bulletin paid fulsome tribute to the heroic pilot who had destroyed his Heinkel rather than let it fall into the hands of the enemy. The relative German codes and grid references remained unchanged throughout the critical months ahead.

By now we had been made party to the secret of radar interception and the disposition of its stations along our coasts, which together with the possible ignorance of the enemy that our fighter aircraft mounted eight guns would give us a measure of tactical surprise. On the rare occasions when we received the reports of air combats, Sir Henry Tizzard would visit us in the evening to analyse them for evidence that our pilots were beginning to hold their fire until this formidable armament could be ranged to maximum effect.

One afternoon Lionel returned from a high level conference of the Air Staff with a serious problem on his hands. In the morning the Chief of Air Staff, Sir Cyril Newall, and several of his Directors had been invited to the private showing of a film *The Lion Has Wings* that had been hurriedly made by Korda,

---

[1] Deutsches Nachricten-Butro, the official agency of the Nazi regime.

probably at the instigation of the Cabinet, to counter the reels of intimidating German documentaries of Luftwaffe operations being shown to diplomatic audiences in neutral countries. As the film conformed to Chamberlain's injunction that our bombing raids were to be confined to military targets it was unlikely to impress anyone who had seen the horrific spectacle of the systematic destruction of Warsaw by German bombers. As Sir Cyril and his colleagues left the cinema they took leave of Korda with forced smiles and polite congratulations. On reaching the Air Ministry they sent immediately for Lionel and disclosed the gravity of what they had seen. One of the sequences was set in the operations room of a fighter station where, from radar reports, aircraft approaching that coastal sector were plotted on a table on which *our* gridded chart of the North Sea was plainly visible on the screen. Not only the radar system but its potential range could be easily calculated by an enemy agent or attaché watching the film. Immediate steps were to be taken to see that this sequence was deleted.

Lionel knowing that I was familiar with film production, asked me to go at once to the British Board of Film Censors and to take whatever steps I thought fit to rectify this appalling blunder — the more extraordinary because the Air Ministry had appointed an officer to act as technical adviser to the production. I demurred, for, having made a clean break with my pre-war occupations, I had no wish to become involved in any way with the industry. Firmly, he insisted that I was the only member of our staff qualified to deal with this emergency.

When I explained my business to the Secretary of the British Board of Film Censors, he was evidently embarrassed and inclined to be unco-operative. I could not, of course, go into the details of my critical mission. We ran the offending reel. The Air Staff was justified in its dismay. The Censor telephoned to Korda. His tone was apologetic; he seemed to be more in awe of the film producers than of the men responsible for the air defence of Great Britain. He put down the receiver and told me that no cuts could be made as prints of the film were being despatched forthwith to Latin America. I told him to speak to Korda again and to make it quite clear that then and there I would cut out the necessary frames and see that any other prints were similarly censored or I would wait until the cutter who had worked on the film could be sent to make a neater job of it under my direction. Again over the telephone the vials of Korda's wrath were poured into the ear of the unhappy Censor. To his credit he stood his ground and transmitted my ultimatum. In due course, a young American cutter arrived and, as fellow professionals, we set to work and agreeably made cuts that in no way disturbed the continuity of the film. And I like to think that I was able to disguise from him the true significance of our surgery.

These two negative exercises of our section added to Lionel's stature when soon afterwards he was faced with an opportunity to force a positive decision that would have a lasting effect on the morale of the Royal Air Force.

The haphazard security precautions at that time were exemplified by the admission of a polyglot film unit to an airfield where two squadrons of Wellington bombers were at readiness to make a long planned attack on the Luftwaffe base on the island of Sylt. It was probably sheer chance that on the eve of the launching of this raid a squadron of ME110s (a formidably armed twin-engined fighter though no match to our Hurricanes and Spitfires) was moved to Sylt. The cost of this operation was out of all proportion to its effect. Of the 24 Wellingtons only 12 returned to their base. As the signals came in, Lionel and I were summoned to the room of the Secretary of State for Air. There we found in conference Sir Cyril Newall, Sir Arthur Street the Permanent Under Secretary, Air Marshal Joubert and our own Air Commodore Buss. Sir Kingsley Wood sat back in the chair at his huge desk; his sharp suspicious eyes behind glinting spectacles made me feel that his only concern was to emerge from the disastrous affair with his political reputation unscathed. How could the communiqué (that Lionel and I would have to compose) be worded so that the best could be made of a tactical blunder and our losses concealed. Newall was plainly out of his depth, appalled by the implications of this defeat. Joubert was calm and ready to give forceful support to a decision reached on sound principles.

Lionel declared that there were two alternatives — to tell the truth or to conceal it. If we took the latter course the Air Ministry would never again be trusted by pilots and aircrews who sooner or later would come to know our losses in any engagement. He argued for the truth with the conviction and forceful presentation of his case as a skilled advocate. I could do no more, as his junior, than endorse the far-sighted wisdom of his opinion. Newall rose from his chair and went alone into an adjoining room. In his absence we re-examined the available evidence. Of the 12 Wellingtons missing, 5 had been making for Holland streaming clouds of petrol vapour and trails of smoke. Their ultimate fate would not be known to the enemy for some time. Newall rejoined us. For a minute or two he sat with his head in his hands. Then, taking the whole burden of decision on himself, he said: "You will say that seven of our aircraft are unaccounted for".

This half truth was, we agreed, justified in this case. But Lionel had established a long term policy that, harsh though it seemed, assured the trust of the Royal Air Force, the people of Britain, neutral observers and oppressed Europeans listening secretly to B.B.C. news bulletins in the accurate reporting, favourable or unfavourable, of our casualties in the great air battles to come. That conference was memorable for me for my first meeting with Sir Arthur Street. Later I would have to disturb this patient and devoted civil servant at all hours of day and night. Some future historian, with access to all the documents relating to preparation of a depleted Royal Air Force for its coming ordeal, may discover him as the Samuel Pepys of our time who wore himself out in realising his vision on which the survival of our nation would depend, and was revealed more clearly to him than to most of his contemporaries.

My first confrontation with the press led me to suppose that journalists could be treated as responsible professionals to whom the truth could be confided and by whom the suppression of news in the exigences of war would be accepted.

Winter came early that year with sharp frosts and heavy falls of snow. We had the weather gauge of the enemy for as a rule depressions and anticyclones approached Europe across the Atlantic. So, at the outbreak of war, meteorological reports ceased to be published, leaving the enemy to make the best forecasts they could from intermittent reports by long-range aircraft and submarines.

The war had not dampened the British enthusiasm for sport. If league football matches had to be abandoned owing to water-logged or snow-bound playing fields the public would expect the sporting columns of the press to forewarn them. One afternoon I found myself facing the assembled editors and deputy editors of Fleet Street and hesitantly, for I was truly unaccustomed to public speaking, explaining that any indication of the state of football grounds would enable the enemy to deduce the condition of our airfields and the effect of the weather on their operational state of readiness. My audience listened attentively, asked only a few questions, and assured me that they could be relied upon not to mention the weather in relation to any sporting fixtures. Afterwards several editors thanked me for my briefing. If this became common practice they would accept censorship as a necessary restriction in time of war.

As the year drew to a close Londoners fell into an optimistic apathy. Like children in a shrubbery playing hide and seek, they accepted the blackout as an inconvenience that hid them from bombers seeking to destroy them. The Nazis were no more anxious than we were to provoke retaliation for the time being.

One day I met Ben Travers. I soon discovered that he, far nearer superannuation as a warrior than myself, felt that there was no future for the arts we served until one way or another the fate of our civilisation was determined. I suggested that he joined us in A.I.6. Temperamentally he was perfectly equipped to cope with the problems that by now were our daily portion. His genial patience and impatience with fools or humbugs would reinforce our skirmishes with obtuse members of the Air Staff and restive journalists, making them see reason in our importunity and on occasion laugh at themselves. Again our Director welcomed an old friend into the fold, for the rather ghostly figure of Ben loomed in a photograph of his fellow staff officers at Chingford in 1918 that stood upon his mantleshelf. Our office was now a congenial annexe to the Garrick Club.

Most of our colleagues lived in London and were fathers of young families. So Ben and I, our homes being in the country, volunteered to hold our beleaguered fort of censorship over Christmas. Both of us believed in our hearts that the joyful fulfilment of our youthful hopes was ended; that those years we romped through in the fields of our opportunity were but a brief period of mankind's convalescence between the recurring fits of epileptic violence that were a European affliction. We shared the tacit understanding that the resumption of our careers became daily more remote. Yet as Big Ben heralded another birthday of the Prince of Peace, lying on truckle beds within reach of our battery of telephones "we wrapped our martial cloaks around us and laughed ourselves to sleep".[1]

[1] *Vale of Laughter* Ben Travers.

Part I
Rout

Tomorrow we of France will enter a night of defeat. May my country still exist when it dawns again .... I want my country to exist both in the flesh and in the spirit when the day dawns. Therefore I must bear with all the weight of my love in that direction. There is no passage the sea cannot alter for itself if it bears with all its weight.

Antoine St. Exupery
Flight to Arras.

I

I was wrenched from sleep by a nightmare of shattering sound — as in a cave amplifying the vibrations of a million decibels. I was about to be splintered like a wineglass by the *vibrato* of a titanic tenor. Fully awake, I realised that the air raid siren mounted on the mansard roof of my attic bedroom was wailing its warning overture to an incalculable drama.

Through the dormer window I looked down upon the little market town of Coulommiers still shrouded in the fading shadow of the night. Day would soon dawn. Above me the cloudless sky was a pale cerulean blue. Across it crept two aircraft gilded by the sun as yet below my earthbound horizon. In their wake shellbursts of anti-aircraft fire tardily saluted them — an enemy reconnaissance heading for Paris. No French fighters had taken off to intercept them from their nearby airfield. It was the morning of May 10th, 1940. Thus, as it proved, symbolically the catastrophe of France had begun.

As an Intelligence Officer at the Headquarters of the British Air Forces in France (Eagle) my duties were clear. First to collate and summarize the day's reports of operations from all our units; secondly I had to censor the despatches of war correspondents accredited to the Advanced Air Striking Force operating under our command. In three months I had gained enough experience to meet the situation with a measure of confidence. There was only one snag. Six days earlier all the journalists had returned to England or to their wives in Paris in protest against disciplinary measures they had forced me to impose upon them.

In March I had been posted to France where I was to preach and implement the gospel of press relations with the Services according to Lionel Heald. My mission had, however, to be fulfilled within the existing framework of the Air Ministry ordinances. The Royal Air Force commendably was more press-conscious than her sister services. It had established a system, admirable in theory, of appointing uniformed and comparatively high ranking press officers to guide and, if necessary, to correct the conduct of war correspondents in the field. Poachers may make good gamekeepers, for usually they are tough enough to punch up their earstwhile fellow miscreants if they catch them intruding on their preserves. In general journalists, though they put on a convincing performance of cynical bravado, are at heart prone to sentimentality, particularly in asserting the freedom of their profession which, in fact, is no greater than the length of the chain which leashes them to their proprietors and editors. The press officers and the correspondents had been Fleet Street cronies of long standing. Their affections for each other united them in regarding me as an unwelcome intruder. Thus the Air Ministry's well-intentioned scheme broke down when the gamekeepers and poachers combined to confound the authority I exercised that might heighten the tensions of their already vulnerable fraternity.

The British Air Forces in France consisted of the Air Component attached to the British Expeditionary Force under Lord Gort and the Advanced Air Striking Force controlled by the Air Ministry and deployed around Rheims where its headquarters (Panther) was established in the cellars of Moet et Chandon. My Commander-in-Chief was Air Marshal Sir Arthur Barratt, one of the first flight of military airmen such as had been my instructors at the Central Flying School twenty-six years ago. He was nicknamed "Ugly" but he was by no means unprepossessing in appearance. He was stockily built and his rather prominent eyes gave him the aspect of a tenacious and faithful bulldog — characteristics that matched this crisis in his career. He was shrewd, forceful, but treated me with amiability. I soon found that with cunning aforethought he had cultivated the society of collaborationists in Paris and had a more realistic grasp of French fallibility than his superiors at home and his fellow commanders in the field. He can have had no illusions as to the confidence of French politicians or the competence of the French High Command. At the same time he must have felt keenly the weakness of his position with the comparatively minimal air forces he could muster to reinforce his allies in the impending confrontation with the Luftwaffe, vastly superior in numbers and equipment and over eager for another quick and cheaply won victory. His Senior Air Staff Officer was Air Vice Marshal Douglas Evill in whose squadron I had longed to serve while chafing under the uninspiring commander of the other one in No. 1 Wing of the Royal Naval Air Service operating from Dunkerque in 1916.

My immediate boss was Group Captain Janus, as I prefer to remember him. He assumed the gruff, rough manner of a stern martinet which in fact masked a gentler nature and, when it came to the test, an inclination to timidity. He welcomed me and approved my declared intentions. He never failed to support me when my actions provoked antagonisms that he bore with equanimity.

My daily routine was to write a communiqué that, having been submitted to Evill, I transmitted to A.I.6 in time to reach the B.B.C. in order that the nine o'clock news could anticipate the news bulletins of the German D.N.B. contrived by Doctor Goebbels' propagandists. At the same time I had to wrestle with the press officers whose charges were growing restive from lack of any news that would make headlines in their respective journals. During the ominous inaction on our front, they were inclined to make mountains of copy out of molehills of authentic news. For instance, I felt it my duty to curb their references to the Luftwaffe evading combat with the R.A.F. The Germans, in fact, were not showing their hand, so that our public at home might be lulled into a sense of false optimism as to the prospects of the impending battle. Again, the Air Ministry rightly or wrongly had set its face against the promotion by the press of "Aces", such as the public were encouraged to acclaim in the last war. Naturally our press corps resented my refusal to allow them to exploit the successes of individual pilots which they sincerely believed would help their readers to endure the *ennui* of the so-called "phoney war". Gradually such restraints induced frictions that I knew would be inimical to our co-operation when the inevitable battle was joined and at the same time I felt a measure of sympathy for their sense of frustration.

The crux of the matter was that I could not confide in them the truth that would have won their understanding. Every day I saw in the map room of our headquarters the forces of the Wehrmacht and the Luftwaffe massing in their order of battle. At the beginning of April our Intelligence estimated that roughly 3,000 tanks and 1,500 bombers and fighters were threatening the frontiers from Holland to Switzerland. Against this the British Army had a few squadrons of light tanks; the British Air Forces in France had some 300 aircraft in the field, many of them known to be no match for their German counterparts. The Air Marshal had no reliable figures as to the strength or viability of the French Air Force.

It was impossible to confide this forbidding discrepancy to a press corps if even two or three of the correspondents were

4

untrustworthy. Unhappily the American representative of the Columbia Broadcasting Company was totally irresponsible. Nor were one or two of the British journalists, avid for scoops in accredited articles, to be relied upon. Only two of our own reporters I could trust absolutely and they, oddly enough, were the toughest and most professional — Gallagher of the *Sunday Express* and Grant of the *Daily Mirror.* Both understood the pressures that I was under and, while exploiting to the full any loophole in the system, faithfully abided by the rules and restrictions imposed upon them.

My relations with our Army G.H.Q. at Arras were close and co-operative, largely due to the amused tolerance and sardonic sense of humour of my opposite number, Major Templer. Together we solved several bizarre problems. The first I heard of General Bernard Montgomery was in a protest by the Chaplain General to the B.E.F. against a pamphlet he had issued to the men in his Division warning them of the dangers and consequences of venereal disease, to which soldiers with no fighting to distract them were particularly vulnerable. The Chaplain insisted that the pamphlet should be censored. Templer, when I told him that my mother in 1916 had boldly anticipated Monty's prophylactic warning much to the annoyance of the Establishment at that time,[1] readily agreed that the only purpose of censorship was to withhold information that might be of value to the enemy. Monty's Cromwellian order would do nothing to lower the esteem of our Forces in the eyes of the enemy.

Once or twice I visited Arras. I can still recapture the vision of the courtyard in the Bishop's Palace on the brilliantly sunny morning when suddenly up the wide steps leading from his Headquarters Lord Gort accompanied by his whole staff, aglitter with sparkling brass and polished belts and field boots arose, as it were, on to the platform like a perfectly directed sequence in a spectacular film or as the subject of a crisp canvas by Meissonier. No sight could have inspired more confidence in the hearts of the British public or, indeed, in my own. Yet every officer in that scintillating group must have known that his hopes for the coming battle were forlorn.

---

[1] By organising in defiance of the Lord Chamberlain, a production of Brieux's play *Damaged Goods.*

Self-censored reflections for Rosalind reading between these lines:

H.Q. B.A.F.F

18. 3. 39.

I left Port Anonymous in a wonderfully antique vessel. The decoration was in the best wild west bar-room style, though it improved as you got lower down. The dining saloon was straight forward Waring and Gillow and above all contained food which was most unexpected. In the main hall a notice in strange script AN POST suggested that the ship had been in the Irish service and it was uniformly dirty enough to make even the Witch of Clonmel feel at home.

My travelling companions were another Intelligence Officer and a very amusing Canadian doctor who had spent the war hitherto in the far north and was glad enough to escape. I turned in very early and fell asleep reading gloomy weekly reviews which suggested that the war was already lost and the whole journey hardly worth while.

The details of the journey can only be revealed when peace comes to a tortured world; by then no one will be the least interested in them. My energies were entirely devoted to shepherding my extravagant baggage along miles of rain swept quays, into lorries, out of lorries and pushing it into trains which were panting to be off. At one point I lost my despatch case which had in it some papers for the Embassy. I was thrown into a sweat of apprehension. A fine start for a budding Intelligence officer. By the time I had thrown all the officials on the train into a state of uproarious excitement after their own heart and had built up a first class hurrah's nest, the missing case was found in a remote carriage, whither one of my colleagues must have carried it in a trance.

The whole journey was great fun. On quay or platform I was attended by perfectly cast film actors (French). I even had Raimu himself as a taxi driver. He was one of nature's gentlemen for with immense daring I made a joke in French. He responded nobly and the streets resounded to his great gusts of laughter and tooting to fit his mood.

I cannot say where I went or what I saw; still less where I arrived. But by the time I had extracted my baggage for the last time, I was glad enough to dump it in a house, even though the house hardly suggested a permanent home. The first impressions were not encouraging. I was extremely tired and very hungry. The officer who was responsible for my reception had apparently been nerving himself for the task in the local pub and was not entirely coherent. Through some lack of personal contact between himself and the driver of the lorry, my baggage was dumped first in one house and then in another. At last I found the house in which I was to sleep in what had been the library of a provincial Frenchman. It contained a massive table and a couple of semi-gothic chairs. The book cases were heavily sealed and even the shoddy grandfather clock had a notice pasted on it, asking me not to open it as it contained the personal effects of the owner. It became a Bluebeard's chamber to me; I longed to tear it open and to see what personal effects one could keep in a clock.

One window was broken, the floor was bare; all the thoughtful owner had left me was a series of very inferior pornographic pictures. These covered one wall; opposite to them hung a series of framed photographs depicting his grandfather's more pompous activities at the time of the Commune.

I went over to the Mess and had a wonderfully English reception. I walked in and sat down to a hastily contrived meal. No-one greeted me or indeed addressed a remark to me of any kind. Needless to say I did not linger after dinner. I got back to find my gear unpacked and my bed made up. I can't say the night was a success. It was very cold and I longed for two or three copies of *The Times* to put under my flea-bag. But as the shutters banged and the wind whistled through the broken window, I did feel that I was nearer the war and from now on could look Pam in the face as far as the rigours of the A.T.S. were concerned. I had arrived in the dark, so the surroundings were still unrevealed. I fell asleep to the tune of frenzied little tootings, which reminded me of Gershwin's *American in Paris.*

19. 3. 40

The next morning I acquired a young batman from Bradford. He is a bright lad and very soon he had got me unpacked and more or less straightened up. The pornographic pictures were consigned to the top of the clock and but for the clammy cold the room began to look habitable.

The day was spent meeting my fellow staff officers, who are without exception a very decent lot. The rest, from a service point of view, is silence. The town is a pleasant, busy little place with, I should imagine, a wonderful propensity for noisome smells in the summer. At the moment the streets are well flushed with rain and the river running through it well charged with mud. Everything is marvellously French and fiddling. The electric light would be more suitable for the deeper and more mystical recesses of a synagogue. The blackout is a light hearted affair; rags of cloth and sacking tacked onto the shutters. Shutters have, of course, come into their own. Every house is fitted with them and they provide the perfect solution as long as the world is darkened; they combine perfectly the functions of keeping out light and letting in air, which would be grand if the air outside my room was not filtered through three dustbins filled with the garbage of ages.

My office is in the eaves of another house. It gets all the sun and is covered with a faded wallpaper which depicts budgerigars mating on convolvuli attended by squadrons of dragon flies. It is of course cold. The chimney is stuffed with soot or nests. Yesterday a French chimney sweep appeared (spotlessly clean, which gave me little hope of immediate relief). After a great to do and much peering up the chimney, he turned to me with a beaming smile and said: "Peut-être les oiseaux!". Having made this charming deduction, he left.

I managed to do some shopping with the aid of signs and a friend who speaks every language but English. He is extremely kind but several months had reduced his supply of adjectives to one, namely "wizard". His French is perfect; but I must say I prefer going my own wilful way with a combination of French without Tears and pantomime. Anyhow I have acquired a splendid yellow tea set, a spirit stove and kettle at a price which would make the most Federal heart despair of Union.

20. 3. 40
My batman has won his spurs by scrounging a supply of coal and lighting the stove in my room so that it has no longer the dank atmosphere of an abandoned yacht. Tonight I will remove my martial cloak from the heap of bedding under which I shivered last night and perhaps the dressing gown may be removed later on.

I spent a busy day and really got down to work. My room was invaded by the chimney sweep and two French lads. After much head shaking and mutterings of "C'est bouché!" they attacked the wall with chisels and crow bars and in no time had it looking as though it had been heavily shelled. One of them went up on the roof and hullooed to his friend who had his head up the chimney. The latter obviously felt the indignity of his position for he turned frequently to me and having freed his mouth of soot declared "Je suis plombier!". I murmured appreciative understanding. I must get him to come and look at the geyser in my billet from which I can only weedle jets of ice cold water. When the wall was practically demolished the trouble was revealed; it was indeed les oiseaux. The major obstruction was removed. A cannon ball with a flue brush attached to it was hurled down the chimney and all was well. My friend the budding plombier took a great fancy to John's photograph which hangs above the fireplace. He, too, was fifteen and he told me with great pride that he had left school and had his certificate.

In the evening I weedled the geyser into life and got a corking hot bath. I regret to say it was the first since I left England and I felt very much better for it.

The nights have been very fine and parts of the town look quite lovely by moonlight. Much of it is very paintable and I hope I shall get a chance to practice my abandoned art on my afternoons off. Today has been brightened by the post. Letters reach here at incredible speed but I gather the service the other way is not so good.

21. 3. 40

A very busy day but an exceptionally fine one. Thanks to the stove the night was not spent in scheming how I could best generate natural heat. As I walked to the office I passed through the market place. The stall holders were very busy setting out their wares and it all looked very jolly in the sunlight.

I had a visitor who, like everything else must be cloaked in mystery. He is in many ways the key to the plan which I hope to put over. He was very pleased and enthusiastic and seemed pleased at my suggestions. I took him out to lunch at a little inn behind the market square. We had an excellent meal served by the proprietress herself. Hors d'oeuvres, trout meunière and

9

delicious cheese, whose nature must remain a dark secret, and a bottle of white wine which would have set the heads of the knowledgeable old boys at the Garrick wagging over its excellence, and all for fifty francs.

The sad thing about the town is that the householders seem to have abandoned all idea of repainting their property for years. This has a certain sombre attraction for artists, for everything is reduced to soft powdery shades. But it does look a bit poverty stricken. I suppose they figure out that with the Huns breaking out every twenty years its hardly worth doing the house up.

In the evening after dinner I went for a long walk with a Wing Commander who is second in command of our outfit. He is a most amusing chap and we stalked through the moonlit streets talking our heads off. After a bit we got out into the country. It looked beautiful, probably due to the discreet moonlight. This place had already been overrun by the Germans once and as I looked back at the town I longed for prophetic vision or Dunne-like perception so that I could see what it would look like this time next year. We did not get back until after eleven and by that time the cafés had emptied and every alley seemed to hold a shadowy group of French soldiers talking to girls, or indiscreetly relieving themselves. Those a little more exhilarated than the rest would pull themselves up into a ramshackle but elaborate salute. It was like passing a succession of Orpens in his best last war style.

22. 3. 40

Today I dressed in my icy billet warmed by the knowledge that I was being transplanted to a new and more civilised house. My new room had a radiator, blue wallpaper, and panelling in the style of Louis Quinze though I don't suppose he would recognise it. On the mantlepiece stand the Brunner boys.[1] The solemn straight gaze of Hugo would keep the wildest libertine from being too familiar with midinettes, one look at Dan, swelling with suppressed giggles, would make the grimmest moment appear comic, Barn's frowning austerity would put courage into the most craven heart, and a glance at Johnnie would send one hurrying off to work to acquire limitless industry marks from the C in C.

On my way to the office I saw that the door of the fine derelict church was open and a few soldiers toing and froing. In

[1] My nephews, the sons of Sir Felix and Lady Brunner.

my best French I asked permission to peer inside. I was rewarded by a really splendid sight. It almost puts parts of Canterbury in the shade and is on a terrific scale. Entirely derelict, the chapels are filled with bundles of faggots and the nave a mass of boxes and barrels. In England it would have attracted scores of earnest Friends. I shall do my best to get inside it again and make some drawings of it.

Everybody was much cheered by the news of Sylt[1]. It seems to have been a well thought out and successful operation. It restored our confidence, for all the other news was devoted to the incredible acrobatics of the French government which are beyond English understanding. However, I gather that it all amounts to very little in the way of crisis.

After dinner I escorted my friends to the new mess which they are starting. It is a very different affair to ours and might well be the home of a banquier splendide. My Wing Commander has a bedroom which looks like a film set for the death of Napoleon. I wish I was with them for it is nearer to our office. But taking things as they are, I am lucky to be where I am. Anyhow it was a joy to return to a room with central heat and to pass a warm night without my entire wardrobe heaped over me.

24. 3. 40

Saturday was a quiet but busy day. Though the nights seem to be as cold as ever, the sun in the daytime is really hot. The chestnut trees are just beginning to break. I was delighted to see a little tree creeper rushing up and down the tree outside my office window. Perhaps he is a cousin of the one at home.

In the evening there was a cinema show in the Municipal Theatre. It was for the English though the film was advertised as *La Chevauchée Fantastique,* which you would hardly recognise as *Stage Coach.* I have seen it twice so I went to bed early. Most of the Staff are getting the whole day off tomorrow. The Wing Commander and I reckon to be able to get off about noon, so we are planning a long walk in the country.

Easter Sunday. A lovely day and the bells ringing like anything. The whole town out and about in their best. I was surprised to see the market being set up. On my way to the office I bought some rolls and carried them off to a charcuterie where the pleasant proprietress filled them up with some

---

[1] A second raid by our bombers on the Luftwaffe base on that island.

delicious looking galantine. As I passed the old church, I saw again that the door was open. This time I was able to have a better look around. I gather it is seventeenth century. The capitals of the columns are decorated with the arms of local dukes, now I suppose forgotten. I was looking at the military stores which littered the floor and suddenly the significance of what they were burst upon me. Chesterton would have leapt for joy. Although desecrated and in the hands of the soldiers, it was entirely full of, what do you think? — bread and wine. Huge barrels of wine filled the ambulatories and all down the nave were tier upon tier of glistening brown loaves. A gigantic sacrament. I long to have time and opportunity to make a drawing of it.

We set off for our walk shortly after noon. We walked for an hour or so through country very like Wiltshire until, having passed through a village with a fine old church, we sat down in some hay and ate our lunch. It was a lovely day. After lunch we pressed on and reached another village. This too possessed a grand old church. We went into the bell tower and became conscious of a sound like the beating of a giant's heart. We realised it was an ancient clock in the tower and looking up saw the two stone weights hanging over our heads.

By this time we were a bit thirsty. We found a little pub. In the main room the lads of the village were playing billiards on a table without any pockets. They seemed thoroughly interested in us and there was a good deal of surreptitious giggling. We sat down in the back room and the proprietress (you notice how few men are left anywhere) brought us some excellent beer. While we were drinking a wonderfully bent old man wearing a cap covered with faded braid passed to and fro. He was obviously the village authority and was I suppose explaining to the lads the idiosyncracies of the English. I think he was still filled with the glory of having rolled the drum and pasted up the notice for mobilisation.

This village had an ancient but delightful public washing place. It was rather like a Roman atrium with the roof running round the sides but open over the shallow pool of crystal clear water.

Although it was Sunday the women were working in a desultory way on the vegetable patches. We now turned for home. At about the twelfth kilometre I developed a blister and was glad enough when, about three kilometres from home, a kindly Frenchman offered us a lift. I got home to find a splendid mail. I weedled the reluctant geysers into giving me a tepid bath. That and the mail read at leisure and the glow of self-righteousness that follows a ten mile walk made life seem pretty good even to an exile.

I dined early at a little restaurant nearby and set off to see some French films at the same theatre as last night's show. The place was packed and it had the air of a huge family party. I sat next to a French soldier who turned out to be a designer of textiles and much travelled in America. The film was a Belgian production and awful. I left after three reels and went to bed early. Nor was I sorry for the blister and stiffness in the old bones made even the camp bed very welcome.

27. 3. 40

The last three days have been extremely hectic although from a point of view of work done very satisfactory. Monday was just an ordinary day's work. I got caught in the evening by a tremendous discussion in my mess. I gathered that nearly all the officers were under the impression that no news which they read or heard was in any way reliable and that even the Air Ministry announcements were far from the truth. The result was that I was kept up far too late trying to prove to them that this was not so and explaining the principles of censorship. It was good evidence of the fact that one of our greatest enemies is Boredom. Fortunately my Group Captain is extremely enlightened and we are trying to devise a means of overcoming this very human weakness.

On Tuesday I went on a visit to a French official with whom I have to work a good deal. We drove through some lovely country. It was a grand day. The sky was splendid with sun and intermittent rain. As we swept past the most lovely old farms, built like fortresses, enclosed with great stone walls and turreted at the corners, I ached for my paints and for a chance to try and put it on paper. Although it was not actually the country of Jean Francois Millet, I passed groups of peasants who seemed to be unchanged. I actually saw one man walking the furrows and scattering seed corn instead of riding about on a contraption made by Massey Harris. We went through one town which had been the scene of a battle in the last war in which the British had fought; a memorial in the Lutyens manner sang out in a sea of plaster and shutters.

My colleague was most agreeable and we chattered away in two languages. His English was better than my French and though the conversation was highly technical we seemed to understand each other pretty clearly. The French are very easy to get on with and their attitude towards us is most friendly and helpful. I gather from old veterans that this is very different to their attitude at the beginning of the last war. I hope it continues so. The thing that strikes one is that they remain human whatever their rank or occupation. They contrive to make their uniforms appear as though they have been hastily contrived for a charade, indeed they are hardly uniforms for no two seem to be quite alike.

We returned by a different road and swept over wide plateaux of farming country. It seemed very like the best parts of Sussex but on a far larger scale. I gather that the farmers do pretty well round here. Even where jerry building has been developed there is not the deadly uniformity of English villadom; the worst French builder seems to insist on his individuality and however awful the fiddling little ornament may be, no two houses are alike.

Before I left, my Wing Commander and I had lunch together at the little restaurant I have found and afterwards went on a bicycle hunt. Neither of us are very bright at French but we became bolder and bolder, even haggling over the price of second hand "velos". At first we were a bit discouraged for we understood that the French for second hand was "ancien". We could not help feeling a little embarrassed at going into shops and demanding an ancient bicycle. The word suggested calamity and frequent breakdowns. Later we found a better word "a l'occasion" and our spirits rose. We saw some dazzling Daisies. At first we thought that so mounted we might make a sensational appearance. But the question of rank intervened. Who should take the front place? As the post of danger it obviously fell to the senior; on the other hand how could he then be sure that his wretched subordinate was really doing his damndest in the rear. We are now coming to the conclusion that a new one might be the best. But I hope that the negotiations are protracted for some time. It forms an admirable exercise for our French and already the cycle shop proprietors begin to laugh at our approach.

By the time you get this you will have realised that today should be forever remembered in the annals of the British Air

Force. Things began to get lively in the afternoon. I stayed at the office until nearly midnight and after hours of anxious pregnancy I produced this morning my first communiqué. As I wrote it with a trembling hand, I thought of you all listening to tonight's wireless and prayed that it would reach your ears in all its virgin beauty. I made one howler which oddly enough was not spotted by anyone here. I used the world "aerial". Apparently this is quite out of order and it is established by custom that one speaks of "air activity" rather than aerial activity. If argument became a junior officer (and it doesn't) I would claim that to talk of "sea activity" instead of "naval activity" would be ridiculous. But there it is and out it goes and I shall know better next time.

30. 3. 40

Oh dear, oh dear, the last three days have been one long rush and as you see the budget has been sadly neglected. You will have realised, I hope, from the vivid despatches which are now reaching you almost daily by wireless and press, that it has been a busy and successful week for all our chaps out here. It was a great moment when with shaking hand I laid before the C in C the first communiqué to be issued by B.A.F.F. and when he put his signature to that now historic document. Needless to say only the *Daily Telegraph* printed it in its original and exquisite form, the rest of the press who as we know have only the public interest at heart, thought they knew better. And from the rubbish they put out, it may well be that they do. However, there it is, and today another has set the wires and cables trembling. The upshot of it all is that our fighter chaps are proving themselves an heroic lot. Even the most hard boiled of their superiors are thrilled with their dash and courage.

In between times I must have done a great deal of travelling but for you it must be an invisible man travelling on a magic carpet over the Never Never Land for all the account I can give you of it. I went by car and fortunately it was a most lovely day. We rolled along over miles and miles of France and for a time (I can see no harm in saying this for all France is scarred) we drove through country which had been the scene of heavy fighting last time. No signs of devastation were visible. A cemetery here and there and the woods having the appearance of a rather seedy fur coat were all that remained. My companion was very well informed and most congenial.

15

Among other things he had been an Observation Officer during the German occupation of the Sudeten land. He was intensely interesting about it all and when you know that he has a son on the stage and is himself an artist, you can imagine that there were few dull moments. I wish I could tell you more but there it is.

I visited the chaps[1] who, though vastly senior in rank, are under my control. They are very amiable and friendly, so that stripes do not come between us, though I am likely to suffer them for their misdeeds. The consummation of my plans is at hand and the work thereafter, if not easier, will at least have the virtue of design and be less in the nature of a charade.

Perhaps I can say that we passed a great French convoy, just like the one which we ran into at Guildford. I was delighted by its appearance of efficiency and road discipline. In one lorry great cookers were steaming away and I imagined them to be full of a delicious casserole of some kind. At every crossroads there were the most efficient military police, their every gesture charged with dramatic appeal.

Looking back on the last day or two it would seem impossible that anything but work was achieved. In fact there have been several significant changes for the better in my circumstances and equipment.

The weather grew very cold and even in my comparatively palatial apartment I was so cold at night that I only got snatches of sleep as first one flank and then other was frozen hard. At last I could stand it no longer and I made up my mind to buy a quilt or a mattress. This in itself was fraught with some danger. I required something to sleep on and my primitive French instinct prompted me to take the shortest route and to ask for a "maitresse" which would have got me nothing more than a bad reputation. My dictionary gave me "matelas" a word which, with my uncertain pronunciation held even greater dangers. In the end I plumped for "pique" and a pique I now have. Last night, after a magnificent hot bath I fell upon my pique and was wrapped in marsupial snuggery. And what is more I slept. I have not been able to leave the office until eleven or twelve. This doesn't matter a bit as soon as I have got all the other administrative work finished.

The pique is all very well. But at this moment outside the office, tethered like a spirited charger, stands my "velo avec changement de vitesse, avec éclarage, avec pompe, avec

[1] R.A.F. Press Officers.

16

sacoche et appareil pour baggage", in fact a splendid bicycle. It is a little shy and self effacing for beside it stands the Wing Commander's and it is, above all, a disciplined and subordinate velo. But there it is and if the worst comes and we are bombed and shot to pieces, I shall be seen flying south upon it even if it is by then "sans pneus et sans sacoche". I think it will be a great joy. It is a real danger here of not getting away or taking exercise and on those trusty wheels we should be able to go far. The whole outfit was the equivalent of £5 (990 fr.) and if I have to part with it (perish the thought at the moment) I ought to get a good price for it judging from the state of the marché des velos a l'occasion of which we are now experts. They are scarce and not so cheap.

My batman continues to be assiduous. The only form of drapes (as they say in the film world) or upholstery available are army blankets. He works miracles of improvisation on this theme. The effect of all his carpeting and draping in this medium is that of a primitive talkie studio. But it is better than nothing.

After trudging over miles of cobbles I have come to the conclusion that they have had a great influence upon the character of the people. I believe that centuries of walking on cobbles have given them their delightfully ramshackle and fantastic manner. You cannot be dignified on cobbles. You must either roll around like a drunken sailor or mince from stone to stone like a pernickety aesthete.

With that inspiring little thought I will close. It has been a good week if cold. Sadly missing you all but conscious that on two occasions of this week I have done my duty, I salute you.

31. 3. 40

Having visited the charcuterie and laid in good supplies of lunch we set off on our most ambitious bicycle ride. It began by a long climb up a hill leading out of the town. We had determined that we would have no shame about getting off and walking when we pleased, but we were paced by a sturdy Frenchwoman and her little boy, who kept on remounting at all but the steepest bits. For the honour of England we felt compelled to accept the challenge and we passed and repassed each other like people in a seven day's race. We reached the top fairly puffing and blowing. The country around here is ideal for cyclists. You climb a steep hill, then career about on an almost unlimited plateau, to end up with a nice run downhill for home.

We went through some charming villages, very neat and nicely arranged round minute "Places" and still looking pretty feudal. Most of them were dominated by a chateau of some sort. We stopped for lunch by a water mill in a valley. A lovely little river ran through it, though the prospect was a little spoiled for me by a discreet notice which said PECHE RESERVE or something like it.

Now and again we came across French military police at crossroads. Here we rested and there was a good deal of handshaking and cementing of allied friendship.

We stopped for some time at an estaminet about half way out on the day's run. We were greeted by a wonderful old virago who would be well cast for a knitter at a revolutionary tribunal. She was very poor in everything but her false teeth which were rich and splendid. We were waited on by her daughter who was very attractive in a gipsy sort of way and who chattered away amiably. Occasionally men with flowing moustaches and squints would come and peer at us. On enquiry the girl told us that there was a colony of refugee Poles in the neighbourhood. The room we sat in was bare in the extreme and the further end of it wrapped in murky darkness. With a show of pathetic pride she made a gesture towards the gloomy recesses and told us that before the war the place was very gay on Sundays. The French country folk must be tigers for self entertainment.

It was a lovely day and the sun was quite hot. We had the wind behind us all the way home and it was more than welcome for by the time we brought the steeple of the church over the horizon we were pretty saddle sore. The cobbles which we had to navigate before we reached home were agony. But our pain was nothing to our pride for we found that we had covered thirty six kilometres, which for the first day's run we thought pretty creditable. I had to go to the office for a bit when I got back and later dined with my fellow cyclist at his mess. We got involved in a terrific political discussion but I was so pleasantly weary that I left them to it and eagerly sought my now snug bed. The bicycles are a great success, they go like anything and are much lighter than English ones.

1. 4. 40

I set off on a long journey with my Group Captain. Alas the details and direction of that journey must remained veiled in mystery. The G/C was a most entertaining companion. He has only recently returned from Palestine where he was the prime mover in the suppression of the rebellion. He is a splendid raconteur and being Scotch flavours the most grisly reminiscences with a certain wistful tenderness. He was most interesting about the Jewish communal (not Communist) settlements. They seem to be all one could wish. Everybody works for the common good and no money changes hands. There is no marriage ceremony nor is anyone compelled to set up house as a married couple until a child is on the way. The mother has to go into a clinic six weeks before the child arrives and remains there until it is weaned. From then on the child remains in the welfare centre, it never goes home to stay though the parents can see it twice a day. They are, however, never allowed to see it when they are dirty or not cleaned up after their work. The education is excellent and bright children can go to universities there or in Europe. He told me lots more about them all but that can wait. He seemed to have an equal respect for the Jews and Arabs and from all accounts he must know as much about them as anybody.

I don't think there could be any harm in saying that one way or the other we went through a lot of country that had been scenes of the fiercest fighting during the war. We swept through village after village whose names are probably better known in England than in France. All of them have risen from their ashes, though one or two still looked as though they were picknicking a little anxiously between wars.

I was astonished and rather horrified by the scale of everything. Vast stretches of bare rolling land, without a spot of cover of any kind and overlooked by slopes and flat topped hills. How anybody fought in such a country I cannot imagine. It must have been hell for everybody. All the fields were beautifully tilled and the young corn beginning to show. I can give no reason for it, but I had a curious feeling that this area would never be fought over again. It may have been the sight of the persistent farmers sowing their crops or the cemeteries, with their head stones drawn up like defending regiments. Whatever it was, it was a very definite instinct. I hope it is true.

We had a long drive and the rest of the day was spent in

meetings and negotiations, so I was glad enough, after a very pleasant dinner at an R.A.F. mess, to sink into a real bed in a hotel in the town we were visiting. It was quite comfortable. It was reputed to be a hotbed of spies and is very much under suspicion, so with a real feeling of melodrama I hid my despatch case under the mattress while I went out for dinner. I must confess that all the people round the bar looked as though they had been made up by Clarksons for the job.

The weather broke that night and during most of the journey home it was raining. The war area looked pretty desolate. We passed what must have been the most spectacular mediaeval castle. Unfortunately the Germans had vented their spite on it and the fine walls and turrets were pierced with shell holes. They are childish people; just like kids knocking down each others bricks from spite.

We had a very pleasant lunch at a well known restaurant in a town on the way home. I found some absolutely perfect burgundy and as it was cold and wet we polished off a bottle; it was almost embarassingly cheap.

As we drew near home I asked the Group Captain whether after all those years service he still had a feeling when returning from leave or absence of any kind, that there was sure to be a hurrah's nest waiting for him to step into. To my delight he confessed that this was so. Sure enough as soon as I got back there were plenty of troubles waiting for me to be straightened out. Journalists crying for my blood and the Air Ministry pursuing me with scorpions. I think that the correspondents have been having things too much their own way. During the last day or two I have tightened things up a bit and they don't relish it. However, we stick to our guns which is the only thing to do; they will soon forget their troubles when they have something to write about.

One of the troubles (and I think this applies throughout the Press) is that there don't seem to be any outstanding men to lead them. When you think that in the last war the Chief Press Officers or their equivalents were men like John Buchan and C. E. Montague it makes one wonder what has come over journalism. They have to be absolutely spoon fed and even then they are constantly complaining.

On top of all this there has been, as I expect you have heard, a good deal of activity. Our chaps have been doing wonders and everybody is delighted at their dash and spirit.

So what with journeying and hurrah's nests the days have slipped by and it is now Friday. In between times I have been trying to write an address for somebody to give to a collection of journalists who are coming over to visit us. Thank heaven I have finished it and I only hope it is what the speaker requires.

One of the things that goes to my heart in this strange country is that they are passionate tree planters. On every hand there are newly planted groves and avenues and even the smallest roads are lined with saplings. You can almost tell the parts of the country which were the scenes of fighting by the age of the trees along the main roads. They seem to plant poplars mostly, though along the river at the back of our billets there is an avenue of pollarded plane trees; I have never seen them treated like this before. At the moment the trunks are the most beautiful colour; pale green where the bark has peeled and russet brown where the patches of bark are left.

Last night I went for a walk along the little river. I think the houses which stand above it must be week-end residences of the well-to-do from the larger towns. There are one or two hard tennis courts sprouting great weeds and a sort of race track but most of the posts which mark the track are collapsing. Everything of that kind seems to have been abandoned until the present job is done.

Yesterday I saw quite a lot of French soldiers on the march. They looked a grand lot of men and in every way smarter and more efficient than last time.

This is about all the news up to date. It seems to have been a very full week but so much of it has been spent in activities which cannot be discussed. It looked for a time as though things were going to warm up altogether, but with the change of weather everything seems to be quiet on the Western Front. It seems a pity that the world can only look forward to a summer as making it easier for them to destroy each other. But that is a melancholy thought to end up with. I feel reason may yet prevail. I shall think of the summers as a time for creeping off in the evening with my rod, Peche Reserve or not.

7. 4. 40

Saturday was a normally busy day. Still beastly cold, so much so that my cycling companion whose blood has been thinned by several years of service in the East has caught a chill and was unable to mount his velo for the Sunday outing. In the evening I went with another chap to dinner at a local inn and afterwards we wandered on to the French cinema. It was a blaze of lights, which looked very refreshing however reckless, and it was absolutely packed. We managed to squeeze into a little private box with a number of French officers and the fun began. The first film was a very second rate American picture. But owing to the fact that French dialogue had been dubbed into it, and very well done at that, the quality of the acting took on a new virtue. It was a most extraordinary effect and one which lead me to think that a great deal of French acting may appear to be better than it really is, owing to the strangeness of the language. After the American film we all streamed out, many of the French soldiery literally so doing for the wall along the river, a most delightful promenade in normal times, was immediately converted into a gigantic lavatory. Nobody seemed to mind. Distinguished citizens and their wives and families mixed freely with what might be called the relieving parties and hardly turned aside from their walk to avoid them. Quite astonishing and rather amusing. It was a gorgeous night of brilliant stars and the whole scene was a strange one. The second half of the film was *Prisonne sans Barreaux,* an absolutely first rate French film with one or two unforgettable moments. I thoroughly enjoyed it and the whole evening (including Mickey Mouse and Donald Duck alpine climbing) was a refreshing change.

Sunday morning was gloriously fine with not a cloud in the sky. On my way to work I found one or two splendid flower stalls in the market and bought a great bunch of anemones for the office. My führer says that Palestine is carpeted with them at the proper season and that they are thought to be the Rose of Sharon mentioned in the Bible, but you probably knew this already. The magnolia in the garden is fairly bursting though quite a lot of the buds have been nipped by the cold.

At noon I put aside the pen and this machine and having visited my charcuterie and having stuffed my haversack with sandwiches I set off upon my shining velo.

I had a lovely run. At first I lost my way and made a wild circuit of the town, but after a good deal of frantic conversations with all and sundry I got upon the road I was trying to find. It ran along a valley by a river. It was perfect velo country, no hills to speak of and plenty of amusing little villages and farms. All the villagers were sitting in front of their cottages in the sun doing their mending; lots of little girls were wearing sun bonnets made out of newspapers; I hope they were properly censored before being put to this really useful service.

I found a suitable haystack and sat down on the lee side of it and thoroughly enjoyed my lunch. The sun was boiling hot and I felt really warm for the first time, at least from natural causes. I pushed on after lunch and found that the road ran nearer to the river and passed a lot of very jolly water mills. The woods were very like those around Whitstable and here and there were clearings where cutting was going on. In one or two of the clearings picknickers were just basking off their lunch. It all seemed very peaceful and homelike except for the fact that one of the parties was composed of two French women and a negress, an outpost I suppose of the Colonial Empire. I ended up in a very pleasant little town. I found an interesting church and sat in it for a bit and rested. For this relief I gratefully approached a statue of St. Nicholas. Beneath it were two boxes, one marked "demande" and "offrandes", very practical. But the demande box wasn't big enough to hold all my supplications so I just dealt with the offrandes; this should have given him an easy Sunday afternoon.

Very rashly I started to walk down the main street which led to the river. I realised too late that it was lined with folk gossiping at their doorsteps. The first who saw me set up the cry "Un Anglais!" This spread like rumour and I had to walk through about 500 yards of scrutiny and comment. I could not retreat and ended by feeling a perfect fool.

I had a brisk run back, completing for the honour of my velo squadron a tour of 36 kilometres and got back in time to issue a communiqué which I hope graced your Monday morning papers. Altogether a very pleasant day and a healthy change from the office.

8. 4. 40

I had a very busy day making the final preparations for the impending Press meeting. The C in C seemed to like my brief for him but I had to break it up into headings. It is very difficult to write a speech for someone else and no one worth his salt could use another's language. But I hope we have arrived at a good compromise. I lunched with one of my Press Officers and a Censor at the little inn which is handy for these occasions. I was offered another dandelion salad. Since I last ate it I have tumbled to the meaning of its French name "pisse en lit". It should make an admirable diet for refugees. They are indeed strange people — none the less I enjoyed it very much.

9. 4. 40.

It seems the Germans have extended the field of their frantic machinations. During the early part of the morning we heard a good deal of rumour, but it now appears certain that they have invaded Norway and Denmark. What a world. It is difficult to see what it means or how it will affect the general campaign. My own opinion is that for a long time they have been coveting the statue of Ibsen in Oslo which contains enough bronze to last them for years. I must say I should like to be there when it is hurled down and replaced with a wooden one of Wagner. He struck me as being a melancholy and overbearing figure which overshadowed our fantastic visit to that unhappy city.

I gather things have warmed up a bit at home which I suppose means late nights and frenzied days for Felix[1] at A.I.6.

II

10. 4. 40

Today my anxieties have been equally divided between the incredible activities going on off the Norwegian coast (of which we knew as little as yourselves) and the skirmishes of a troupe of War Correspondents who came to attend a conference. I cannot help feeling that the situation of the Norwegian army was no more desperate than my own when for some considerable time, before senior and better men than myself took charge, I stood with my back to the wall parrying the attacks of embittered journalists. My weapons were attempted charm alternating with intimidating silences; and all the time I was in a sweat of terror least my words should appear in garbled form elsewhere. My fears were, I believe, groundless. They were a very decent lot and most of their grievances are the product of boredom and inactivity.

I had to arrange the room for their reception and I tackled it with the enthusiasm I would expend upon a movie set until in the end it looked ready for the signing of peace or the drawing

---

[1] My brother-in-law, Sir Felix Brunner.

up of a new and more formidable treaty of Versailles. I understand the meeting was a great success and that they all went off happily. The C in C spoke admirably; he was quiet but authoritative and cleverly mixed a number of home truths with invitations to mutual co-operation.

All through the day we had been the prey of rumour and wireless sets that crackled and banged to such an extent that the English news sounded like a distracted Englishmen trying to read aloud while a Frenchwoman (some overpowering French wavelength) was trying to quarrel with him and her supporters were letting off Chinese crackers in the street. The result was that by the evening we had no very clear idea as to who was in Norway or what fleet had been sunk. At nine o'clock, however, I heard the first real news, which was thrilling. It really sounds as though we have conducted a brilliant naval operation and that the Navy has come into its own. I can hardly bear to wait until Winston tells the world. I was so thrilled that afterwards I crept off to a deserted room which houses a piano which includes all the charms of a Jews Harp and a banjo and thumped away triumphantly. The fact that the instrument was completely out of tune only added to the modern and martial theme of my strummings. I was interrupted by a call to the office and having dealt with the trouble, went to bed for the last time as a man of forty two fantastic years.

11. 4. 40

Of many strange birthdays this has been the strangest. It was a lovely day and I arose early and after breakfast set off blithely to order my dinner from the redoubtable M. Pellerin. I had invited six of my more genial colleagues to the feast and was determined to put as bold a face upon the occasion as exile permitted. On my way through the streets I came across an auction which was being held in a narrow alley outside a deplorable house. On a bench were the most pathetic collection of household goods and death alone could have been the motive for their disposal for most of the things could have hardly been given away. A most distinguished looking man with a fine white moustache and melancholy eyes pronounced panegyrics over battered pots and pans while his assistant, a thin and eagle eyed clerk searched the faces of the crowd for any hint of a bid. The bidding appeared to be a matter of centimes but was none the less keen and, of course, there was a good deal of mockery and laughter. I could have watched it for hours.

I interviewed M. Pellerin in his kitchen. He is a splendid figure, very like the monster with a black moustache who appears in Charlie's early films. At first he was a little cold, unwilling I suppose to believe that his art was truly appreciated by an Englishman. There was a good deal of shrugging of shoulders, lips pursed in incipient raspberries and vague "Que voulez-vous". Finally I appealed to him to treat me to his chef d'oeuvre. Immediately he warmed as one artist to another. It appeared that his triumph was in some way connected with ducks. He disappeared and returned with a brace of plucked ducks and began to rhapsodise on the miracles he would perform with them although they were a trifle old. His wife and the competent and tireless waitress hovered around us and sang confirmatory choruses to his more extravagant suggestions. All was settled; the wine was chosen and was to be slowly brought to the proper temperature in the course of the day. As I left he called me back. In a voice charged with friendship and emotion he offered to make me a glacé pralinée. The chorus rose into a crescendo of gluttonous approval and I bowed my way out with repeated remercis. I had already had the price of the dinner in fun.

But, alas, events of which I cannot speak and if I could would bring tears of frustration to my eyes, developed in the course of the morning which made it clearer and clearer that we would be compelled to abandon the feast. My colleagues were kindness itself and insisted on carrying me off to their mess for lunch. The importance of the events in question was entirely overshadowed as far as I was concerned by the thought of my having to go and confess to M. Pellerin, who by this time would be in transports of creative art, that the dinner was off.

Shamefaced and losing all my little French in my embarassing plight, I struggled to tell them how desolated I was and flung in repeated and consoling "c'est la guerre". They were most understanding and greeted my offer to pay for any trouble they had been put to with merry contempt. So there was no birthday dinner for me. But M. Pellerin is an artist and I am quite sure that having taken up his palette he would not lay it aside. I feel certain that some unworthy Frenchman has guzzled the ducks and smacked his unworthy lips over glacé pralinée that should have graced my birthday table.

No good weeping over melted pralinées. The rest of the day was busy enough and we were cheered by the news that dribbled in from the North and seal was put on our pride in the Navy by Winston's admirable speech which we heard at about five o'clock. They do seem to have done magnificently and the picture of the *Renown* crashing at twenty four knots through a heavy sea, loosing off broadsides at the two German cruisers was a spectacular one.

In the evening another compassionate colleague carried me off to dinner at *his* mess and on the whole I spent a very happy day though more entertained than entertaining. But it was the sort of day when nobody quite knew what the next hour would bring forth so on the whole the postponement of the feast was wise enough. It would have been worse to have had to abandon a half eaten feast than to have had none at all.

I have been lent Maurice Baring's *R.F.C. H.Q.* which is most interesting. It is fascinating to compare the job which he was doing twenty years ago to our own conditions in which we are doing very much the same work. In it he gives a charming definition of a gentleman: "One who loves God and has beautiful manners". I think M. Pellerin is a gentleman.

12. 4. 40

Today was a quiet one and something of an anticlimax as far as we are concerned. In order to preserve the illusion of youth I had my hair cut and it speaks well for my French which, as the late Secretary of State would say, is rapidly accruing, that I emerged from a highly efficient and lavishly equipped hairdresser without a tonsure or a permanent wave; in other words such hair as is left looks more or less normal.

It rained pretty well all day. During the afternoon a body of French troops marched along the road, gloriously out of step but beautifully equipped. I think that the greatest change one sees in them is the condition in which they keep their horses. This particular company or whatever it was, was followed by six splendid looking animals; they looked just like a string of race horses and each one had a smart looking blue cloth on its back. I hear on all sides that the French army is the last word in efficiency.

So ends what has elsewhere been the most spectacular week of the war. A few days ago some anti-aircraft guns opened up in the middle of the night, but in my jaeger bag and pique I sleep so soundly that guns of heavier calibre will have to be used if I am to be aware of them. I expect Felix has had a frantic week. I am a little jealous, for the activity which broke out here has died down and though my dripping pen has been poised ready to record it, little worthy of record has come my way.

22. 4. 40

After an influenza black-out, the budget is resumed and the publisher hopes that his readers will not be so inconvenienced again. Nor, he hopes, will he be and warns all comers that only death is worse than M and B 693 or whatever the number of the foul stuff is. Our doctor is of the service variety, no young specialist recruited from Harley Street, and I gather that this wretched remedy is a godsend to the service sawbones for it kills or cures most of the ills to which the unhappy soldier is heir to.

Springing lightly into the first person, I am glad to say that Saturday saw me returning to feeble health but none the less health. A kind friend who is liaison officer with the French and something of a fin de siecle Parisian brought me back from one of his excursions a bottle of METATONE which is worth all the vin in the pays to me. Now shot through and through with strychnine and Vitamin B I am rapidly gaining ground and shooting out communiques with the old vigour.

On Sunday practically everybody went to Paris to see a football match between the R.A.F. and the French. The R.A.F. tactfully lost and honour was satisfied all round. I was invited to spend the day at a very nice Mess up on a hill at the back of town. Here I basked in the sun and wandered about a gigantic and feudal kitchen garden which had been most successfully cultivated by its new owners. The house is very pleasant eighteenth century with some really lovely pieces of empire furniture in it. The garden is just like a theatrical setting; in fact when I came out upon the terrace after dinner and saw it flooded with moonlight I said almost automatically "Act Two: the same the following night". I had a most restful day, went to the office about five in the afternoon and recorded the deeds of our really miraculous chaps and returned there to dinner. After dinner I had a nice strum on their grand piano.

The weather really seems to have taken a sudden and determined turn for the better. It has been very hot and looks like remaining so for a bit. I suspect we shall be pretty boiled here in the summer. But who knows, by then war may have broken out in the Antarctic and we may transfer our whole H.Q. to the Great Barrier Reef.

I have one very good piece of news. A new Mess is being started up on the hill near here. I have been invited to join it and I accepted with alacrity. I have not had time to visit it yet; I have been very busy and all the resources have been called upon to cope with ordinary business. I gather it contains real beds and two pianos; I ask no more. My fellow messmates are a very nice lot and at least two of them well versed in French shoppery and cookery, so we ought to make a good show of it. Flu in a camp bed is not a very successful affair; in fact I shall be glad enough to sleep a bit higher off the floor in however strange a French bed.

23. 4. 40

This looks like being a very busy week. Monday and Tuesday whirled by, a mass of correspondence and hectic evenings getting out communiqués. Lovely weather, though it is breaking up a bit now.

I visited the new mess and it turned out to be a trifle disappointing. It is true that the house is on a hill well above the summer stink line, that it possesses two pianos, one a grand, and some real beds, but it is rather a gloomy chalet and for some extraordinary reason all the bedrooms lead out of one another and apart from the fact that it looks as though I might have to share a room, the constant toing and froing of people at all hours of the night through one's bedroom might be a bit disturbing. The house appears to have been the resting place of a retired French colonial officer. Faded photographs of the owner in pith helmets of ancient design, arrays of spears and arrows on the walls all marked POISONED give the impression that at any hour of the night one might be invaded by fuzzy wuzzies on the war path and murdered in bed. So unless I am offered a bedroom with a passage to it I shall stay in my own queer quarters.

Nothing much has happened outside the ordinary run of business. I had a visit from a French colonel connected with the Censorship. He was exactly like Eddie Knoblock dressed up for a charade. His English was not very good but he delivered his opinions with the utmost gravity. We got on famously and I think he will be very useful. On meeting and parting we did some spectacular saluting and heel clicking and I hope he went off in a happy frame of mind.

There are some lovely gardens behind our mess. They belong to a monastery, the remains of which (Henri IV) are quite a feature of them. The river runs round and through them. As I came through the little park on the way to the office this morning, the river banks were lined with French recruits who were being taught to salute by the most kindly N.C.O.'s. The recruits were wearing caps with red tops. Some were doing saluting practice and here and there were little bunches of them grouped around a rifle on a fixed stand doing elementary musketry. Those who were standing at ease were laughing and chatting away with the washerwomen who were hard at work in their little pent houses on the opposite bank. With the bright green grass and the Corot like trees, pale feathery green with bursting buds, the whole scene looked like a painting by one of those nineteenth century French artists who illustrated that vast life of Napoleon we used to have at home. I stood for a long time watching them all; it was fascinating.

Last night I went with my Wing Commander to dine at our little cafe and was thoroughly enjoying a sole Normande when the telephone found me even there. So between courses I had to walk about half a mile, attend to some business and return for the cheese. In spite of this interruption we had a very pleasant evening and afterwards went for a bit of a walk, modest enough for the legs are a bit feeble.

27. 4. 40

The Budget has been interrupted for two or three days. I woke up on the morning of the 24th to find a really dud looking day so I determined to set off on a long journey which certain circumstances had made necessary as soon as it looked as though I could leave the camp without fear of having to put out a communiqué. I have really had the most thrilling travels though I must confess that I shall be glad enough to get to bed tonight even though the bed is a camp one and I am duty officer in the Group Captain's room.

One of my jobs was to visit one of our advanced squadrons and one whose heroic exploits it has been my privilege to record. Since I have alluded in my communiqués to the fact that our actions have taken place in the neighbourhood of Verdun, I think I can safely say that my journey took me through this extraordinary area. As I drove East, evidences of the last war became more and more frequent. Although the fields had been miraculously tilled and levelled, here and there you would still see pieces of shell pitted ground which had been too much for the reclaimers. There they were like scars on the bright green fields with a decent veil of rather stunted little birches trying to hide them. Here and there were still lying bundles of rolled up and rusty barbed wire; a curious rambler seems to flourish in these devastated places. At this time of the year anyway it looks exactly like ancient wire and lies thickly on the ground.

Verdun is most impressive. I suppose the town itself was badly knocked about; but there are still quite a lot of old buildings and a rather fine gate and the houses along the river front all look fairly antique. The country around still looks pretty grim. As you come out onto the hills above the town there are two villages on each side of the road which consist of entirely gutted houses. There seems to have been no attempt to tidy them up or to rebuild them.

The chaps at the squadron were the grandest lot. I'm afraid I can't tell you much about them. You have to read the nonsense the journalists write about them. When I got there they were all sitting in the diminutive mess censoring letters. The young Squadron Leader made me most welcome and a superb high tea was rustled up for me. I was glad enough to get it for I had been travelling hard and long. It all carried me back to the old days. They might have been a reincarnation, they were so exactly like a squadron of twenty years ago. To my middle aged eye they appeared to be living in profound discomfort. As I prepared to leave, feeling a little guilty at driving off to the comparative flesh pots, I took a last look at the rather bleak landscape and primitive surroundings. Half apologetically, I said to the Squadron Leader; "Well, It's not so bad here: it will be quite nice in the summer." A light of joy and pride came into his eyes. "No", he replied: "It's wonderful isn't it .... magnificent!" His enthusiasm was most moving. He was the type of chap that only England can produce. Extremely modest yet with great self assurance and with tremendous presence for one so young. I gather he got his first Hun on his first trip as leader of a flight. I left them all with very real regret and felt I would rather be an Intelligence Officer with them than back at H.Q. But I dare say they would find me painfully anti-diluvian.

We had a rather sticky time on the way home. Early on we had to be diverted for some reason or other from the main road. As a result of this we got completely lost in the neighbourhood of Mort Homme and Douaumont. It was growing dark and I have never wandered about such haunted country. Everything looked either blighted or blasted. In the hollows and in the larger shell holes, wisps of mist like some noxious gas had begun to collect and the whole atmosphere was most uncanny. I thought of that fiim *Miracle before Verdun* and was soon ready to imagine thousands of resurrected dead advancing on us through the stunted and unwholesome looking trees. It took us hours to get back to something like civilisation and it was nearly midnight before I tumbled into a bath in a fairly decent hotel half way home.

The next day I got back here. I had hardly got settled down and was preparing to get to work on the results of my visit when who should ring up but Patrick.[1] It was a real joy to hear his unmistakable voice, the more so as I was faced with one or two problems upon which his advice would be the most valuable help. He wanted me to come and join him at a nearby but unmentionable city. It all fitted in very well, so as soon as I knew that I should not be called upon for a pronouncement I lit off to join him. I got there in time for dinner. He had arranged for me to stay at his hotel. It really was grand to see him again and to pick up a few threads that had got a bit frayed. We fairly chattered away over a gorgeous meal that was arranged for us by a colleague of his, a most charming chap whom I hope to see again. Of course we sat up far too late but his advice was all I hoped for and I was glad to find that he supported me in certain actions I have got to take. He really is very wise. Incidentally, we began dinner with the most fascinating dish. It was called "Crudités" which is a good start and it consisted of a great dish of uncooked vegetables which included mushrooms, celery, tomatoes and even Jerusalem artichokes. They were served with a lovely sauce and made the most clean and refreshing start to a gargantuan meal.

I had a very comfortable night and for the second time revelled in a real bed and a bath that did not demand patience

[1] Alan Patrick Ryan, B.B.C. and Dept. Political Warfare.

and skill to weedle tepid water from it. I stayed with Patrick the next morning and we tramped about the town pursuing our subject. I left for home about lunch time. On the way back we had a blow out, so while this was being dealt with I had a bit of a blow out myself at a little village inn. So home, or what we call home, to find myself plunged in work but much refreshed by the interlude with Patrick.

III

At the end of April my forbearance with the journalists and their tolerance of my impositions broke down.

I received an urgent summons from Squadron Leader J. W. C. (Hank) More to visit him at his airfield on the plains to the eastward of the formidable defence system at Verdun. He was in command of one of our two fighter squadrons armed with Hurricanes. I found him deeply concerned about an unforeseen threat to the morale of his pilots. In action they had proved themselves undaunted by their skilled and experienced opponents. More was faced with a subtle and psychological threat to their well being.

The war correspondents who, on the whole, lacked the decorum and discretion of those attached to our G.H.Q. at Arras, had settled down (as, indeed, I think most of us had done) to the continuance of the war of attrition that had ended in 1918. Many had their wives living in Paris. Most of their newsgathering was done in the restaurants and bars of Rheims. When our pilots were on leave there they were fêted by journalists who in exchange for expense-acccount champagne, hoped to get stories with a "personal angle" from their young guests who, not surprisingly, were soon split into two factions — those inclined to reticence and with a distaste for such intrusion on their privacy, and others who enjoyed such entertainment and the publicity that they were assured would be given to their exploits. More soon detected the divisive effects of this disparity of response to such treatment that the press officers had been unable to control. More was a Cranwell trained officer of exemplary distinction. Later in the Far East he was captured and died when a Japanese prisoner-of-war ship was sunk.

Immediately I issued orders that in future pilots were to be interviewed only by appointment and in the presence of a press officer. This proved to be the last straw. To a man the journalists went on strike leaving the press officers, whose uniforms prevented them from deserting in the face of the enemy, sullen and united in their resentment of my high handed action. I had no regrets, for More's appeal had been dealt with swiftly and effectively.

There was, however, bound to be an angry reaction in Fleet Street. The wrath of outraged editors and influential proprietors would be vented against my Air Marshal. Therefore, I suggested to him that he should invite the correspondents at Arras to a conference at Coulommiers to be followed by visits to units of the Advanced Air Striking Force. He asked me to write a discourse for him on the whole affair. The result was, we agreed, too rhetorical and contrived and would be more effective if he gave the gist of it in his own words.[1]

In due course the contingent from Arras was assembled in our conference room. Among them I was delighted to welcome Evelyn Montague, whose sister Rachel was an old friend and whose father, C. E. Montague, I revered as the most perceptive drama critic of his time writing in the *Manchester Guardian* for his father-in-law C. P. Scott. The meeting began on a note of slap-stick comedy, for as he entered the room the Air Marshal slipped and fell flat on his back. But thanks to his commanding eye of Mars and the good manners of his guests, not a smile diminished the dignity of the occasion. He put the case for our actions clearly and concisely. He reminded them of the dictum of the first press censor in the previous war, my uncle Sir Edward Tyas Cook, himself a distinguished editor, that "if the censors and journalists get on together too well neither were doing their job properly". He also urged them to respect the purely domestic activities of his officers and men. Recently he had entertained some of our pilots to celebrate a remarkable day's work. It had been an entirely private affair. The reporting of such occasions made their repetition more difficult.

"The strain on fighter pilots" he added, "is inevitably a very great one. When interviewing or visiting them in times of stress I would ask you to intrude as little as possible upon their

[1] See Appendix A.

privacy or to interrupt the relaxation which is essential to their health and spirit."

He had already answered the questions that his audience had to ask as to the provocation of their absent colleagues. Afterwards they assured him that they had no sympathy for their behaviour and that they deplored the accounts published in some of the dissident newspapers as misrepresentation of the facts. When I returned to my office I found a note to the effect that I had been promoted to Flight Lieutenant in the field. It was a generous reward for such a rearguard skirmish.

The following day Lord Trenchard, the patriarch of the Royal Air Force, visited our headquarters and lunched in our mess. I heard an assiduous staff officer ask him if he would like to visit the Maginot Line. "No, thank you," he replied, "I think I'll wait until I can see that and the Siegfried Line at the same time!" A few hours later the battle began that in five years time would make it possible for his prophetic whim to be gratified.

Self-censored reflections

29. 4. 40

I am now overwhelmed with the fruits of my travels and spend my time writing or trying to write concise minutes and resisting an inherent temptation to tinge my arguments and proposals with dramatic and irrelevant details. I cannot help feeling, that I am really the last person in the world to be doing this sort of thing. Communiqués, yes; but battling with importunate war correspondents on paper, no. However, here I am and I shall continue the good work until I am thrown out on my ear.

Thus was Sunday morning spent. My cycling colleague tried to lure me out for an afternoon ride. But the legs are not really themselves and the wind is still a bit short in the congested tubes. So I did not go. Instead, after lunch I went and watched a splendid football match between a French cavalry team and our own chaps. The field was in the park behind our mess. There was quite a decent crowd but I took my stand behind the French goal keeper in the hopes that he would put a performance like the man who does the turn on the music halls. I was disappointed; he was just a jolly good goal keeper. It was an excellent game and very well refereed by a corporal in our office who took on quite a new character in a splendid and most impressive blazer. We won, three goals to one, but it was a very even match.

2. 5. 40

Once again the Budget has got behindhand owing to extreme pressure of business. On the other hand business has so occupied the time that there is little news. All I can remember of the lighter moments of the last three days is a torrential rainstorm, a pleasant dinner with my Wing Commander followed by a cinema and an Ensa concert of doubtful quality.

On Monday I, or rather my faithful batman, moved my things to a new room in the attic of the same building. It is a pleasant little room with a nice big window and lots of cupboards, so that I have at last been able to unpack and to cease for the time being diving into a suitcase with the inevitable chaos which results from this odious practice. Being at the top of the house the room is a haven of peace and I no longer feel that I am sleeping on the platform of a busy terminus, I have sacrificed the use of a great mirror that was the feature of my last room. Now my little hand one with awful powers of magnification hangs on the wall; I find the sight of myself like a close up in a rather drab film in the early hours of the morning a little unnerving. But I sleep like a top and that is all one can expect.

Cobbles are death to shoe leather, consequently the time came when my shoes had to be repaired. To my astonishment they were superbly done by a little local cobbler. I always imagined that the people of France walked about on cardboard footwear. My shoes could not have been done better in Piccadilly. This is a great relief; I do love being properly shod.

Spring is here. The trees are sprouting, the market becomes richer in flowers and the haberdashers are displaying the white robes of candidates for confirmation. On Tuesday just as we were getting ready for lunch a torrential rainstorm broke over the town. I never saw anything like it. The streets ran rivers (which will do them no harm from a sanitary point of view) and the crossroads became great muddy lakes. But on the whole it is warmer and soon we ought to have more settled weather by all accounts. The result of this storm was that when I went to the market the next morning to get some anemones for the office, they all looked sadly battered and I had to content myself with some pink carnations and some vague white flowers. Somehow they don't really look right and give the office the air of an actresses dressing room.

In the evening I dined with my Wing Commander at M. Pellerin's hospitable café. He threw an excellent meal during which we discussed feverishly but without heat the relative merits of promotion by favouritism or seniority. I was all for the former and feel more convinced than ever about it since this excursion into service circles; he took the opposite view so the dinner was a great success and although we went to see a rather poor American film *(Golden Boy)* we picked up the argument again afterwards and mooned through the streets improving our themes all the way home.

Yesterday was an exhausting succession of crises. Certain steps I have had to take to regulate the hitherto fantastic antics of the war correspondents are likely to be the source of trouble. So I spent the day putting the case on paper and waiting for the enemy to deliver their attack. It did not materialise on this front so I suspect that they are assembling their forces on the home front. This has given me time to make my dispositions and to prepare to take arms against oceans of trouble if need be. The maddening thing is that at times like these our energies should be consumed in such pettiness.

Self-censored reflections

4. 5. 40

This morning I came down to breakfast to be greeted by the first salvo of the enemy's broadside. The Air Commodore in our mess got back from London last night and brought with him a copy of *Truth* which contained a bitter paragraph headed "R.A.F. Gags Press". The paragraph reproduced in garbled form the order which I issued on the 2nd so they had not let the grass grow under their feet. As usual it was a complete misrepresentation of the facts but it can be guaranteed to throw the requisite fuel on the fire. When I got to the office I heard that all the correspondents have now returned to England so I expect Fleet Street has been busily preparing for action. I see in *The Times* and also in *Truth* that some papers have behaved disgracefully over the rumours of the death of

Peter Fleming in Norway. I hope this expression of disgust developes. The sooner the public realise that the sole interest of the Press is to sell their wretched rags and to cut each others throats in the process, the better. All but the small minority are out for nothing but their own ends. They protest and whine if they think you are holding up the news and call heaven to witness that the public have the right to be told at once, but if you go one better and see that the news gets on the air the night before, they scream of injustice. Anyhow the decks are cleared for action and I am ready for all comers.

The day has been ominously quiet. I hoped we might have some action so that I could prove our ability to get out quicker and better news without the correspondents being here. The weather is very muggy and we had another quite severe thunderstorm yesterday; all this helps to promote an atmosphere of suspense.

Sunday: A lovely day. But, alas, although the sinews and vitality are all that could be wished for, I cannot go a-veloing. To start with I am duty officer, I am expecting a visit from my opposite number at G.H.Q. (needless to say a full Colonel but a charming one at that) and owing to the departure of the correspondents in their childish petulance I must be ready to hurl out swift and stirring news, should anything occur. So there it is. But I am somewhat consoled by a magnificent bouquet of lilac and tulips, price 3 francs, which I picked up in the market on my way to the office. The air is full of the clashing of bells calling the faithful to Mass and the birds are singing like mad.

7. 5. 40

Alas, Sunday did not turn out to be a day of joyous veloing. I had forgotten that I was Duty Officer and in addition to this not too onerous duty I had to entertain my opposite number from G.H.Q. It was a lovely day and I contrived to steer my guest into the sun on every possible occasion and in between times got a good deal of fresh air. He is a most amusing and energetic man and absolutely full out to give us all the support we need in the coming struggle.

He brought with him another senior staff officer whose brother was a fellow member of the Garrick but now, alas, is serving a prison sentence for manslaughter resulting from a car accident. I found myself sitting next to him at lunch and became obsessed with the need to avoid any subject relating to the law. When, unexpectedly, he asked me if I knew his brother I was immensely relieved as he was evidently pleased to talk about him. To the credit of the Committee weathering one of those stormy factional rows that from time to time have enlivened the Club, it decreed that imprisonment for manslaughter was not a breach of "conduct unbecoming a gentleman" that, according to the rules, would justify expulsion from the Club. When we parted I asked our guest to remember me kindly to his brother who was a bit of a card, quite good company but I always felt would land himself in trouble sooner or later.

I had a very quiet night as D.O., in fact so quiet and passed in such deep slumber that, the clerk having forgotten to call me at the usual early hour in order to get certain jobs done before my relief came on, I woke with a start at 8.30 and had to scramble into clothes and feverishly write out a report before it struck nine. However calm was restored by a gorgeous hot bath which my cunning batman weedled out of the geyser. Night duty especially in times of quiet is amply rewarded by the leisurely toilet which follows it.

The flies have been getting a bit above themselves lately. In an effort to deal with the situation I visited the local Woolworth and was sold, what do you think, an "attrape mouches" in other words a fly paper. It hangs above my head as I thump this machine. In quiet moments I lure the mouches onto its glutinous surface by singing this little quatrain, composed by myself in the original French.

> Mes petits mouches
> C'est une bonne bouche;
> Descendez s'il vous plait
> Sur mon papier.

It isn't really a quatrain; but no matter the results are terrific.

Monday was a fairly busy day. As yet the storm of the correspondents has not broken. The silence may or may not be of sinister import. The weather was rather muggy and threatening at first but in the afternoon the clouds vanished and towards evening it became altogether lovely. As a precaution we had brought our velos up after lunch. About six o'clock the call of the wild became irresistible so we sloped off and had the most lovely run through the country up on the hills nearby. It was really perfect. The peasants were still at work in the fields and here and there were the most Rowland Hilderish groups of threshing parties. The sun was getting low and as we came to each village the lighting effects were indescribably beautiful. Towards dusk we reached a village about five kilometres from here and fell into the Cafe de la Place and drank some cool light beer and watching the reeling departure of a conscript who had made the most copious farewell libations. He embraced all his friends in turn and bestowed profuse alcoholic kisses on all the company. We all left the cafe together and only the coldest English aloofness prevented my being decorated in the same manner. We had a grand spin down into our town, dined at another little cafe (not a patch on our friend Pellerin) whose proprietress told us tales of the German occupation in 1914, of how Sir John French and General Foch had both lunched there and how the Germans had been tricked by a wag who put up a road sign which grossly underestimated the distance to Paris. Altogether a very refreshing twilight and we both felt as though we had snatched a day's leave from a grudging and exacting war.

Tuesday. Another lovely day. This morning the *Daily Mail* and the *Telegraph,* as you probably saw, came out in the open with two articles which were the grossest misrepresentation of the truth. For the writing of those articles Mr. Noel Monk and Mr. Lawless (well named) should be disqualified from returning to France as correspondents. If the inaccuracies contained in a report of a letter which they have in front of them are any criterion of their qualifications as war correspondents they might just as well report our actions from a desk in Fleet Street or from the bar of their favourite pub. I only hope that someone in the Air Ministry deals with them thoroughly. My gauleiters' eyes were a-twinkle at the prospect of battle. After ruling the Arab and Jewish press in Palestine for several years the Monks of this world are small fry. Everyone who matters here stands firm. The situation is interesting and developments will be watched with immense interest. Today a whole bunch of correspondents are coming down from G.H.Q. and I am expecting some pertinent questions from them.

What with one thing and another I was kept at the office

until fairly late and after dinner I wandered off to the faded Louis Soi-disant-seize room with the Henri Quartre piano and had a nice time to myself with *La Fille avec les Cheveux du Lin* only it sounded more like tarred hemp.

Wednesday. A most interesting day. Giving the lie to the statements in the London papers that there were now no correspondents with the R.A.F. I corralled a dozen or so representing all the leading papers from elsewhere. They were to come to a meeting and were to hear a talk from the C in C on general subjects. Up until the last moment I suffered from jitters lest they should fail to turn up. I spent the morning getting everything on the top line. The advance guard turned up in good time but I had a few anxious minutes as the main body were late. However they all arrived at last. Amongst them was Evelyn Montague, representing the *Manchester Guardian*. I immediately introduced myself and we managed to have quite a bit of a gam before the meeting started. He is a first rate chap and altogether the correspondents were a far better type than those who have given us all the trouble. Question time came along and the subject of the departed journalists was tactfully introduced. The C in C gave a first rate and most reasonable explanation of the whole affair and the childishness and folly of their colleagues was laid bare and quickly recognised as such by all of them.

I was tremendously relieved when they went and it was realised by everyone that the meeting had been called at just the right time, for there had been some doubts expressed, and reasonably so, that it was a bit of a risk.

I had only just got back to the office and was breathing easily when I was sent for by my G/C. He told me that the C in C was delighted and that I had been promoted on the spot to F/L and that the other elevation would be accelerated! I must confess that I was thrilled, chiefly by the undisguised joy of the G/C who is passionately keen on the work of his section. He has been splendid throughout and always ready to back us up if he thinks we are right.

So all is well that ends well and it was worth being debagged to be raised in such dramatic circumstances. I think when this has all blown over things will be much easier and the correspondents if they behave will having nothing to complain about in the way of getting news.

I was kept fairly late at the office. As I had only been told of my promotion by the G/C I kept it to myself and will do so until it appears in orders. So there is no celebration. After dinner I picked up my Wing Cmdr. at his mess and we went for a long walk in the starlight. Somehow or other the sky seems to be much wider than at home. The Great Bear seemed so dwarfed that it was quite hard to find and the Pole Star was playing a very second fiddle to a dazzling Venus. I suppose this is due to the far greater scale of the landscape. The fervour of our arguments was almost as great as those at the same time going on in the House of Commons and the results just about as indefinite. I suppose all this open self criticism is good for the English soul and a prelude to great effort. I am only afraid that those foolish Germans may mistake it for dissension though if this tempted them to some miscalculation, it would not be a bad thing. Whatever may be said at home, experience out here has taught me that in all essentials we are on the top line and in complete agreement with the French.

On that bright and hopeful note I will close the budget and get it off before anything occurs to interrupt its passage home and, oh, that I could get in the envelope as well.

8. 5. 40

I have received an invitation to dine tonight with the C in C. It means a journey and by all accounts an excellent dinner. So I shall pack up a bit early, put on my best tunic with the single stripe and appear before him in decent humility. By the way, the promotion and debasement business has reached a wonderful pass. Determined to be in all things correct I decided to have my stripes removed in order that no one could point the finger of accusation at the V.R.'s as an unruly lot. The first tunic was debased, the second went to the camp tailor. It was returned with a rather impertinent message to the effect that he could not mess about with any more officers' tunics for a fortnight as he had so much other work to do. So here I am a Flight Lieut today, a Flying Officer tomorrow, bewildering to all but myself who at heart am an Air Marshal.

My visit to the C in C did not begin well. I was kept late at the office after all and a message asking my fellow guests to pick me up went astray so I got left behind. At last I got a car and dashed off at frightful speed, arriving about twenty minutes late. Dinner, however, had not begun. The guest of the evening, a colonel of the French Air Army had only just arrived. I never saw anyone with so many medals. His four rows included the Medaille Militarie, the M.C. and the D.F.C.; he appears to have been an ace of some distinction with a fine string of victories to his credit.

The C in C's house is an attractive place. I gather that it is the weekend resort of some magnate; the rooms are large and tall and the windows, which look out over a lovely valley, are large and wide in the Californian style. In fact the whole house reminded me vaguely of Beverly Hills. Dinner was excellent. I sat between two soldiers, one a sapper and the other a gunner, both of whom knew Kit[1] very well and spoke of him in glowing terms. I sat opposite the C in C and next to an Air Commodore who had been Air Attaché at Berlin during the same period as Captain Gould had been Naval Attaché. He was most interesting and seems to have been under no illusions as to their aims as early as '37. The C in C was an excellent host and the conversation did not hang fire. The French colonel spoke English very well though now and then almost out of politeness to the C in C, who likes to plunge a bit in French, he stuck to his own language.

After dinner we played an amusing variation of darts. Later a five franc note was stuck on the dart board and, having bought three darts at a franc a time, we were invited to win the five francs by hitting the note once. It was incredibly difficult though it looked a gift. The French Colonel won in the end, not only the five francs but all the pool as well, so everybody was delighted. By the time we had finished the game and talked for a bit it was midnight, so we listened to the news which was not very cheerful. South Norway has been evacuated and once more it looks as though command of the air wins every time. If only we had woken up to the fact sooner. Last war we went into it only just having grasped the importance of military training and this time we have plenty of leeway to make up in the air. And the maddening part is that we are by nature born airmen and given the stuff to use can see off these wretched Huns at any time. On the way home the soldiers discussed the news a bit gloomily and our mood was heightened by flashes of intermittent lightning and heavy thunder showers. All the same it had been a very amusing evening.

---

[1] My brother-in-law Brigadier C. G. Woolner, M.C.

43

IV

When the Luftwaffe and the Wehrmacht began their assault on the Netherlands and Luxembourg, the newspaper proprietors (responding, I later learned, to prompt action by Lord Beaverbrook) sent their correspondents back to their posts. They were by no means crestfallen and I was unrepentant. Rapidly the exercise of censorship got out of hand as the French Ministry of Information insisted on submission to its censors of all despatches. I did my best to mediate between the press officers and the bewildered bureaucrats in Paris who themselves were under constant pressure from schizophrenic politicians. Events moved so rapidly that my main pre-occupation was to provide A.I.6 with as accurate and timely reports of operations as I could muster. These were not subject to French censorship. Whether or not out of pique provoked by the hysterical accounts of their reporters of my obtuseness, several newspapers did not print our official communiqués. These may have been brief but they were to the point and, in so far as we could ensure, truthful. All too soon chaos and security precluded their composition or publication.

One morning I attended the Air Marshal's conference in our operations room. The maps showed that the British Army had reached their positions along the River Dyle in Belgium — complying with the strategy of General Georges but leaving behind them a line of defence in depth that they had been labouring to complete throughout the winter. Remarkably their advance had been unimpeded by the Luftwaffe. This, I suspect, prompted Ugly Barratt to comment grimly:

"Now they have got us where they want us. ..."

Then, as if to confirm his appreciation, we received news of the German thrust from the Ardennes across the river Meuse between Mezieres and Sedan. Near our headquarters was a small airfield that was the terminus of the Spitfires making their daily photographic survey of the German frontier. Now their pictures confirmed the rapid building of pontoon bridges at Mezieres and the massive movement of troops and tanks across them.

The next day Barratt, after inviting the dazed General Vuillemin to send French bombers in support of the operation, committed all his available bombers to destroy the bridges and

Jeanne d'Arc pleurerait . . .

Dans le discours qu'il a prononcé au début de l'année 1940, le cardinal Verdier, archevêque de Paris, s'adressant à tous les Français, a dit : « Amis de la paix ! Notre Jeanne d'Arc pleurerait, si elle voyait comme le sang français coule encore . . . » Jeanne d'Arc lutta et mourut pour la défense du sol sacré de la France contre les pirates anglais et une poignée de Français alléchés par les fausses promesses britanniques. Mais l'histoire a rendu justice à cette héroïne, elle a été mise au premier rang des grandes Femmes de France et l'église l'a canonisée.

Dans la grande guerre 1914/18 un million et demi de Français — sans compter l'armée coloniale — durent mourir pour l'Empire britannique. Ce sacrifice est vain, car de nouveau la France a dû courir aux armes pour l'insatiabilité du capitalisme anglais. Le nombre des morts de la dernière guerre a eu, entre autres effets désastreux pour la France, celui d'aggraver le problème angoissant de la dénatalité. Dans cette guerre mourra un nombre de Français encore bien plus grand qu'en 1914/18, car cette guerre — écoutez bien les discours de Mr. Daladier et de ses chefs anglais — doit être menée jusqu'à l'extermination.

Mais qui sera exterminé? Ce ne seront ni les banquiers qui réalisent les grands bénéfices de guerre ni ceux qui font les grands discours! Ce seront au contraire les jeunes ouvriers qui donneront leur sang, les paysans, la masse des petits rentiers, toute la population ouvrière de la France.

Ceux-là seront les victimes de 1940. Ces millions d'hommes sacrifiés n'engendreront plus de fils. Autant de générations qui manqueront à la France lorsque les chefs impérieux de la Grande-Bretagne lui imposeront dans 20 ou 30 ans une nouvelle guerre. Mais une guerre — même victorieuse — ne pourra jamais rendre la France plus forte. Elle ne peut que l'affaiblir. Réfléchissez un peu !

Il est impossible que l'on puisse vraiment gagner cette guerre, quand on n'a pas encore fini de supporter les conséquences de la guerre précédente. Contre cette vérité concrète, tous les beaux discours des ministres anglais, toutes les ressources de la dialectique politique, resteront inopérants.

En terminant son discours le cardinal Verdier disait : « Nous sommes prêts à supporter tous les sacrifices, afin de sauver, pour l'avenir, le noble sang de la France ».

Ici Monseigneur le cardinal se trompe. Par de tels sacrifices inutiles la France future sera un pays sans hommes, sans soldats, sans puissance et sans bonheur. Les Français ne doivent pas se laisser duper par des phraséologies politiques vides de sens. Le martyre des millions d'hommes serait inutile. La France ne peut vivre que quand ses hommes vivent. S'ils se sacrifient il ne restera, pour l'avenir, de la France qu'un symbole:

le Tombeau

Airborne Subversion. A leaflet showered on France by the Luftwaffe, April 1940.

harass the river crossing. Within an hour or two he had lost three quarters of his striking force in France. Twenty-eight French bombers, as obsolete as many of our own, were all that Vuillemin could muster; their pilots pressed home their attack with reckless gallantry. At the end of the day their group was reduced to one aircraft.

Soon, our Air Marshal had abandoned his advanced headquarters at Chauny, had lost all contact with the Air Component now in disarray as they began a withdrawal for which they were totally unprepared, and had no more than 30 serviceable bombers and less than half his fighter force — a graver mathematic in that it meant that Fighter Command had lost a quarter of its strength for home defence.

None of these desperate actions had hindered the onrush of Guderian and his tanks towards Arras and Boulogne. Though we did not know it at the time our headquarters and indeed all the groundlings of the Advanced Air Striking Force were saved from certain capture by an attack mounted near Rethel against the over-extended southern flank of the German advance by Colonel de Gaulle. Isolated and limited though it was, it deflected an enemy thrust towards Paris. As no provision had been made for transport in the event of an unimaginable retreat from Coulommiers, and as we had no means of defending ourselves on the ground, all but a very few of us would have been rounded up as prisoners.

In order to see how the Press Officers were faring I went to Rheims. There was little we could do to clarify the situation. Our airfields were now under constant attack by enemy bombers. At Panther[1] plans were already being made for withdrawal. While my opposite number there gave me the gist of the situation I looked down into the cellars below me where ancient employees of Moet et Chandon were going through their daily ritual of giving a bottle of champagne a half turn in its cradle. The next day a large bomb fell upon the main road above them, shattering thousands of bottles of what Peter Fleming unmockingly might have called "the precious fluid".

By this time, thanks to our Air Attaché, Air Commodore Douglas Colyer, who had ruthlessly commandeered a consignment of Dodge trucks ordered from America by the French army, we were no longer potential prisoners in Coulommiers. Our headquarters occupied a number of villas along the road that led from the town eastwards towards

[1] HQ. A.A.S.F.

Rheims. For days past I had watched from my office window the contagion of panic spreading through a demoralized population. At first a few cars with shields of mattresses on their roofs came down the road heading for Paris. As their numbers grew and their pace was slowed by large horse drawn farm wagons piled with household goods on which whole families were uncomfortably perched, the residents of the houses opposite our own came down and offered food and drink to the refugees in evident need of it. As the westward flowing flood slowly abated, one by one those houses were shuttered and abandoned as their infected owners took to their cars and followed in the wake of the uncontrolled evacuation. Lacking direction from their Government and distrusting its communiqués, those in the path of the German advance took to flight and so created chaos on the roads that were the lines of communication of the armies that should have defended them. Thus by dropping leaflets and by fifth column propaganda the invaders made the invaded their unwitting allies.

Our headquarters was preparing a withdrawal to Troyes. From the back gardens of our houses columns of smoke arose as our now useless files and registers were committed to the flames. I was ordered to Paris to maintain liaison between our Embassy and the B.A.F.F. and, if possible, the flow of official communiqués to the Air Ministry and the copy of the frustrated journalists through the tortuous channels of the French censorship that became increasingly obstructive as the military situation steadily deteriorated.

When I reported to Douglas Colyer, who throughout had never failed to appreciate the difficulties of my task, he directed me to an office in the Place de la Madelaine occupied by a cell of political warmongers directed by Sir Campbell Stuart from Woburn Abbey. He had no idea what it was up to other than providing leaflets to be dropped over Germany, clearly less effective than those showered by the Luftwaffe on French troops on the frontier depicting Joan of Arc weeping over her dead countrymen or licentious British soldiers seducing their abandoned wives and daughters. There I met the touring company of Stuart's melodramatic productions led by Paul Willert, a genuine francophile, capable of shattering one's most cherished illusions with a caustic wit mellowed by a wry smile. In support of him were Lord Strathallan his exact foil, sensitive, vulnerable to harsh realities and quite unfitted for skull-duggery however fatuous, and, in theatrical terms, menace personified by a shadowy figure to whom the others seemed to defer. His name was evidently a *nom d'espionage.* I was not surprised to hear, after the war, that he had been murdered by the cook on his yacht in the Mediterranean. I was allotted an office lately vacated by Noel Coward who earlier had been posted to New York to undertake another fanciful and, as it proved, abortive mission. He must have been well aware of the folly of sending him to Paris where nobody would take players seriously outside their stage doors.

I was all the more delighted when, soon after my arrival, my old friend Patrick Ryan came to Paris to attend to the clandestine radio operations that were probably the most practical weapons in the armoury of this now irrelevant political warfare. And on his heels came Hilary St. George Saunders to be our representative at the French Ministry of Information. So however futile our particular activities at this juncture may have become, Willert, Ryan, Saunders and myself were an effective outpost of the Garrick Club and made the most of the convivialities that even in the deepening twilight Paris could still nourish.

Self-censored reflections

10. 5. 40

A day that will undoubtedly go down to history. I appeared in orders as a Flight Lieut and Germany immediately recognised the threat by invading Holland and Belgium. You can imagine what a day it has been. It began at about 5.0 a.m. and has gone on ever since with one long rush. I have been doing what I can to help out other branches while I have been waiting for news, though you may well say in all conscience there is enough.

The dirty dogs. I must say my heart turned over when I heard that an air fight was in progress over Amsterdam. Quite apart from the wretched Amsterdammers I was haunted by the thought of a Heinkel falling among the Vermeers. And now on the wireless I hear that incendiary bombs have fallen on Canterbury. The consoling thought is the picture of Babs[1], armleted and determined attending her dug out. In spite of the terrific operations in progress, this little town remains calm and when at three o'clock I staggered off for lunch I found M.

[1] Margaret Babington, Steward of the Friends of Canterbury Cathedral.

Pellerin serene in his white apron only too willing to throw up a splendid and restoring confection. And we certainly needed it.

It really is almost intolerable. I am simply bursting with news but all of it is taboo, though you will read or hear almost as much as I could tell you anyway. We now have to walk about with tin hats and gas masks and if the heat continues or increases I shall perish of apoplexy walking up our hill. Of course the weather is quite lovely and the whole effect of spring a mockery of our folly — not ours perhaps, for the Boches have forever condemned themselves as unprincipled barbarians. Last night as I wandered off to my billet, very late, I saw the most lovely crescent moon. My pocket was full of French change which accumulates until it weights one down, but appears to have no real use when one is shopping, so I turned it like mad and wished like anything. The morning's news, I may say, was not the fulfillment I asked for, unless it can be said that the opening up of the war brings the end of it nearer.

12. 5. 40

The last three days have gone by so fast that they have all melted together in one long hectic rush and here we are on Sunday with an uncompleted Budget and a late one at that.

You can well imagine what it has been like. Information pouring in and constant readjustment of my own plans to meet changing conditions. However, touch wood, things seem to have straightened out today and I have everything under control. The best joke is that my renegade journalists have now returned but on my conditions and, though we will give them a very square deal, they now know exactly where they get off.

Bedtime is limited and when I am in my cot not always tranquil, for the mournful air raid siren appears to operate from directly under my pillow and could hardly be ignored by one deaf from birth. Meals are matters of chance but as usually happens adverse conditions produce their own charms and I have had some very cheerful meals in some of my colleagues' messes when time has been too short or too late for me to get back to my own.

This must all seem to be trivial rubbish when perhaps the most decisive battle of all time is being fought out elsewhere, but as you know, my lips are sealed and I must avoid any mention of affairs in case I get led on too far. Anxious as times are and hard as the work is, it is made very light because all the chaps I work with are so calm and cheerful. My leader is a tower of strength and it is my ambition to repay his help and consideration. I dream of waking up one morning and seeing a parachute jumper (preferably dressed as a woman) landing in the park nearby. It is too early for anyone to be about. I creep out and after stalking him for some time, I capture him with extreme guile, whole and in full possession of his gadgets and letters of credit. Marching him before me I appear in my leader's office and hand him over with my compliments.

I cannot bear to think of these wretched creatures falling about all over Holland but I expect the Dutch are not backward in treating them as they deserve to be treated when they are caught. I only pray that Holland emerges from the struggle without being razed to the ground but with these blasted aircraft falling apart all over the place, the odds are against it.

I must not spend any more time on this. The weather is lovely and the market this morning yielded me some beautiful red and white tulips and yellow daisies. So for all the confusion the office is not entirely bleak. I expect next week's Budget will be a bit scrappy but here goes this one. And so we live.

14. 5. 40

It is now nine o'clock on the second day of this incredible week. Outside the office it has been two days of glorious weather with the birds singing to beat the band and cool moonlight nights of intense quiet follow them. Inside the office a steady stream of news comes in of what may well be the most critical days we have ever had to face. Each bit of paper curtly announces some action which must have meant heroic gallantries to those who took part in it. It is quickly read, forgotten by the time another batch comes in, and relegated to a file. Occasionally a car goes by the window loaded with household goods of a refugee from some distant front. Comic things occur from time to time; for instance, at a most critical moment your letter arrived enclosing an invitation from Who's Who for any additions to the silly little list of past accomplishments for the coming year. The temptation to be facetious was almost irresistible; and yet it is comforting to know at a time like this that some overworked clerk is waiting anxiously to hear of any new recreations I may have taken up during the last few months.

Watching it all from some distance but having every scrap of information gives one such a vivid picture that it feels as though you are watching a slow motion film of two gigantic railway engines approaching one another with inevitable collision. Sometimes I can hardly believe I am really here. I have just picked up an old copy of the *National Geographic* in the Sergeants' room. In it there was a picture of the Oakland-San Francisco suspension bridge and the thought that I had crossed it only a few months ago seemed equally mad. The only realities are in your letters and they are fairly lapped up.

I was most interested in the bomb dropping affair near Canterbury. I can guess the target. The Dean must have swept about the Precincts glowing with self-righteousness.

Things are in such a state that any poor wretch who leaves an aircraft by parachute in extremity stands a good chance of being lynched by the infuriated populace wherever he is.

My journalists are behaving themselves pretty well but most of them are fairly obtuse and the antics of the B.B.C. man so unpredictable that I have to watch him like a lynx. You can give them rules to guide them and explain the reasons until you are black in the face, and they will go straight off and blow the gaff without turning a hair.

15. 5. 40

The general hurly burly and anxieties of today have been brightened by a farcical incident in which I have fortunately been able to play an important though lucky part. At lunch I was told by our mess secretary, who is one of those near Frenchmen who were found in England and commissioned as interpreters but whose interpreting is given through a barrage of alcoholic vapour, (what a parenthesis for a communiqué writer) that a girl had reported to the Mairie the following story.

At eleven o'clock or later last night a man had knocked on the door of the café at which she worked and lived, and in guttural tones had asked the way to another hotel in the town. He was dressed in a suspicious looking uniform and a hat or helmet of German style. Believing him to be a parachute jumper she shut the door in his face. The following morning she reported the incident to the gendarmerie and by the time I heard the story rumour had added the discovery of the parachute. But the girl's report was not received kindly by the authorities. The head of the police and the Mayor himself upbraided her for her lack of patriotism for her delay in reporting the incident and giving time for the wretch to escape. "Est que c'est la facon que vous defendrez la Patrie?" and so forth, with growing indignation until I gather the girl was chastened and alarmed at the position in which she found herself.

Later in the afternoon I happened to be in our central room and was regaling the gathered officers with this rich addition to our growing stock of parachute stories. A soldier who has recently joined us started to laugh. He declared that he was the man who had knocked at the door of the café and had asked the way to his hotel which, being a newcomer, he had lost. What a situation. Immediately my colleague of the Bath Club, a linguist and one whose work brings him close to the Gendarmerie, rang up and explained what had occurred and begged that the patriotism of the girl might no longer be in question. Profuse explanations and interchange of compliments and all was well. We only asked if the officer could be sent his parachute as a souvenir.

Such a silly incident is worth its weight in gold in the midst of so much staggering solemnity. This and the writing of a long despatch has kept me busy and amused and another day has whizzed by. Thank heaven (or heavens) the weather shows signs of breaking which means protection for our bomber boys and mud for the Huns, perhaps. I am knocking this off to the rumblings of distant thunder.

16. 5. 40

The weather did not break after all and I was woken up by distant gunfire to find a most gorgeous morning. So another hectic day began. During yesterday the stream of refugees in their pathetic cars steadily increased. On my way to the office I passed one that seemed to epitomise the whole sorry business. The roof of the car was piled high with bedding and bicycles. Inside it sat the driver, a grim tired looking man of about forty, beside him sat an old lady her face grey and the texture of marble. She sat rigidly upright staring in front of her though her eyes were still seeing the scenes she had so recently left. Behind them, wedged in between an indescribable welter of household goods was a little girl of about five, peering eagerly out of the window and obviously pleased and excited by so much unexpected travel.

Later in the day we saw a refugee lorry go by, full of beds with people asleep in them!

As though trying desperately to compete with the general situation, nature has filled the air with the most incredible flying beetles, the like of which I have never seen. They whizz by the window in hundreds and are busily engaged in eating the leaves off the very pleasant tree outside.

I may have said so before, but during the last days I have thought a great deal about the A.R.P. effort in England. Comic as it was at times, I do believe that it may contribute enormously to pulling us through. There is no doubt that no other country has anything to compare with it nor is there any doubt that a country well prepared and disciplined for this peculiarly unpleasant form of war has a very good chance of reducing its moral dangers. Whoever really got it going and officials like our Mr. Martin, the Sanitary Inspector (and I expect there are thousands like him) may be well rewarded for all their efforts. Bombing is robbed of half its terrors if sensible protection and adequate services are available. And, of course, it depends for its success on moral rather than material damage.

This days' addition to the budget looks quite idiotic as an account of the day's happenings; but there it is and the gaps can be filled in when we all meet again. It's very cheering to have a word now and again with A.I.6 and to hear the friendly voices of Ben and Felix.

20. 5. 40
HOTEL SCRIBE,
PARIS.

I am going to get this off to you together with a very scrappy Budget while the going is good. I don't know how or when it will reach you.

You will have gathered that I have been on the move. By listening and watching the map you can imagine the position in which we find ourselves. On Friday I was ordered to leave and to come here to take charge of the Paris situation. Bishop, my S.S.P.O.[1] turned up from nowhere and carried me off in his car. The S.P.O.'s were the last to leave a certain city, though perhaps the jackdaws are still there.

[1] Senior Service Press Officer.

52

The S.S.P.O.'s appearance really brought tears to the eyes. He is quite elderly and his uniform always looks rather like one which has been hastily thrown upon a super at Drury Lane. Now he has a tremendous revolver (and needs it). He wears it over his tunic but it insists upon falling over his hips with the result that the tunic bulges out above it and a little frill of skirt sticks out all around beneath it.

So armed we got here and the first thing I heard was a complaint from the A.P.M. about the despondent talk and gossip which the correspondents were handing out in the more popular bars of this city. So, like a skilled cow puncher, I rounded them all up, put them in one hotel, chose the best as a leader, put them under military discipline and started all over again. The same night I put out, through Ward of the B.B.C. who by the grace of God fell into my hands, a broadcast (particularly designed for the English news in French) which was designed to hearten the French people about dive bombing and the air menace generally.

I have parked myself in the outfit in which Noel Coward was the bright gem. But I found there a charming man, Lord Strathallan, quite young and very agreeable and another man who is a member of the Garrick, Paul Willert. They have all been most kind and helpful.

It has been the hell of a to do all round but things are straightening out. It is all very bewildering and the Germans new tactics seem to have knocked people a bit endways. I think that the French, at the moment, are like a man in the ring, easily his opponent's equal who, while taking things a bit calmly during the first round gets a tremendous whack on the nose which partially stuns him. That has been my impression during the last few days. In the meantime, the Mad Hitler has taken a pretty big bite out of the bread and butter.

Paris is very quiet and calm. I walked straight into an alerte and the streets emptied quietly and completely. It is a lovely city and perhaps has more character at a time like this. The Cabinet seems to change every five minutes. I am moving in such circles that I get pre-information of almost everything and it usually turns out to be right.

There is no doubt that there has been a lot of communism and defeatism and, as usual, politics seem to have undermined the efficiency of everything. But they seem to have to go through this stage always so I suppose we must not take the situation too seriously. I lunched yesterday with a man who had just left Knickerbocker, the American correspondent. In his opinion Roosevelt is already lagging behind public opinion as regards coming to our help. This, of course, must be by design, so that he can appear to have his hand forced. By jove, we can do with a little help.

I am very well — ashamedly so, seeing what our chaps have been through ...... Don't worry and remember that now the gun has gone off we are so much nearer the end.

21. 5. 40
c/o. AIR ATTACHE,
BRITISH EMBASSY, PARIS.

..... I hardly know what to say about these last strange days. I have really been to busy to think very much; only when alerts sound and suspend business does one think about the extraordinary situation. The general mood here, which of course goes up and down, is of the old Austrian type — the situation is desperate but not serious. I am in close touch myself and through other contacts with more or less formidable government circles (which change from day to day) and the general feeling is that those in the saddle are a good lot and are not likely to throw their hands in.

But it has been a tough and anxious week. I've been able to arrange one or two heartening broadcasts for the French about the R.A.F. and its work during the last few days. They are funny people the French; they know only of their army and they think only of our effort measured in army terms. So I hope that by stressing the magnificent work of our chaps they will realise what we have been doing.

Yesterday, while 16 Heinkels circled about in the sky above us, we fell into a fantastic discussion. My two colleagues are probably marked men if the Huns picked them up. We explored avenues of escape for them and for the office staff. It all seemed very unreal and mad.

A day or two later I was ordered to attend a conference at Coulommiers. When I reported to my Group Captain I found him planning a bombing operation against a target specified in a top secret signal from the Air Ministry. I arrived too late to hear the details and assumed that it was based on information from the Foreign Office which at that time was the post office of the secret service whose reports were distributed to the Services concerned. Among those present I recognised the stocky figure and pugnacious visage of Tubby Long who twenty-five years ago had been a friend and fellow pupil at the Central Flying School at Upavon. He was not a member of our staff and as he left the conference abruptly we greeted each other but briefly.

Soon after my return to Paris I began to receive peremptory signals from the Air Ministry where evidently consternation reigned as the result of sensational reports published in the press of the bombing of a secret target in France. How had the war correspondents known of this? I replied that, as I had only accidentally had pre-warning of the operation and of its apparent secrecy, I had judged it wise not to call attention to it by telling the censors to suppress any mention of it. Soon I discovered that one of the pilots engaged in that sortie had told Reuter's correspondent of its secret nature. Scenting a scoop the latter filed a despatch that began:

28 MAI 40
SPECIAL TARGET BOMBED EXHERE STOP TARGET
IN CLEARING AT NEARBY WHERE TRANSPORT
PLANES STOP DEFENDERS SURPRISED BOMBERS
OUTCAME CLOUD ETRAIN WHOLE STRING
BOMBS ON TARGET STOP RAID FOLLOWED
LONDON TIP THAT INTERESTING HAPPENINGS
PROBABLE AT TARGET PILOTS UNKNOWN STOP
BOMBERS GIVEN FIGHTER ESCORT WHICH
OFFHELD TWENTYFOUR MESSERCHMITTS
DURING ACTUAL BOMBING STOP

Naturally the national newspapers made the most of this agency report. The Air Ministry accepted my explanation, but I was puzzled by an apparently routine operation even if it had been a response to secret intelligence. Thirty-four years later I came to understand the cause of such a sharp and, indeed, fearful reaction from London. For an assignation between Field Marshal Goering and his generals in the field at a chateau behind the rapidly advancing front line may have been one of the first signals intercepted by the operation of the Ultra decoding apparatus which later Field Marshal Alexander described as adding a new dimension to war[1].

[1] See *The Ultra Secret.* E. W. Winterbotham. Weidenfeld and Nicolson. 1974.

Luckily in the heat of battle and the elation of victory, the suspicions of the enemy had not been aroused. And perhaps it gave the very few privy to the Ultra secret a pretext to limit the circulation of its intercepts to all but the Prime Minister and the Commanders-in-Chief of our forces on our several fronts.

On my return to Paris I had to deliver a communication from my Group Captain to the chief representative of our secret service in France. He was referred to as "D" and that *sotto voce*. Colyer directed me to his secret habitat in the Rue Charles Flocquet near the Eiffel Tower. I was genially if cautiously admitted by an Irishman, Green, perfectly cast as an Abbey Theatre style conspirator. I had not long to wait in the reception room before the comedy in which I had become a supernumerary actor began. I was joined by a man who, evidently regarding me with suspicion, with no exchange of courtesies sat down upon a sofa. Tactfully I took my stand with my back to him at the window. Then, to my delight, in its reflection I watched him rise, extract some papers from an inner pocket, and hurriedly stuff them under the seat of the sofa. He had barely regained his composure when I was ushered into the presence of D. I had to admit that his appearance as an *émincence-gris-d'espionage* was disappointing. Though dressed as a commander R.N.V.R. he was every inch a provincial bank manager and as such received me with guarded courtesy. Later I learned that he had earned preferment in his strange profession as a master of the art of forging documents.

I was anxious to deliver my message as quickly as possible and to be about my own equally, at this juncture, futile business. But D was not evidently pressed for time. He rang a bell on his desk and, on cue, an elderly colonel entered stage centre. D invited me to hear his latest penetration into enemy secrets. Thereupon the colonel hesitantly sight-construed a manual issued by the Wehrmacht on the use and maintenance of its 120 mm howitzer. Clearly nothing would deflect D from his desire that I should be entertained by this recitation. I began to feel like an English opera singer being instructed in the meaning of a recitative from Götterdämmerung. At last the colonel closed the manual and smiled expectantly as though anticipating the applause that his scholarly if tedious performance certainly deserved. At a nod from D he retired into the wings. After the disclosure of his latest acquisition, the matter I had to convey to D was evidently small beer. My interview had lasted so long that when Green saw me off the premises his affability implied that henceforth I would be *persona grata* should I wish to call again. Happily I never did so, for within a fortnight the house would be the headquarters of the Gestapo.

One of the first visitors to my office was Captain André Maurois seeking permission to visit units of the Advanced Air Striking Force. I was keenly aware of his integrity as a true patriot. Gladly I sent him on his way. No sooner had I done so than it was conveyed to me by those claiming to be in the know that he was not be trusted and that his political allegiances were suspect. This typified the atmosphere of suicidal intrigue that permeated the corridors of evaporating power during the last days before the reign of Germans was harshly imposed on the just and unjust Parisians alike. My faith in Maurois was not misplaced. The creator of Colonel Bramble went straight to the heart of the matter. He asked "Hank" More to let him read the squadron log book. The entry for May 10th began "A lovely day ..." In his first contribution to *Paris Soir* Maurois quoted this as evidence of the underlying lyricism of the Englishman at war — immutable since he had first recognised it in 1915 and indeed as Shakespeare had discerned it in his contemporaries. His pieces in *Paris Soir* portrayed the spirit and performance of our pilots with greater penetration and authenticity than those of any other journalist in France.

Each day brought its strange encounter. The most elegant of my visitors was Mrs. Reginald Fellowes. In happier times she had been a popular and influential hostess in London and Paris. Now, it appeared, she commanded the services of a French Radio network. She asked me to invite André Maurois to broadcast his impressions of the Royal Air Force in action. Immediately I consulted the most knowledgeable and level headed war correspondent, Edward Ward of the B.B.C., as to the wisdom of doing so, and together we briefed Maurois and presented Mrs. Fellowes with a *fait accompli*. In turn she asked if she could do me any such favour. She could indeed. I was by now convinced that the demoralization of France had been largely achieved by the Stuka dive-bombers striking terror into the hearts of soldiers and civilians alike. Experience had taught me that in fact the banshee shriek they emitted as they plummeted on their target was more demoralising than the blast of their bombs; and that as they flattened out they were vulnerable to any stalwart soldier armed with an automatic weapon. Here was an opportunity to try and counter the legend of their invincibility. Mrs. Fellowes agreed to put one of the studios of her radio station at my disposal. Ward readily agreed to collaborate in this attempt to cut the Stuka down to size. He spoke French fluently and was a master of the microphone. Together, the following evening, we went by appointment to Radio 57. A taciturn concierge admitted us with evident reluctance into a large dimly lit studio filled with shrouded orchestral instruments. Tersely he informed us that when the red light came on we would be on the air. In this surrealist setting Ward stood ready for action with our script. The signal was given and he began his broadcast. He was nearing the end of it when we realised that we should have time in hand. I had brought with me a copy of the *Illustrated London News* containing a stirring piece by Arthur Bryant. When our script ran out I handed this to my companion and he construed it with such *brio* that any listeners we might have had must have been rallied by it. Though, as we left the studio, we ruefully mocked at the futility of our performance, for the next day or two several Parisian newspapers printed columns culled from our radio improvisation.

Less agreeable was my confrontation with two equally socialite and beautiful ladies who had been working at a Church Army Hostel in Rheims. I had been told that they had arrived in Paris, pardonably distraught, and were alleging that the NAAFI units had been abandoned by the R.A.F., that several of their staff had been killed, and that their manager had declared that he would never serve the R.A.F. again. Before going to see them I asked our Provost Marshal in Paris to arrange a meeting with the NAAFI official in charge of its transport. He told me that there was no truth whatever in these stories and that he was prepared to issue a statement contradicting them. On hearing this the ladies, contrite and abashed, agreed to my suggestion that they should return to England immediately and do the best they could to repair the damage their careless talk may have done to the reputation of our airmen fighting against overwhelming odds.

I could not, alas, counter such insidious rumours with heroic truths. I could not, for instance, tell these gossips of the armament officer at Rheims who, under constant bombing attacks, had managed to load stores of poison gas, held in readiness to retaliate if the Germans used it, onto a commandeered goods train which took it safely to Nantes and so to England. Had he not succeeded in this gallant task or had the gas been released under bombardment the Germans might not have hesitated to use it with devastating effect on the beaches at Dunkerque.

On the morning of May 28th the waiter at the Hotel Scribe where I was quartered dumped my *petit-dejeuner* on the table by my bed and, flourishing *Le Matin* in my face, with melodramatic emphasis announced:

"Les Belges se rendent!"

From that moment I felt that the campaign, regardless of M. Renaud's passionate and optimistic exhortations, had lost all reality. My concerns seemed trivial against the background of our army's retreat and the long drawn out anxiety of its evacuation. The conditions governing my liaison with Eagle and Panther, now in more or less orderly retreat, and the care and control of the correspondents grew increasingly chaotic. The latter, to their credit, did their best to serve their newspapers by keeping in touch with our squadrons, but these were operating almost day to day from different airfields hard to find on the antiquated maps at our disposal. As the situation worsened the French censors became increasingly obstructive and, as communications began to break down, the transmission of copy was so long delayed as to render it un-newsworthy. Miraculously, as the Germans swept towards Boulogne, our lines to the Air Ministry were still open, thanks to the English girls operating our Exchange in Paris. The denouement was, perhaps, predictable. The doyen of the Press Officers, lost his head and had been persuaded by his service and civilian colleagues pursuing our elusive formations, to bypass the French censorship, to ignore my admittedly waning authority in Paris and to appoint his own censor and send the correspondent's copy in the official "bag" to the Air Ministry. The first I heard of this flagrant breach of standing orders was from Lionel Heald. When I reported it to Colyer he immediately told Panther that the bag was not to be used for such a purpose. I was pressed to order the delinquent Wing Commander home. As an officer his conduct certainly merited court martial. Yet feeling that his heart, as it were, was not in his military tunic and that he was subject to pressures beyond his endurance, I took no action and in the prevailing confusion his folly was happily forgotten.

V

Our units were now so out of touch with each other and with our Headquarters that, as I saw it, the only issue of importance was to ensure that the withdrawal of our remaining Air Forces in France was carried out under the smoke screen of security. Our bomber strength was withering away; our two fighter squadrons were still in action, usually against enemy formations four times their number, but the strain was telling on the pilots whose task remained to cover our retreat to the Atlantic ports. Roughly, throughout the campaign, they had destroyed twice as many enemy aircraft as they had lost. The German reaction to their skill and élan was slow, for the indoctrination of the young Luftwaffe pilots had been so thorough that a survivor from a Heinkel shot down by a Hurricane, when being interrogated, could only repeat like a parrot: "The Heinkel is faster than the Hurricane .... the Heinkel is faster than the Hurricane!"

Parisians were becoming accustomed to air raid sirens though as yet no bombs had been dropped upon the city. When, during an alert, from the window of my office I watched the crowd in the Place de la Madeleine nobody paid any attention to it. But, if a shower of rain fell, the girls in their pretty spring dresses ran panic stricken to the entrance of the metro.

Of all the thankless and futile duties by now undertaken by British officers in Paris that of attempting to approve or to censor the reports of our journalists to the satisfaction of the French Ministry of Information was the most exasperating. At the Hotel Louis le Grand where the Ministry conducted its frantic business, the fluctuating mood of its government — its expressions alternating between alarm and despondency laced with patriotic assurances of vainglorious hopes — made it impossible for them to define or to fulfill their responsibilities amid the prevailing chaos. Happily my colleague, the R.A.F.

The last R.A.F. convoy to embark from Brest, 16th June 1940.

SS 'Lady of Arran' sails from Brest.

The last of France
(long after Ford Madox Brown)

'SS Canterbury' overhauls 'Lady of Arran' on passage to Plymouth, June 16/17th
1940.

censor Flight Lieut Johnstone, carried on as best he could with exemplary calm and good humour that soothed our bewildered Press Officers who, in turn, mollified our frustrated journalists.

On Sunday June 3rd with the idea of giving us both a congenial break in our frantic routines, I invited him to lunch with me at the Pavilion Bleu in the leafy tranquility of the Bois de Boulogne. The sky was cloudless. We choose a table set in the shade of the trees outside the restaurant. In the midst of our meal I heard for the first time the distant throbbing drone of hundreds of unsynchronised aircraft engines. As it grew to a thunderous crescendo we looked up to see the sky scintillating with huge formations of bombers. The noise of their engines was overwhelmed by the deafening explosions of their bombs that fell with deadly accuracy on the Renault works at Billancourt, a few hundred yards away across the Seine. A near miss or two were uncomfortably close. We rose from our table and were astonished to see that all our fellow al-fresco lunchers had fled and were huddled together for protection beneath the glass canopy surrounding the restaurant — all but one semi-intoxicated Englishman who staggered towards us, flung open his jacket to reveal a row of medals and, like the Ancient Mariner, began to spin an incoherent yarn as to how he came by them. His maudlin monologue broke the tense silence that followed the end of the bombardment. He reeled away to accost a more appreciative audience among the crowd emerging from their fragile shelter. The unopposed bombers were lost to sight in the smoky haze that hung over their target.

The waiters, to their credit, imperturbably resumed their service with no concern, apparently, but to satisfy their patrons whose appetites were unimpared. Over coffee and remedial brandy, Johnstone and I discussed the implications of this long awaited attack and the probability that the end of our farcical Parisian endeavours was in sight.

That night the French Government declared Paris to be an open city and the next day left the capital for Tours. Our Embassy had to follow them. Only the Ministry of Information remained in the Hotel Louis le Grand to which I and my colleagues working there were anchored. It was not difficult to evade their censors in the general confusion. The American correspondent Knickerbocker succeeded in betraying the flight and destination of Reynaud and his cabinet. This naturally enraged all concerned, though no doubt the enemy were forewarned of their intentions. I was able to report the situation to A.I.6 and, thanks to Ben Travers, to my family, before I lost touch with them indefinitely.

For two days I had little to do but watch the smoke of burning oil tanks smudge the northern sky. Paul Willert had packed his fellow conspirators off to Tours so he and I still had access to the office. That evening I felt impelled to say farewell to Maurice Chevalier, for only a decade ago in Hollywood we had shared such happy times with Douglas Fairbanks and Mary Pickford as their weekend guests at Pickfair. The stage doorkeeper at the Folies Bergères, though eyeing an English officer with undisguised hostility engendered by the spreading legend of our desertion of France, reluctantly went to ask M. Chevalier if he would receive me. He returned and led me through narrow passages thronged with lightly clad shepherdesses now not very joyful but awed if not frightened by the dangers that threatened them. Luckily Chevalier was resting between his turns in the revue. He received me with touching friendliness but as one welcoming a ghost from a now irretrievable past. Behind the mask of his makeup I could detect with sympathy the fear of a great actor whose career, after years of labour and now at the peak of success, was in jeopardy.

It was, of course, not an occasion for reviving fond memories of an innocent age that had seemed so indestructible. His debonair charm had deserted him. Gravely he took my hand and accepted my condolences and the hopes I expressed that, as an artist, he would survive the impending catastrophe. So, as the curtain fell on Paris, I parted from the player who, more than any other ambassador, had represented the gaiety of France to millions of filmgoers throughout the world.

Next morning the stream of refugees in cars carapaced with mattresses thinned to a trickle. As the din of traffic dwindled Parisians stood in the streets listening to the thud of distant gunfire. It was time to be off but I could not leave until our staff at the Ministry of Information were on their way; they could not budge until their French colleagues had thrown up the sponge. I managed to telephone to my Group Captain at Troyes. To my relief he promised that a car would be sent to pick me up in the Place de la Madeleine before midnight. Many restaurants had closed but Viels was still open and there I shared a farewell meal with Paul Willert and Alexander Worth.

During the afternoon I became anxious. Unable to telephone, I went to the Hotel Louis le Grand to see how things were going. As I entered the hall I saw Hilary Saunders at the top of the palatial staircase, like a rock projecting from a river in spate as the French staff surged down it in precipitate flight. Striking, as he saw me, a Napoleonic pose, he declaimed:

"It's a rout, my dear boy, it's a rout!"

All was well, our staff was on its way to Tours.

After dinner I returned to the Place de la Madeleine and began my hopeful vigil sitting upon a bench near the flower stalls which had lent such colour to the view from my office window. There was an ominous quiet in this neighbourhood usually as thronged by night as by day. Even in the short cut I had taken through the Rue de Sevres the wraiths, who normally loomed from the pools of light under dim street lamps into the shadows murmuring husky invitations as they drifted by, were not abroad in this night of apprehension.

Paris had been declared an open city, that is to say open to the Germans. I wondered whether they or my rescuer would arrive first. I knew only too well how hazardous such journeys as his against the stream of refugees could be. I was no doubt under observation by the German agent who had probably kept watch on our office for weeks past.

As the time went by I tried to imagine my escape on foot, in uniform, and much too tall to be inconspicuous. Nor was I sufficiently glib in the language to pass myself off as a native. Perhaps I should make for the nearest harbour, steal a small boat and sail home. Certainly I had not enough money to bribe my way through the Germans who would soon be between me and the coast. Just about midnight a gallant member of our staff turned up in a very small Austin van. While we were loading my gear into it a lanky English officer approached us and asked for a lift. I could not refuse though I was daunted by his height. The only way to accommodate him was to put our luggage in the front seat and to clamber with him into the back where, like foetal twins in the womb, we were entwined throughout the long night journey — only stretching our cramped limbs when jams of tanks or refugees or air raid alerts brought us to a halt. We arrived at Troyes just before dawn.

Self-censored reflections

12. 6. 40
BLOIS

Somehow or other I must get a letter off to you today. The last three days have been a complete nightmare. On Monday the Air Attaché told me that the French were falling back to defend the Citadel of Paris and that I must leave as soon as I could. This was all very well but of course I had to get all my chaps away first. Although he and I knew that the French Ministry of Information would be off like scalded cats before dusk, up until noon they were doing a good deal of "boy stood on the burning deck" stuff. This meant that I had to arrange for transport for the others on spec and, if necessary, stay myself at the Ministry after they had gone in order to save R.A.F. face. Telephones were by this time most erratic. By six o'clock the transport which I had asked for had arrived; the lads pushed off and such a flap had developed at the Ministry that I was able to think about my own arrangements. I have the vaguest recollection of a hasty meal at a cafe near my office with Paul Willert and Worth of the *Manchester Guardian.* I remember asking for a sandwich and being abashed by getting a French loaf cut in half with a few pieces of ham in the middle; not an easy form of food to negotiate in the middle of the kind of conversations which the situation inspired.

Shortly after midnight, when I had almost given up hope, my transport arrived in the form of a small Austin van. It was driven by an heroic colleague from B.A.F.F.

It was a fantastic journey and it lasted until four in the morning. The roads were packed with refugees going South and convoys and tanks moving North. Indescribably eerie and whenever a block stopped the stream urgent and high pitched shouts expressed the anticipation of being strafed. This we fortunately avoided; why I can't imagine. The misery and pathos of the stream of refugees, now beginning to be swelled by the evacuation of the capital, was decently veiled by darkness. The roadsides were lined with cars which had been halted while their exhausted owners slept.

We reached our destination at dawn. Kind friends were waiting up for me and in a very short time I had put up my camp bed and was fast sleep.

..... So ends the Paris interlude. I cannot yet realise that within a few hours it will be the centre of a terrific struggle.

I spent the next day reporting here and there and getting an idea of the new dispositions. It was nice to see the chaps again but, as you can imagine, everyone was pretty hectic and there was not much time for small talk. The following morning I bagged a car (which my Group Captain has told me to stick to and to shoot anyone who tries to take it away!) and now I am rushing up and down Hornblower's river trying to sort out once more the tangled skein of press and censorship.

I really feel quite a campaigner now. I put up my camp bed when and where I can and eat food when it is obtainable. The shifting population makes eating a problem. They descend upon towns like unhappy locusts. There was no bread or milk obtainable yesterday morning in the town which I had graced for the night.

The refugees fill one with sorrow and sympathy. It is really dreadful to see and move with families crammed into cars piled high with mattresses and with bicycles tied all over them. Lorry loads of patient, hopeless peasants; waggons filled with household goods pulled by the owners' beloved horses with one or two more following behind. I have seen them outside farms being loaded with furniture and sacks of produce and then trudging off slowly and almost aimlessly, breaking the continuity of the motor traffic. The theme of this appalling symphony is the whining of engines and the blowing of strident horns. I have seen no one either excited or impatient. They wait in queues outside cafés for meals and stand around petrol pumps which never cease working until they run dry, waiting their turn for the transfusion of the life blood of their escape. As they move South they spread the infection of escape. First of all the villagers watch them apathetically as they pass, then they stand idly and begin to wonder about themselves and soon they are packing up and joining the stream.

I haven't the slightest idea where I shall end up. I have a roving commission which is absorbing and carries me all over the place. But at least I am busy and, I hope, being useful.

VI

In the morning my Group Captain told me that I was to take a Hotchkiss car with a driver and to keep Eagle, Panther and the British Embassy in touch with each other and at the same time to keep an eye on the French Ministry of Information if it had reached Tours and was in operation. My driver, Riley, an Australian, was just the man for the job — no nonsense about rank and entering fully into the spirit of our roving mission. For the first day I had with me a French officer, Colonel Thomas, our one time liaison with General Georges at Meaux. But now the General's Headquarters had gone none knew where, and with it my companion's occupation. He proved an entertaining fellow traveller as far as Tours where we hoped to find the French Government in being. He seemed indifferent to the fate of his country, determined only with justifiable pride to make our journey a *tour gastronomiques de force* — memorable for the superb lunch we shared at Amboise.

At Tours I found all confusion. Hilary had arrived there safely. The British Embassy was in a chateau near Clery. There I found Douglas Colyer established in a huge dovecote with his wireless unit operating on an upper floor. He told me that if I needed a bed at any time (or a floor for my valise) he could accommodate me in a nearby shooting lodge.

I found our Embassy in the chateau and in some disarray. The furniture was covered in dust sheets, the Ambassador was in the only bath and his staff embarrassingly unshaved. They complained that their sole communication with the outside world was through their Air Attaché and his wireless apparatus. Returning to Tours I told Hilary of their predicament. Thereupon he, with his imperturbable affrontery, found a French signals unit and took them to Clery to lay on telephone lines from there to the French Government. Naturally proud of his achievement he presented himself to the Ambassador who dressed him down severely for betraying his whereabouts.

I set out to find Panther and found the remnants of the Advanced Air Striking Force starting on the last lap of its retreat — bombers on their way home while Numbers 1 and 73 squadrons stayed as long as possible to cover our evacuation. I returned to Tours. The nearby airfield had been heavily bombed. The French Government, attributing this to Knickerbocker's betrayal, left hurriedly for Bordeaux followed by our Embassy and Hilary Saunders. The indignity of the flight of our diplomats had been mitigated by a little romantic relief. A young secretary had only recently returned with his bride to Paris on what our statesmen would now term a "working honeymoon". Thus there was general concern for the safety of the happy pair as they took the hazardous road to the south. None had cause to suspect that the bridegroom, Donald Maclean, was already far gone in treachery. Their hasty flight from France was but the beginning of a tragic journey that ended in the open prison of Soviet Russia where the unrepentant defector had leisure enough to take a long hard look at the ideology that he and so many of his intellectual contemporaries at Oxford and Cambridge had been persuaded to embrace by perverted missionaries of Communism.

Douglas Colyer was still in his dovecote. He directed me to the shooting lodge (evidently the love nest of the son of the noble owners of the chateau) where I found Paul Willert and Thomas Cadett, lately Paris correspondent of *The Times.* They invited Riley and myself to share their frugal meal. I dossed down on the floor, but not to sleep, for Cadett began an inspired recapitulation of French military ineptitudes and political treacheries that had led to the humiliation of a great nation. He paced up and down fulminating against his editor, Geoffrey Dawson, who had eliminated unpalatable truths from his despatches, and so deceived not only the British public but misguided foreign readers who believed that The Thunderer was the voice of the British Government. Weary as I was, I was spellbound by a tirade that I would remember for years to come.

I awoke from an all too brief nap to find that our hosts had already departed for Bordeaux. The previous evening Willert, assuming that I might reach England before he did, had entrusted to me an oilskin pouch, containing, he impressed upon me, most secret documents which he asked me to deliver to a named official at the Foreign Office. Now I found that very considerately he had left me a large can of petrol, knowing that we might find it hard to come by on our unpredictable peregrinations. Colyer had told me that my Air Marshal was on his way to Angers.

My first concern, however, was for a long suffering Johnstone at the French Ministry of Information who, having no R.A.F. transport, might be stranded in Tours when all but he had fled. Thither I returned to find the bridge over the Loire crammed with traffic stampeding southward. Leaving my car on the north bank, I began my search for Johnstone on foot. In due course I found him confronted by the locked doors of the house abandoned by the retreating Ministry. As we recrossed the bridge, I saw the staff of our Air Attaché driving slowly towards me. They told me, as I perched on their running board, that they were heading for Bordeaux and cheerfully urged me to follow them.

We returned to our lodging at Clery. Riley asked if, in view of our future contingencies, he could service the car. I decided, therefore, to spend the night there. At dawn the next day we set out in search of our headquarters, keeping to the north of the river.

We were half way to Angers when we were stopped on the outskirts of a village by civilians armed with shot guns. They were preparing to confront German motor-cycling troops reported to be heading in their direction. In the village we were welcomed by a dapper and undaunted cavalry subaltern and invited to join him for coffee and croissants outside a nearby café. He told us that he had set up machine gun posts covering the approaches to the villages from the north and declared his intention to delay the advance of the enemy as best he could. This was my first encounter with any semblance of local resistance. As we parted with friendly exhortations, I refrained from telling him that on our way from Tours we had seen no signs of the French army.

As we were nearing Angers, I happened to look back up a side road and through the gates of a drive leading to a large chateau with a number of R.A.F. vehicles parked outside it. We were in luck. In the chateau I found our Headquarters staff and my Group Captain in a state of agitation. When I told him of my breakfast companion's expectation of the imminent approach of the German Army, he ordered me (why me? I wondered) to go in and tell the Air Marshal. Ugly Barratt was his usual urbane self, and he received my intelligence with composure. Yet within half an hour the whole Headquarters was on the road to Nantes in a series of convoys, one of them led by myself and Riley in our Hotchkiss. Evidently my Group

Captain had been trying to dissuade Ugly from setting up an Headquarters and urging him to retreat towards Nantes and Brest but without avail.

About half way to Nantes, acting on the principle that the first duty of an officer is to see to the welfare of his men, on reaching a stretch of road well screened by trees, I stopped my convoy and told the men to take an half hour break to eat their lunch ration under cover. Hardly had they begun, when we were overtaken by another convoy led by my Group Captain. He stopped and upbraided me for my folly and ordered me to get along at once.

I had heard in Tours that the War Correspondents were heading for Nantes. So before I reached there I had decided that I must do what I could to ensure that they got away safely from France. Leaving my trucks on the outskirts of the town I began to search the area near the quays. By great good luck I caught sight of the correspondent of one of the "quality" newspapers with his wife in a side street. He told me that they had found a small cargo boat in the harbour and would soon be sailing for home. Was there, I asked, any room in her for his colleagues? He said that he was not interested in their escape but told me that I might find them in a nearby hotel. Evidently the cameraderie of Fleet Street was wearing thin. I ran them to earth, but they were not particularly pleased to see me and assured me that they would take their chance of getting a lift from a nearby airfield. Later I gathered that my concern for their escape earned me the soubriquet of Scoutmaster Irving.

Rejoining my convoy, I led the way to Brest. It was growing dark by the time we reached Vannes. In the square I saw a promising hotel-restaurant. My men had had nothing to eat since noon. The friendly proprietress was ready to provide supper of omelettes and coffee for them all. They were tucking into this when again my Group Captain interrupted our meal and in front of the men ticked me off for dereliction of dutiful flight from the enemy. Happily he hurried away leaving us to finish our supper in peace.

Not far beyond Vannes we overhauled a vehicle drawn up on the roadside. It had evidently broken down, bore no identification symbols, but was attended by an R.A.F. Squadron Leader and three sergeants. In the moonlight I recognised Tubby Long by the wart on his prognathous jaw. When I asked him if I could help him, he told me that the truck was full of radio equipment and that it was of the utmost importance that he should get it safely to England. I assumed that probably he was at the receiving end of a number of radio transmission sets left behind with agents in areas occupied by the enemy. Thinking it tactful to ask no questions, I offered to escort him to Brest if he could get the van running again, which as I spoke, the sergeant succeeded in doing. I suggested that if it broke down again we could transfer the most compromising equipment in it to my car which could accommodate all of us. He readily agreed to this. I handed over my convoy to a Flight Sergeant ordering him to report to the Group Captain when he reached Brest and to explain the reason for my absence. A few minutes later I took station behind Long's vehicle which was evidently not at its best. So we crawled to the outskirts of Quimper.

Before entering the town we drew up in the stillness of the moonlit night. With electric torches we studied the map in the hope of finding a way of avoiding it. Then, from the shadow of a nearby house, a lad clad in white shirt and shorts aproached us. He offered to guide us through the suburbs and across the River Odet by a bridge outside the town and thence onto the main road to Brest. Standing on the running board he did so and seeing us safely on our way he wished us good luck and vanished as angelically as he had first appeared. I felt then and still do that this was something of a supernatural encounter. Had I confided my suspicions to my tough companions, full of strange oaths and incipiently bearded like myself after two days and nights on the run, they would have laughed me to scorn. Yet who but a guardian angel would have so waylaid us at 2 o'clock on the morning of France's final capitulation.

Thereafter, Riley and I kept station as rearguard to Long's faultering van and, indeed, to the remaining British Air Forces in France, though in fact the only pursuer we feared that would inevitably overtake us was the dawn.

Thirty-five years later I found that my diagnosis of Tubby Long's engagements was incorrect. The Ultra Secret had at long last been revealed. Winterbotham, who had brought this miracle of radio espionage to fruition had sent two special liaison units, trained in the interpretation of its intercepts, to France — the first to Lord Gort, the second commanded by Tubby Long to Air Marshal Barratt. I had therefore been shepherding through that night men and equipment that, had they or their truck fallen into the hands of the enemy or of the by then hostile French authorities, might have aroused sufficient suspicions to jeopardize our use of the most effective secret weapon we possessed, and tipped the balance in our favour to win the long drawn out struggle, that, in spite of this incomparable advantage over the enemy, we did by a very narrow margain. So I learned why, perhaps, I was mentioned later in Barratt's despatches, for no other services of mine could have conceivably merited this.

The sun was well up when we reached the crossroads above Brest where the men of our Headquarters staff were standing, sitting or lying asleep in no sort of order. As soon as I arrived my Group Captain told me to take charge of the party while he and two of his staff officers, one of whom was his brother-in-law, went in search of a ship in the harbour in which we could embark for England.

Soon after he left two JU 88 German bombers evidently on reconnaissance flew inland from the direction of the harbour. The blue of our uniforms must have stood out on the bare ground on the hill top. I felt sure that we would soon be a target for dive bombers. As evidence of composure artfully assumed I shaved. Looking around I could see no cover but a well-trenched potato field. After an hour or more I began to wonder what had happened to our Group Captain. Four hours later another officer of the Intelligence Staff appeared from nowhere in a state of indignation and alarm. He had found another R.A.F. contingent wisely dispersed in a thickly wooded park, The Bastion, nearer the town under a Wing Commander Grierson, who, as a regular officer, was angered by the dilatory action of the Embarkation Officer. I thought it wise to get my men back into their lorries and drive to this refuge and to ask Grierson to take them under his command. Riley and I then set off to explore the harbour. On our way I took him to lunch, we had had no breakfast, at a nearby restaurant. It was full of French naval officers who did not disguise their contempt for their absconding allies.

At one quay we found alongside the *Lady of Arran,* a packet boat of the cross-channel type, with a smaller one of the same kind ahead of her. As I approached the latter, the Group Captain and his companions emerged rather sheepishly from a deckhouse. Evidently they had expected to be well clear of Brest by now. I told him what I had done and asked if I could take any orders to Wing Commander Grierson. I was told curtly that it was none of my business and was ordered to get aboard the vessel astern. With some compunction I obeyed the order. We drove the Hotchkiss to the end of a gangplank leading to an aperture in the ship's side. A friendly French officer came up to us and helped us unload our gear. I left my valise with bedding, winter wardrobe, books and a treasured martial greatcoat on the quayside. I rewarded our friend with the gift of the Hotchkiss. Riley went ahead with the rest of our gear including a tin box containing all the records of my tempestuous relationship with the Press. Just as I was entering the ship, a package flew past my head and burst against a bulkhead ahead of me, scattering its contents over Canadian soldiers carpeting the floor in attitudes of exhaustion that suggested a scene in the nether hell of Dante's Inferno. Gingerly I collected the scraps of paper that lay on or among the unconscious sleepers and returned them to Paul Willert's oilskin pouch. The French officer had found it on the back seat of car and mercifully had hurled it after us.

On deck I found the officers of the 12th Lancers. They had lost all their inadequate tanks. But each was as spick and span, shaven and polished as if ready for parade at their home barracks.

We sailed later that afternoon. The ship was piloted through the narrow entrance to the harbour at a snail's pace; magnetic mines had been dropped there earlier by those JU88's. Later I heard that No. 1 Squadron, still in protective action, had shot at least one of them down. Hence, perhaps, our immunity from attack at the crossroads. Once through the narrows we headed out to sea, preceded by the ship bearing my impetuous Group Captain home. To my unworthy amusement we rapidly overhauled her and left her astern. Later we were overtaken by the swifter *Canterbury* in which, I hoped, Grierson and our men were safely on their way.

All my shipmates expressed a sense of relief and hope following the news of the surrender of the French Government. Now, for better or worse, we would have to fend for ourselves. No doubt the French felt as bitterly of our withdrawal as we did of their half-hearted resistance and overt collaboration with the enemy which had left us in no doubt of their brilliant strategical and tactical exploitation of our inferiority in weapons, training and logistics.

As night fell I went below to lie on the iron springs of an upper berth above the Commander of the 12th Lancers Colonel Lumsden. Like my Patron Saint, I found no comfort on that grid iron. Thus I had plenty of time to contemplate the failure of my mission. I concluded that I had found no solution to the problem of Press censorship in the face of defeat — inevitable from the outset to those aware of the odds, military and political, against us but, perforce, incommunicable to the as yet undisciplined journalists.

I felt that my Uncle Teddie would have taken a lenient view of my conduct. Censorship can be, of necessity, the suppression of truth, for truth in war may be a strategic hazard. Who could gauge the effects of making the British people aware of the deficiencies and defeatism of our allies, of the inadequacy of our own Air Forces untrained to support an army, of the danger of leading them to suppose during the phoney war that the Luftwaffe was timidly avoiding confrontation with the R.A.F. If such news was to be denied the newspapers little remained to be reported but trivial gossip and deceptive half truths. Happily the relations between the Services and the Press would mature as victory slowly became assured. And when the liberation of Europe was at hand the results of Lionel Heald's patient efforts here and in the United States to this end justified his faith in the compatibility of security and the freedom of a responsible press.

I had upheld the main tenet of Lionel's doctrine. At the outset I had no difficulty in persuading my superiors that the communiqués issued by our Air Marshal were to be neither equivocal nor evasive. In the strenuous days ahead the morale of our air crews in the cause they fought for was sustained by the knowledge that they and the world at large were perfectly informed of the successes and failures of their operations and of the losses these entailed.

Normally I have an insatiable appetite for reading at any time when otherwise unoccupied. Bereft of reading matter, I was tempted to explore the contents of the oilskin package that I had so nearly left behind. It proved to be a vividly illustrated dossier on the peculiar sexual practices of a German minister or diplomat whose importance made him a target for attack by such squalid ammunition. I remembered how twenty years ago I had seen Pemberton Billing in the dock at the Old Bailey successfully exposing the seamier side of diplomatic relations and so warning the nation that statesmen, politicians and public servants who laid themselves open to blackmail of this kind were guilty of treason. Evidently, behind the courtesies of protocol, less squeamish practices were keeping us abreast with these sordid but necessary manoeuvres.

At the same time I contemplated what, had the ship been sunk and my body washed ashore, its lifeless arms still clutching the unopened package, would my grieving family have made of the sodden collection of pornographic photographs found among the effects of the deceased, faithful unto death.

The package, however, served me well. Disembarking at Plymouth I was hurried to a transit camp nearby where many inmates, I discovered, had been kept for several days. Immediately I sought out my Group Captain and told him of my urgent mission to the Foreign Office. Perhaps he was impressed less by this than by the fear that I might report his conduct that now I felt sure he regretted. He kept me close to him and so to the earliest train to London. As we parted at the portals of the Foreign Office, Whitehall around me suddenly dissolved into a swirl of mist and water. For the first time in my life I had nearly fainted from exhaustion. But I remained upright, the miasma cleared, and having been directed by a porter to a gloomy corridor on the first floor, was met by a supercilious young secretary who regarded my dishevelment with evident distaste — for I was still armed and helmeted having left all my ceremonial gear on the quayside at Brest. I handed him the package. The contents cannot have been unexpected, for he handled it with disdain and without a word of thanks returned to his office. So I had carried the nauseous news from the Place de la Madeleine to Whitehall.

I had a brief but warm welcome from my old office mates at the Air Ministry. Lionel was ready enough to let bygones be bygones as far as the misdemeanours of the Press Officers was concerned. He gave me 48 hours leave.

Rosalind, our daughter Pam and I had a joyous reunion over lunch at a Danish restaurant. They disguised their anxiety as to my whereabouts during the past ten days. Pam, in a uniform smarter than my own now plainly travel stained, was off duty from her teleprinter at the War Office.

Before going home with Rosalind to Greys, I returned to the Air Ministry and spent the afternoon writing a memorandum[1] in which I stressed in the now likely event of the Germans attempting an invasion of these islands, the importance of local defence by volunteers armed and trained, however crudely in the arts of sabotage. From what I had seen at close quarters, had such resistance been organised in France Rommel's blitzkrieg would have been brought to a standstill. The first and last sign of it had been in that village on the road to Angers. Without mentioning it to anybody, I sent this paper to Patrick Ryan at the B.B.C., asking him to forward it to Major Dallas Brooks, an evidently highly-placed Intelligence Officer whom I had met with him at dinner at Paris.

The following day Rosalind and I went to Winchester to put our son John's fears for me at rest. The College was playing its annual cricket match against Eton on such a summer day as only England can enjoy. As we stood in the shade watching the leisurely progress of the game I turned and saw that the man standing beside me was Douglas Evill.

Only a few days ago I had submitted to him at Troyes my last communiqué for his approval. He like myself must have been keenly aware of the incongruity of our rapid translation from the chaos of the defeat of France to the tranquility of this ancient college where both our boys were enjoying perhaps the last days of its centuries of cloistered quietness. Uppermost in both our minds was the grim prospect of another generation doomed to resist the Teutonic disruption of everything to which that summer afternoon gave an illusion of immutability.

---

[1] See Appendix B.

Part II
Repulse

This England never did, nor never shall sit at the proud foot of a conqueror.

William Shakespeare
King John

I

Returning from leave, on my way to the Air Ministry I sought an early lunch at the Garrick Club. The only occupant of the long table in the coffee room was Peter Fleming. He, too, had recently escaped from a similar if less decisive *débâcle* in Norway. From his half-mocking and self-deprecatory account of his adventures I felt that we shared a realistic concern as to the outcome of our now lonely challenge to the Nazis unless not only the nation but our depleted armies learned the lessons of the defeats that we had witnessed, took the measure of our formidable and resourceful enemies, and braced ourselves to resist invasion by tactics beyond the conception of conventional military minds.

Towards the end of our meal he suggested laconically that I might like to join him in organising an underground army in Kent and Sussex that, recruited from local volunteers, might effectively harrass the Germans if they gained a footing there. I readily agreed and briefly summarised the paper on this subject that I had written on my return. He told me that he had been invited to undertake this urgent task by General "Bulgey" Thorne, now G.O.C. of XII Corps that would have to defend these shores as best it could against an apparently invulnerable enemy now drunk with the heady wine of successive victories at comparatively little cost. So we parted on the understanding that, if a way could be found around Service protocol, I would report to the General and thence to Peter at his necessarily secret headquarters.

I went straight to Archie Boyle and Evelyn Baring. To my surprise they told me that they had received my report from Dallas Brooks, that there was an establishment for one R.A.F. Staff Officer at XII Corps, and that under that cover I could be best employed in accepting Peter's invitation. So, with their blessing, I bade farewell to Lionel Heald and proceeded, as we now put it, to Tunbridge Wells.

There I was greeted by the General's portly A.D.C. — but as a fellow theatrical rather than as an addition to his staff. For this officer was Henry Sherek, lately an impresario of promise but now as ardent a soldier as ever took the field. Our common love of the theatre made it easier for me to gain audience with the General on a matter that I could discuss with nobody else.

Bulgey Thorne was deeply concerned for the success of Peter's project which he had initiated and welcomed my participation in it. Our relationship became informal when I learned that our mutual friend, Harold Dearden, had been Medical Officer to the battalion of Grenadier Guards that Bulgey had commanded in the first world war. I was given a desk in an office of the Intelligence Staff which I shared with two military Air Liaison Officers — "Togs" Leaf and Mervyn Vernon, who had no more idea than myself of the text book duties we were to perform. It was, I thought, an ominous sign that, in the event of an invasion, at this level practically no provision had been made for air operations in immediate support of the army. Moreover, bearing in mind the instant capture of the impregnable fortress Eben Emael by German glider troops and the dive bombers that were on call by the Wehrmacht with devastating speed and precision, I had no doubt that if the forward airfields at Hawkinge and Lympe could be captured by air-borne troops as the Dutch and Belgian airfields had been, these would be rapidly reinforced by regular forces, light artillery and ammunition transported in JU52 aircraft designed for the purpose.

The south-eastern shores of our sea-girt isle are indented with platforms aproned by sandy beaches which invite invasion by maritime enemies. Over the centuries we developed a naval excellence that defeated or discouraged violations of our insularity. The last few months had shown how vulnerable our old fortress could be to enemies well trained to capture limited objectives and exploit their advantage with ruthless efficiency. Though our soldiers in retreat from France were unaware of it, the German air staff had taken the measure of the punishment our fighters had inflicted on the Luftwaffe attacking Dunkerque. For them, in their confident arrogance, this might not prove a deterrent; for us, it raised the undiminished morale of the Royal Air Force on which, for the time being, the fate of Europe utterly depended.

Such speculations were forgotten when I reported to Peter at his headquarters in a small farmhouse, The Garth was conveniently tucked into the foot of the densely wooded hillside above Godmersham. Already he had the organisation of what was then called XII Corps Observation Unit well in hand. His brother, Richard, had arrived from Scotland with a company of Lovat Scouts to train the bands we raised in the use of arms and in night operations. A whimsical and warlike Sapper, Michael Calvert, skilled in the use of the most modern explosive devices, would inspire and equip our volunteers to practice with relish the arts of sabotage. Already Royal Engineers, put at Peter's disposal by our General, were constructing well-hidden underground shelters at strategic points, similar in all respects to the one occupied by Peter Pan and Wendy in the Never-Never-Land designed by the painter William Nicholson, with entrances and vents concealed by tree trunks and other natural features and large enough to accommodate a dozen or so saboteurs and stocked with several weeks supply of food and ammunition.

The services I could render Peter were, thanks to my local knowledge, to find leaders to raise and command groups of volunteers and to procure for him, with the help of Boyle and Baring, R.A.F. wireless operators and the necessary equipment to keep him in constant touch with the General in any circumstances.

My first task was predictably easy. In Kent and Sussex the invaders would be harrassed by stouthearted countrymen bearing such names as Neame, Foreman, Day, Body and many others still enjoying the affection and respect of their neighbours as for many generations past. We were all working against very limited time. To this end, having enlisted the local patriarch (and none failed to respond to the challenge) I got from him a list of trustworthy men I could invite to join him. I allowed myself half an hour for each interview — ten minutes to sum up the temper and discretion of the man; ten minutes to explain that the proposition I was about to put to him must, for the sake of his fellow volunteers and his family, be a matter of the utmost secrecy and that betrayal of it would put his and their lives in jeopardy; ten minutes to describe the intensive training he would undergo while the Germans on the other side of the Channel were deploying their forces for the invasion, and the name of the local leader to whom immediately he should report.

By now the Home Guard was gaining strength so that, in effect, our recruits were an elite of that force whose comrades were totally unaware of their desperate commitment. For the most part they were farmers, gamekeepers, foresters and land-owners familiar with the natural features and conditions of the area where they worked. Consequently their training went forward rapidly as they in turn were able to contribute practical suggestions of value to their instructors. None of this would have been possible had they not, at the outset, been inspired by the authority and amiable bearing of Peter Fleming.

I was ten years older than Peter when, while I was staying with Tom and Ellinor Pellatt at their Durnford School,[1] I became aware of his effortless assumption of responsiblity as head boy enjoying the privilege of driving the donkey cart loaded with picnic provisions to its idyllic retreat at Dancing Ledge. Particularly vividly I remember years later meeting him in the foyer of the Carlton Hotel on his way to interview Von Ribbentrop for *The Times,* appearing to regard this as a grotesque assignment but one that I knew he would fulfil with a wit and perspicacity beyond his years. When by the happiest chance my brother-in-law bought Greys Court from Peter's mother, Mrs. Val Fleming, and my sister set about making it a perfect home for her four boys, he was building his own at Merrimoles on the neighbouring estate. Earlier I had designed the settings for Somerset Maugham's play *The Circle* in which his wife, Celia, had entranced London audiences; so one way and another we had associations that cemented the kind of easy going friendship that with studied nonchalance he preferred.

So, as the period of precious breathing space passed and in the evenings we mustered at The Garth to report progress and plan the next day's duties, I was able to observe through the lenses of near middle age the attitude of my younger companions to their present commitment. I have chosen the word commitment carefully for this was contrary to Peter's nature. He had, after all, to the delight of his readers recounted his Brazilian and other adventures with a sceptical and amused detachment that mocked the heroic overtones of earlier travellers' tales. He had served *The Times* well as correspondent and leader writer; but if its editor, Dawson, believed that he was grooming a possible successor, he was the more deceived in imagining that his *protégé* would commit himself to such enslavement. As soon as he left Oxford he had joined the reserve of officers in the Grenadier Guards; but neither at this nor any other time did he show any inclination for conventional regimental service. Nevertheless, it was plain to me that he was deeply and probably fatally committed to his

[1] See *The Precarious Crust*

present adventure. I felt he regarded this as the climacteric of his life. Yet he disguised so skilfully his own account of it, even from his godson who was to be his biographer, that in the eyes of many of his friends and of the critics of that book the extraordinary promise of his brilliant youth seemed never to have been fulfilled. I, on the other hand, was and remain convinced that Peter was consummating a vow to avenge his father the Germans had slain in the first war and his youngest brother Michael, who had died of wounds only a few weeks earlier as their prisoner in France. He had not deceived himself or his fellow saboteurs as to their slender chances of survival if the invasion transpired. What had justified his and our own conviction that it seemed inevitable?

As the R.A.F. Intelligence Officer at XII Corps Headquarters I received daily reports of the rapid redeployment of the Luftwaffe along the coast line that, like the "Half Moon" of the Spanish Armada, semi-encircled our island. Our sparsely held front from Caithness to Lands End was menaced by two German air fleets of bombers and fighters. These were mainly concentrated in the Pas de Calais. Meanwhile hundreds of barges that had been the traffic on the canals of Holland and Belgium were photographed by our Spitfires assembling in the channel ports of France from Dunkerque to Le Havre. Our interpreters had detected the modifications to their bluff bows to provide ramps for putting ashore their cargoes of men, tanks and ammunition. The Battle of Britain had not yet begun in earnest. The German dive bombers were harrassing our coastal shipping with the support of heavy artillery mounted above the narrows of the Channel on Cap Gris Nez. Our General had been informed by the Admiralty that, if the Germans attempted a *coup-de-main* on the Kentish Coast immediately, owing to the number of destroyers lost or in dock following the evacuation from Dunkerque, he could not count on naval support for at least ten days. I kept Peter up to date on all such information.

Meanwhile as we recruited and began the intensive training of our volunteers he could not fail to assess the scarcity and inadequacies of the troops at Bulgey Thorne's disposal. Even to me, as I quartered the area, the absence of artillery or armoured vehicles was only too apparent. One day I found Colonel "Boy" Browning with a company of Grenadier Guards wired into the village of Sarre with less exhaustible supplies of its famous cherry brandy than of men and ammunition — the only strong point in Thanet and supposedly responsible for the defence of the key airfield at Manston. Bulgey, very much aware of the need to conceal our weakness and to sustain civilian morale, ordered the hasty construction of "pill boxes", at strategic points. These, perforce, were built of bricks and were no more than impressive stage properties that one shell from an 88 mm gun would have demolished, as anyone can verify today who comes upon such weathered relics while rambling on the Romney Marsh. The only mobile and partially armoured reserve at the General's disposal was an independent Brigade of Guards stationed at Croydon under the command of another old Dunfordian, Pat Bradshaw. My wonder and admiration for the mystique and professional zeal of the Brigade, that perhaps blinds us to the perfection of its military prowess by the elegance and panache of its public performances, was excited by an invitation, at this very time, to take part at their headquarters in a paper exercise on the strategic and practical possibilites of capturing the Cherbourg peninsular *with air support*. As I made my inadequate contribution to this discussion I recognised in the front row a young Sapper officer — the son of an old friend whom I had known since he was a child. He listened with rapt attention. Four years later almost to a day, he was killed in action near the village of Ranville with the 6th Airborne Division stubbornly holding the left flank of the 8th Army after D Day.

I have perhaps laboured the point of conjectures long past. I feel in honour bound to do so because I believe that as this crisis receded the effect of anticlimax on Peter's character was profound. At peace with himself in the immediate prospect of death in action defending his country and freedom with innate devotion, a new and almost unwelcome lease of life left him restless and without ambitions common to men of his quality and talent. Thenceforward, this Celtic D'Artagnan (as Lady Violet Milner dubbed him) cultivated a pose conveying the impression that he regarded his occupations as soldier, author and landowner as something of a lark. None who responded to his leadership at The Garth would have been deceived by this disguise. Certainly, though he affected a contempt for an enemy he despised but never underrated, his seriousness of avenging purpose was, like Hamlet's, never in doubt.

As the Battle of Britain intensified, other duties limited my visits to The Garth and further participation in Peter's strenuous daily exercises. My last fling was the acceptance of a challenge by Peter to guide him and a small armed party from Godmersham to Whitstable avoiding all roads but the crossing of the highway from Canterbury to Faversham. This was a crow's flight of fifteen miles. For a normally sedentary forty-three year old uncertainly marching under cover of hedgerows, copses and woodlands, it was, as Peter I think meant it to be, a trial of my own strength and bump of location as much as a tactical exercise for his partisans. All, however, went well. As we ate our pack lunches sitting on a wall in the garden of our abandoned windmill home my aching feet were forgotten in contemplation of the happy years that Rosalind and I and our children had snatched in the now rapidly receding truce in hostilities to which my generation seemed condemned.

Later Peter invited me to witness proof of the prowess of what he now styled his Auxiliary Units. Not far from Wye the headquarters of a territorial division were in a moderately stately home. Without prior warning, Peter planned to lead a night attack upon it. All went without a hitch — sentries were easily surprised and overpowered, night duty staff held at knife and pistol point, booby traps set and a bomb with a simulated acid time fuse planted under the G.O.C.'s very desk. The following morning the justifiably irate General summoned us to an inquest on the night's work. We met on the spacious terrace of the house overlooking a formal garden centred on an ornate fountain in a placid pool. The General's indignation fanned his critique into a blazing tirade, condemning the affair as an impertinent folly and totally unrealistic in terms of a military exercise. At that moment he was interrupted by a loud explosion when, to our delight, the disintegrating fountain soared upward in a cloud of spray. Calvert had not denied himself the pleasure of demonstrating his destructive art in the medium of plastic explosive with genuine time fuses. Honour was satisfied and any official protest by the General was smothered by the exigencies of secrecy.

So honourably was this secret kept that a few months later General Sir Bernard Paget, G.O.C. of the newly formed South Eastern Command to which I had been translated, sent for me. He understood that I was, for some extraordinary reason, the only officer who could explain to him how arms, ammunition and rations sufficient to sustain a force of 500 men for six months had been drawn from the command depots in the area without apparent authority and unreceipted. Peter was by that time on active service in the Middle East. The General was deeply impressed by the explanation I gave him and thereafter kept a friendly eye upon his Auxiliary Units. For months to come Sappers would be recovering uncharted milk-churns filled with gelignite that Calvert had hurriedly planted under road and river bridges in the path of the enemy's advance from the coast that would later be blown if necessary after dark by his graduates in detonation.

II

My R.A.F. duties were various and curious. They included the examination of crashed German aircraft and reporting modifications to armour plated protection for their air-crews, nursing a fellow Intelligence officer in danger of a nervous breakdown due to close confinement in a lodging house in Tunbridge Wells with a German pilot who, as a skilled and amenable engineer, spent his days reporting all he knew of the organisation and equipment of the Luftwaffe and could only be taken out for exercise by night, rescuing fighter pilots tangled in tree tops by their parachutes, and trying to reconcile our soldiers and airmen whose hostility towards each other now and again exploded in brawls when they confronted each other in pubs and night clubs. To grapple with this and with security problems the Air Ministry had hastily organised its own police force. In order that its authority and terms of reference should be clearly defined, I promoted a conference between representatives of the R.A.F. and military police and security forces in the Town Hall at Tunbridge Wells. All went well until an obtuse officer of M.I.5, whom even Dr. Watson would have detected as late of the Indian Police, claimed to have the prerogative in almost every duty that was to be assigned to his R.A.F. colleagues. Although the meeting ended in confusion, I was able to inform his superior, Kenneth Younger, of the rift in our security lute which, thanks to his intervention, was soon played upon in inter-service harmony.

Two incidents remain memorable. I was in search of a German bomber reported to have crashed near Ashdown Forest. On my way I found a farm with its barns ablaze and in the yard the farmer and his wife weeping for the loss of their son killed by a futile bomb. Leaving them inconsolable, I found the wreckage of an ME110 in the smoking pit it had gouged out of a neighbouring field. The only human remains I could identify were five booted legs. This was signficant because normally these aircraft carried a crew of two — it was conceivable, therefore, that some high-ranking Luftwaffe officer had been on this sortie. While I was considering this a lorry was driven into the field. From it emerged an army chaplain followed by the driver and his mate bearing a brass bound coffin worthier of the dead farm lad than of his murderers. I suggested to the indignant priest that they should be buried by filling in the grave they had dug for themselves. Later I thought that this display of archaic chivalry towards a dead foe was totally irrelevant. To compare the German armed forces with our own was dangerous nonsense. The airmen whose bodies were to be interred with such reverence were the willing servants of a regime that had rehearsed its tactics by bombing Warsaw and Rotterdam under a Dictator who was already the architect of the gas chambers. Our fighter pilots had little fellow feeling for the enemy they were so desperately holding at bay. Until we as a nation squarely faced the prospect of defeat by ruthless forces of evil our survival, let alone the liberation of Europe, was uncertain.

Another incident was of historic significance. I received a message from Colonel Macnamara, commanding a detachment of London Irish, asking me to come immediately to his headquarters at Mount Ephraim near Faversham. He had just fought the last action against a foreign foe on English soil since the abortive invasion of South Wales by the French in 1792. An hour or so earlier a JU88 had made a forced landing more or less intact on Graveney marshes about half a mile from the sea wall behind which not so long ago I had crouched at dawn waiting for the wild duck homing from their feeding ground at low tide. Half a dozen of his men were posted at the Sportsman Inn where the coast road turns sharply south for Faversham. When they saw the aircraft land on its belly, they buckled on their equipment preparing for a leisurely rounding up of the crew. Between them and their objective the marshes were gridded with dykes. They had scarcely left the cover of the inn when they were greeted by bursts of machine gun fire. The Germans had taken up a posture of defence. Retiring to the inn our soldiers reported the situation to their Colonel who soon joined them with reinforcements and organised a text book plan of attack. Although under heavy fire, as his left and right flank made feint attacks, the Colonel led his centre in a dash that took the enemy by surprise, his batman in the assault shooting off the ear of one of the prisoners.

When I reached Mount Ephraim the Colonel took me to the room where they were held for the time being. Alas, I knew no German so I could not interrogate them before the arrival of an officer from M.I.9. All three affected surly arrogance. I remarked that the man with his head bandaged typified the fanatical and unregenerate Nazi. As it happened he was the only one who carried a copy of the New Testament in his pocket. Which, I wondered, of his appearances was deceptive.

Returning to General Thorne's headquarters I rang up Lionel Heald and asked him to persuade the Air Staff to send a signal to the General congratulating Colonel Macnamara and his men on their victory in this minimal but historic action. There was no response. Another opportunity to promote harmony between the R.A.F. and the Army had been lost.

One day my colleagues Leaf and Vernon took me to Hever Castle to lunch with Lady Violet Astor who had welcomed their suggestion that I should join them. I had, in fact, never heard of Hever Castle, and the only Astor whose name was familiar to me was that of Nancy, wife of Lord Waldorf Astor, and then only because she, as a Member of Parliament, seemed to be carrying the torch of the role of women in public affairs lit by my mother and her fellow pioneers before the first war. I had I suppose heard from our old friend, Harold Child, deputy dramatic critic of *The Times* and Bruce Ingram's right hand man on the Literary Supplement, of Major Astor, Chief Proprietor at Printing House Square.

Violet and John Astor became our close and life long friends. Just as we rarely recapture the impact of our first viewing of a well-loved picture, so familiarity is apt to blur the image that quickens our affections for true friends at first encounters such as this which, in the context of my life, had unforeseen consequences.

Violet's blue eyes, which as depicted by de Lazlo were inherited from her father, Lord Minto, were the media of her expression that she used to great effect. They invited sympathy, blunted sharply perceptive comments on those who earned her strictures, and with an almost imperceptible glance signalled her disapproval of a remark that offended her inborn sense of propriety or presumed upon the good nature that she regarded as prerequisite to good manners. Occasionally her assumption of naivety led one to suspect her strict adherence to the rules of behaviour she espoused. Once, when her weekend guests in the drawing room at Hever were discussing a recently published book of travel by a lady of their acquaintance, she astonished them by remarking: "Of course, you know that she murdered her husband!" Later, when I reminded her that a recent libel action had been won against a hostess whose dinner table conversations had been reported by a guest and expressed my concern for her indiscretion, she turned her blue lamps of innocence upon me and pleaded: "But she did, didn't she?"

At first meeting I was deeply impressed by her composure. This, without doubt, was the outward sign of moral courage, for she was not naturally self-assured. It was a protective instinct she had, as it were, developed in adversity. Her father was one of the few aristocrats of his time to whom privilege entailed the obligation to serve the Crown, that is to say his country. She had spent her formative years in Government House, Ottawa, and her adolescence as his constant and treasured companion during his Vice-sovereignty in India. At that time discontent prevailed throughout the dominion and assassination was its expression. Bombs had been thrown at her parents driving in their carriage, luckily mistimed. Yet her mother recorded at the time of her first marriage that she had never seen a bride "so composed on her wedding day". Violet was well aware of the risks of being driven with her father in an open carriage to the cathedral, though not that a bomb had already been found among the flowers adorning it.

Harsher tests of composure lay ahead. Five years later her beloved husband, Lord Charles Mercer Nairne, was killed in action leaving her with two children; and of the thirty officers on her father's staff who had been her companions at sport and partners at vice-regal balls ten would meet the same fate.

When on social duty she could assume an almost intimidating decorum. But *amour-propre* was not her first love. She was a tom-boy when, as a teenager, she won the Calcutta Steeplechase on one of her fathers' horses. Perhaps the shocks and restraints that life would impose upon her naturally extrovert nature generated inner tensions of which only those very close to her were aware.

Thereafter I called several times at Hever on my way back to Tunbridge Wells after visits to the extremities of my parish in Sussex. Usually I found her alone in her moated castle; but for her down-to-earth attitude to the battle raging overhead her isolation might have inspired Tennysonian sympathies. Once I found her undismayed by a bomb that had burst only a few yards from her drawing room, regretting only the topiaried yew-tree it had demolished. Later we supped together, dwarfed by the emptiness of the great banqueting hall, to the baneful whine of falling bombs — not very near but their discord curiously amplified by the exponential horn of the Tudor chimney expanding to the great open hearth. Though she never expressed it, I became aware of her only fear — that of a mother with four sons at risk, in this second calamity that threatened all she cherished.

III

One of my journeys westward was in response to an urgent message from a military unit based at Lancing College. Above, the battle of Britain was at its height; below, a bumper harvest was being reaped under blue skies laced with vapour trails. The College was the headquarters of what then passed for an armoured brigade, equipped for the most part with commercial vehicles hastily plated with sheets of iron loop-holed for small arms fire. The Intelligence Officer was Gerald Gundry, a fox-hunting man famous in the shires and M.F.H. to be. Troopers of the 17th Lancers kept constant watch from observation posts on the downs. One of these on Steep Down overlooking a cluster of barns in a hollow, reported that shortly before dawn a Lysander aircraft had circled the area, swooped low over the buildings and dropped a package. Five minutes later a black limousine with a white roof drove up the track leading to the Steyning-Shoreham road. From half a mile away three men were seen to leave the car, hurriedly search the area, retrieve the package and drive off in the direction from which they had come. The operation was repeated the next morning. I interrogated individually the troopers who had witnessed this, purposefully affecting scepticism. But I failed to find a loophole in their evidence which tallied in every detail. Moreover I knew that the enemy had captured several Lysanders during the campaign in France.

I reported all this to my R.A.F. superiors at G.H.Q. Home Forces. It was agreed that a Wing Commander Kaye should join me and that together we should keep a dawn watch from a concealed position on the track the car had followed. Marcus Kaye proved to be the best of company and, as it turned out, we would be working close together for the rest of the war. He was the son of the Headmaster of one of the biggest Jewish schools in London. His manner and appearance was Chaplinesque. An R.F.C. pilot in the first war, he had been shot down and captured. Though he had managed to escape several times, the Keystone Cops of Germany always recaptured and punished him, but like Charlie, his cocky and indomitable spirit had never been broken. Before we began our watch we arranged with Fighter Command that all British aircraft would be kept out of the area. Meanwhile the C.I.D. in Brighton were co-operating in every possible way to follow such clues as I had been able to give them.

On our first visit to Steyning before we began our vigil, we visited the local Observer Corps to make certain that the orders from Fighter Command had been circulated. To their credit, the Observers on duty were suspicious of us and in no time at all we were arrested and imprisoned in a nearby police station. Before long, however, our friend Squadron Leader McEvoy, representing Flighter Command at the Air Ministry, bailed us out. Our vigils, however, proved fruitless. All the troops had to report were a series of radio intercepts from German aircraft in the near vicinity that to us were unintelligible. So the hours we spent together in ideal surroundings as the sun gilded the vast fields of corn around us served no purpose but to discover our mutual philosophical and political convictions and to cement a long-standing friendship.

Marcus returned to his headquarters. I decided to continue the watch for a dawn or two. Returning along the track for the last time, as I reached its junction with the main road a car identical to the one described by the troopers coming from the direction of Steyning was just about to turn off towards me. I held my course and forced it to back on to the main road and so kept in the lead. Though I was armed, it had been impressed upon me that I had no powers of arrest and must call upon the Field Security Police, with whom I was in close contact, to take any such necessary action. I knew that sentries were posted on the Shoreham end of the bridge over the estuary of the River Adur. I calculated that if I reached the post the car behind me would be brought to a standstill and that the sentries would hold it there until the Military Police arrived. To my dismay, as I turned towards the bridge, the car stopped for a moment and then continued along the road that I had not realised led off to Worthing. So my dutiful observance of protocol had, perhaps, ruined the chance of arresting the conspirators. For the number of the car which I had written on my map proved to be a fake one — in fact that of a two seater owned by a woman doctor in London.

Later I was summoned to a meeting at Scotland Yard. There I found representatives of the Special Branch, M.I.5 and the Air Ministry. I was grilled even more severely than I had cross-examined the troopers, so much so that by the end of the interview I felt that I was under greater suspicion than the circumstances that had brought me there. I left feeling deeply frustrated and that no action would be taken to investigate what Kaye and I were convinced was a line of communication between the Nazis and an underground subversive group in England — a kind of fifth column that I had seen so successfully employed in France.

After lunching at the Garrick Club I met in Garrick Street of all men, Tubby Long. I told him of the affair in detail and of my resentment of the negative attitude of the meeting at Scotland Yard. He listened patiently, a taciturn realist punctuating my narration with grunts of appreciation or surprise. His only comment was: "I shall take you to see Winterbotham at once". The name meant nothing to me. He led me to a house in Queen Anne's Gate to which apparently he had right of entry. We climbed the stairs to the top landing. By some unseen agency a panel of the papered wall opened to reveal a door. He asked me to wait a minute. For a moment the scene recalled the farcical performance at "D's" *ménage* in the Rue Charles Flocquet. This was dispelled when I found myself alone with a robust and friendly man of about my own age in the uniform of a Wing Commander. His manner was courteous and, though modest, inspired trust in his ability to circumvent the tortuous channels of service bureaucracy. He heard me out with sympathetic attention, showing particular interest in the German radio signals picked up by the signallers at Lancing College. He dismissed almost apologetically my inquisition at Scotland Yard as of no account. He thanked me for the information I had given him and assured me that all necessary steps would be taken to deal with the situation that he appeared to take seriously. I left him confident that the matter was now out of my hands and in those of a man capable and willing to follow it up.

I felt that I should inform Archie Boyle and Evelyn Baring of what I had done. When, in their office at the Air Ministry, I told them of my visit to Winterbotham, Evelyn sprang from his chair and locked the door. Then Boyle warned me, with severity, never to mention that officer's name again. Nor did I, until years later I was discussing this affair with Douglas Colyer, assuming that as Air Attaché in Paris he would have known of Winterbotham's activities. I found that he too had no idea of their nature. Indeed he was as surprised as I was to discover that Winterbotham had initiated, organised and, insisting on unprecedented measures of security, distributed the revelations of the Ultra Secret.

I felt it to be my duty, as soon as possible, to visit the soldiers at Lancing College and to assure them that the vigilance of their outposts on the downs now had the official attention it deserved. I was spreading my sleeping bag on the floor of Gerald Gundry's room when a signal was received putting all British Troops on alert, followed by another giving the terse code word "Cromwell". This meant that the German invasion was thought to be imminent. There was nothing we could do until further specific orders called for action, so we turned in to catch what sleep we could. I woke at first light and was dimly

H.Q. 35 Wing. Centre in front row: Wing Cr. Maclean, Group Capt. Donkin. June, 1944.

Mustangs reconnoitring N. French coast.

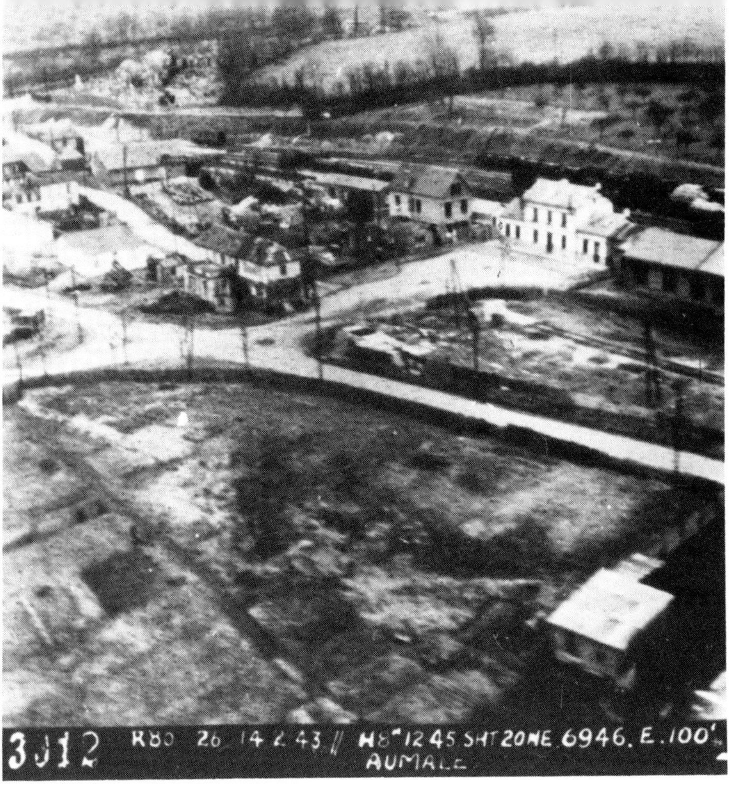
3012 R80 26 14 2 43 // H8" 12 45 SHT 20NE 6946. E. 100'
AUMALE

Low oblique photographs of Aumale.

Radar array near Boulogne.

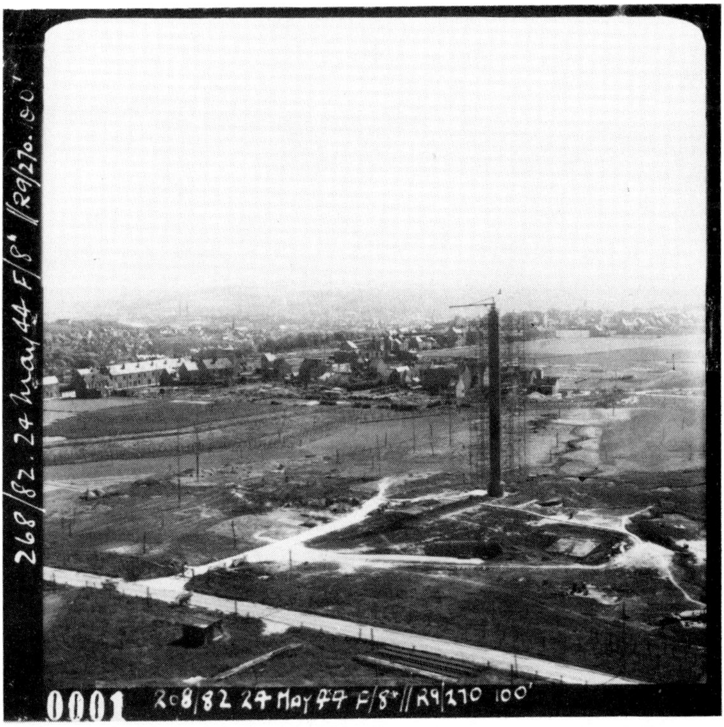
268/82. 24 May 44 F/8" //29/270. 100'
0001 268/82 24 May 44 F/8"// R9/270 100'

conscious of Gundry, fully dressed, leaving the room. To my shame I dozed off again but was re-awakened about an hour later when he returned. I could scarcely believe that, as I tried to collect my wits, church bells all over the country would be ringing the alarm, that in the south countrymen would be ordering their families to stay indoors as, armed with shotguns and rook rifles, they prepared to defend their homes against parachutists, and that Peter's auxiliaries would have gone to earth. "Well," I asked him, "Has it begun?" "Has what begun" he asked as he pulled off his dew-soaked gum boots. "The invasion, of course!' "Oh, *that,*" he replied with unaffected *sang froid:* "I really don't know. I've been out exercising our beagles." A few hours later orders came for a general stand down. While the beagles were exercised Sealion[1] sank into a coma from which, mercifully, it never awoke.

Soon afterwards Göring diverted his bombers to night attacks on London; the day to day conflict with our fighters and attempts to put their air fields and control rooms out of action had inflicted unacceptable losses on the Luftwaffe. The portly clown who had assured his Führer that he could win air superiority over Southern England was nearer to achieving this than, fortunately, he realised. He was deceived by Air Vice Marshal Park's brilliant deployment of 11 Group's depleted squadrons and rapid improvisation of control rooms when his main installations were put out of action. At this critical time I was proud to know that the voice of the controller most trusted by our fighter leaders in combat was that of Ronald Adam, the actor who had volunteered to help in creating the high standards of performance that later distinguished our Canterbury festivals of drama and music by playing Henry II to Russell Thorndyke's Becket in my grandfather's version of Tennyson's play.

Some time passed before, during a weekend visit to Hever, I met my host, John Astor. He, too, inspired friendship at first sight. I found his natural reserve no bar to frank communications and soon discovered that we shared many interests — notably painting. He was a founder member of the school of "Sunday Painters", though he would have deferred artistically to Churchill and to his old friend, Harold Alexander, as bolder executants than himself, and readily conceded that the latter was the most accomplished of them all.

---

[1] *Sealion* was the code word for Hitler's invasion of Great Britain.

The House of Astor was founded on the rock of Manhattan Island. On the land it owned buildings rose and fell and rose again ever higher and higher built by ground leaseholders who developed it at their own risk. John's father, William Waldorf Astor, had shocked his clan by entering politics. In the short run he found the rough and tumble of Washington and the vulgarity of public life and of the press which battened on it much to his distaste. He had no difficulty in procuring the post of Ambassador to Rome where he expressed his disgust for the present by collecting relics of the past, shiploads of which he transported to England where, in due course, he intended to settle.

John's mother died when he was seven years old. An innately diffident boy brought up by a lonely and inarticulate father might have been driven into emotional isolation and so robbed of fulfillment. Mercifully his father had been granted British citizenship the year before John went to Eton. There and at Oxford followed by service in the 1st Life Guards he made the most of opportunities afforded to him to excel in sports he loved and to enjoy the companionship of contemporaries from whom unconsciously he had assimilated the peculiar and essentially English demeanour of a democratic aristocrat. Indeed he came to personify the denouement of a tale of expatriation beyond the bounds of Henry James' imagination.

So, at first meeting, the impression John made upon me was that of a kindly Englishman of military bearing with a sense of humour underlying his stern reserve whose character, after years of service and suffering in the first war, had been moulded, cast and refined in a metal impervious to erosion by pretensions to social aggrandizement or to what in those days was expected of one so endowed in terms of "success".

As it happened, at that first meeting my communications with John were all too brief for, as we finished dinner, the drone of German bombers and distant thud of guns caused us to withdraw not to the drawing room but to the roof. There on the leaded ramparts loomed a figure which appeared to be the embodiment of Tartarin de Tarascon — tall, stout and wrapped in mufflers into a conical but vigilant fire watcher. I was introduced to Monsieur Chambon, the legendary chef of Hever, who in happier times when John and Vi lavished hospitality on their friends, had expressed his genius in an incomparable cuisine with the help of a platoon of female aides who as novitiates in his culinary rituals gladly accepted the stern discipline he imposed upon them.

Though few bombs fell near the castle that night, the horizon was aglow with fires. I knew by now that John was seeking a few hours peace and quiet after a week of watch-keeping with the staff of Printing House Square where defiantly *The Times* went to press through night after night of continual air raids. It was typical of him to spend his press-man's holiday at the side of his firewatching chef who, earlier in equal defiance, had conjured a delicious meal from the meagre rations at his disposal.

I left the castle shortly after dawn. Here and there along the road through Penshurst to Tunbridge Wells columns of smoke from smouldering farms and barns rose like pillars supporting the ceiling of thin cloud. On my way I overtook a farm worker trudging eastwards. I stopped to offer him a lift. He got in and sat beside me without a word, teeth clenched on a clay pipe charged with pungent tobacco. To break the prolonged silence I remarked: "It was a rough night, wasn't it?" Slowly he took his pipe from his mouth and, after a pause for contemplation, he replied: "Ay — 'e came a tidy frost." I knew then that Hitler's hopes were vain.

Two months later I was paying an early morning visit to my opposite number at Kenley when the station commander, Group Captain Victor Beamish, in his cumbersome flying kit burst into the room and went straight to the direct-line telephone to the Air Ministry. He and his Wing Commander had just returned from one of their private sorties in their Spitfires over France in search of enemy aircraft. Visibility was poor. Suddenly through the murk he had seen white streaks of foam in the wake of a strong naval force heading eastwards between Cherbourg and Le Havre. He was a Scotsman, and the Gaelic lilt of his vowels confused the officer to whom he was speaking who was already astounded to hear the first report of this challenge to our control of the Channel, as to whether it was a strong force of E (coastal motor) boats or U (submarine) boats escorting two large warships that must be *Scharnhorst* and *Gneisenau* making a dash from Brest, where they had been virtually immobilised, to Bremen. Over this flotilla swarmed shore-based fighters giving constant air-cover. Then began a day of desperate encounters and humiliating defeat — or so it seemed. The enemy had jammed our radar for hours past, Bomber Command had not time to rearm with armour piercing bombs, half a squadron of torpedo carrying aircraft of the Fleet Air Arm had been lost in the hail of anti-aircraft fire from heavily armed ships with all their guns trained to port, and by noon the weather had closed in to shield the battle cruisers from tardy bombing attacks. But for Beamish's chance sighting they might have passed through the narrows without detection.

In his book *The Hinge of Fate* Churchill dismisses this action as an "episode of minor importance"; in his perspective of our global commitment and with the hindsight which revealed that both ships had been put out of action for several months by mines laid before they reached their home port, he was right. But to many of us this defeat of our unco-ordinated services was deeply depressing and incited us to further rebellion against the apparent acquiescence of our superiors in schisms that rent assunder any prospect of dislodging the Germans from their ill-gotten gains in Europe. What other reversals lay in store for us? What further threats to our already harrassed traffic through the Biscay and the Mediterranean? So far the prize of Gibraltar had been denied them by the vacillations of Franco; Portugal might remain inviolate as a convenient playground for agents and double agents trading on the lust for espionage of the Intelligence Services striving to outwit each other but often defeating their own ends.

Victor Beamish personified the calibre of our station commanders at that time. In spite of his precarious health he had become a doughty fighter leader. By accident I had witnessed a scene that gave me a deeper understanding of the esteem in which he was held by all who served him. One morning I was in his Intelligence Office when he entered quietly and asked my colleague how many officers had been there the previous day when he had sharply reprimanded him. Mystified, my friend ventured ten at a guess. Beamish then ordered a sergeant to find ten officers to report to him there immediately. When one by one they arrived showing signs of apprehension, Beamish having counted them said:

"Yesterday I ticked off your Intelligence Officer in front of ten others. I now know that I was mistaken in doing so and I want as many of you to hear me apologise to him".

The "episode" in the English Channel had sharpened my doubts about inter-service relationships that all too soon proved to be more serious than I had imagined.

At the turn of that critical year the War Office established a South Eastern Army Command with headquarters in Reigate. To it was attached an Air Staff manned by a Group Captain, a Wing Commander Operations and a Squadron Leader Intelligence to which post I was promoted. Our Group Captain, "Dizzy" Desouer was inclined to non-conformity, easy going, with a dry wit and a readiness to let his subordinates get on with the job. He had commanded one of the first Auxiliary Fighter Squadrons trained before the war that, perhaps, turned the scale by reinforcing the regulars during the Battle of Britain. Candidates for his squadron were not recruited but elected. Qualifications entailed a week-end at Lympne Castle where their host was the suave and inscrutable Air Minister, Sir Philip Sassoon. Should they pass muster as well-mannered if boisterous guests and hold their liquor with geniality they were accepted for week-end training. If such graduation seemed bizarre, the means were perfectly justified by the skill and courage of the end which in all too many cases was the abrupt termination of the youth of their candidates.

Our Wing Commander, Bill Murray, was typical of the generation of officers trained at Cranwell in doctrines that had been initiated at the Central Flying School, Upavon and adopted by Lord Trenchard when the Royal Air Force became the Third Service in 1918. Too many senior R.A.F. Officers were still subject to allegiances or prejudices engendered by their earlier service in the army or navy. In fact the Royal Air Force would not create its own image until the alumni of Cranwell and its own staff college became its hierarchy.

The task which Bill and I had first to undertake together was to mitigate the total ignorance of our soldiers of the air affair. The immediate and most serious consequence of this was that troops on the coast were wasting our sparse supplies of ammunition by firing at aircraft beyond their range and, worse still, at our own crippled in action returning across the Channel. To remedy the first, Bill was inspired to produce a metal roundel about the size of our identity discs with a slot cut in it of such a proportion that, if held at arms length, indicated that an aircraft would be out of range until its wing span filled the aperture. The General approved this ingenious device. But how was it to be produced and issued without delay? Knowing well that the "usual channels" were sluggish, I sought permission to visit General Macnaughton commanding the Canadian troops in this country. He may have been a political general, but he was an academic scientist, likely to appreciate our purpose and free to implement it on his own authority. I found him amiable and co-operative. In a few days thousands of these discs were produced and distributed to all units manning our coastal defences.

This had to be followed up by action that not only would instruct the troops in elementary aircraft identification but would cure me for ever of a pathological fear of public speaking — probably a form of stage fright inherited from my mother. With a hastily contrived mobile exhibition illustrating in simple terms the marked difference between our own and enemy aircraft, I lectured on the subject to every unit stationed between Dover and Brighton. The results of our combined operation were as rapid as its conception and execution.

All too soon Bill Murray was released for the more active service he craved. His successor was none other than the companion of my recent downland vigils, Marcus Kaye.

Our Air Staff would control and direct the operations of the newly formed 35 Wing composed of two squadrons to be trained in visual and low-oblique photographic reconnaissance. For the first time army commands were thus assigned direct though limited support by the Royal Air Force. Since South Eastern Command would be responsible for opposing an enemy invasion (though the prospect of this grew fainter month by month) the Army/Air co-operation had a livelier purpose and sense of urgency than elsewhere. Our squadrons were conveniently placed on the airfield at Gatwick. We were partially responsible for a Spitfire high level photographic squadron operating from Oxfordshire and about to embark on the mapping of northern France. The recent calamitous campaign in France had been conducted on French maps printed in 1858. Meanwhile two Canadian Squadrons, Numbers 400 and 414, were being trained for reconnaissance duties and would be under our operational control. All our squadrons were equipped with American

Tomahawks, the tail end of a consignment to the French Air Force, fighters that were no match against those of the Luftwaffe. The operations of our squadrons called for a high degree of individual skill and judgement from pilots who gradually became masters of techniques that would be prerequisite to our successful return to Europe.

By a happy coincidence this first experiment of a combined Army/Air Staff got off to a good start. Readers of my earlier volumes may remember our family association with Luke Paget. As Vicar of St. Pancras he had married my father and mother and recalled his affection for them at their respective funeral services; he had joined Rosalind and myself in holy matrimony, and had christened our first child, Pamela. I had arrived at Reigate to find that our G.O.C. was his nephew, Sir Bernard Paget, who in 1940 had taken over command of the expedition to Norway at two hours notice only to be faced by having to conduct the withdrawal of our troops from their hopeless predicament with minimal losses.

A day or two later he sent for me and, thanks to his uncle, our relationship became less inhibited by our relative ranks than in the normal course of duty. He asked me, knowing I was a painter, if I would design the sign for his new command. I was glad to do so but what had he in mind? A tiger's head was his ferocious choice. Though I did not admit it, I had never studied tigers. What to do? A visit to the Zoo was impossible at such a time of hectic organisation. But I remembered that John Astor in his studio at Hever had a magnificent tiger skin with a mounted head — a trophy of his service as A.D.C. to a viceroy in India. As the wives of officers were not allowed in the command area I could only join Rosalind when rarely I got 48 hours leave. Thus I often spent Sundays with John and Vi and most of them in his studio where he very kindly offered me the use of his paints and canvases. So the following Sunday I spent making studies of his tiger, sufficient for me to take back to my office in Reigate where I would stylise them into a design for the block makers of the badge. The General approved my design which, I think, was the first tangible evidence of true co-operation between our services.

Earlier I had been preparing to settle into a billet in a small house within walking distance of my office when John Hare, the military liaison officer with our Air Staff and responsible for his colleagues assigned to each of our squadrons, told me that he had found very comfortable accommodation in a house above Reigate Heath belonging to Arthur Rank. There was, he said, room for another officer and asked me to join him there. The name Rank meant little to him. My immediate reaction was to decline his invitation. I knew that Rank, as an ardent Methodist, had promoted production of religious films. Those I had seen were of a quality that, if they did not match that of our Canterbury plays, were sincere in content, well cast, and confidently directed. Not suprisingly the film distributors of Wardour Street were disinclined to waste screen time on profitless evangelism. Being a stubborn Yorkshireman and a flour miller of considerable means he decided to meet the challenge by acquiring a chain of cinemas in which he could exhibit any films he chose. His motive was entirely altruistic. Nevertheless the knowledge that he was involved in the film production that I had reluctantly abandoned would sharpen my nostalgia for the work which I had so much enjoyed. John Hare ridiculed my reluctance and, as I found him a congenial companion and was grateful for his concern for my comfort, I packed up my gear and drove him up to our new quarters. Arthur Rank's wife, Nell, gave her "billets" as she called us a warm welcome. She proved to be a kind and most considerate hostess. Though sharing her husband's Christian pre-occupations she leavened them with a keen sense of humour and an impatience with pretension or pomposity of any kind. She arranged for her children's old nanny to bring us our breakfast in our rooms at an early hour. We seldom returned to our billet before bed time when we would catch a glimpse of our host immersed in files and papers as he finished his day's work, or playing bridge with his lawyer, Woodham-Smith, and business associates who had come to confer with him. After a week of prodigious labour, for he was partially responsible for the distribution of the nations dwindling food supplies, he regularly fulfilled his duty as a teacher at the local Sunday School. I managed to conceal my connection with films for a time though, by declaring my commitment to the Canterbury Festivals, I could discuss with him sympathetically his desire to use the medium for his Wesleyan purposes. He seemed to be a very simple man, still subordinate to his father in the direction of their flour-milling enterprises and as yet unaware of the power his wealth would enable him to exert upon the mandarins of the film industry whose arrogance in Wardour

Street was curbed only by their uncomfortable proximity to
Carey Street.

It is no exaggeration to record that, as soon as our squadrons
were retrained and fully operational, 35 Wing began the
continuous reconnaissance of the enemy occupying the coast
of Europe from Den Helder to Le Treport — the latter an
arbitrary line of demarcation between the areas for which
South Eastern and Southern Commands would be responsible
for the co-ordination of intelligence reports. With Sir Bernard
Paget's permission and support and in co-operation with his
own intelligence Staff we set up a room in which the rapidly
accumulating results of our photographic sorties were
interpreted, annotated and displayed. In fact this room was the
only harbinger of our ultimate intention to liberate Europe
from the Nazis though, as my friend Ralph Arnold, the
General's A.D.C., later confessed in his autobiography, he and
most of his fellow staff officers could make no sense of our
activities. Fortunately, two of them immediately recognised
the tactical value of our close surveillance of the enemy across
the water. They were Archie Chisholm, whose monocle and
dégagé manner disguised the acute and subtle operator who
had been largely responsible for the political manoeuvres of
the British Petroleum Company in Persia, and Goronwy Rees,
a Fellow of All Souls College, who took a witty and
mephistophelian delight in provoking the amiable antagonism
of romantics like myself. Their whole hearted support and
pertinent interest in our undertakings were a ray of sunshine in
the cool climate of military indifference. One night after a
spirited conversation over dinner in our mess during which I
tried to parry Goronwy's tempered thrusts of cynicism with
my property sword of romantic idealism, as I dropped him at
his billet on the way to my own, his parting shot was:
"Laurence, if I held your views I would cut my throat
tonight!" Many years later his innate sentimentality led him to
be spellbound by the unmitigated blackguard Burgess to the
ruin of his academic career at the hands of his Welsh masters,
and to dramatise his imagined betrayal by his friends whose
affection had not been cooled by his failure to fan it from time
to time by breezy reminders of his stimulating existence.

IV

While I was at 12 Corps the presence of an eccentric and dynamic General in our midst had made itself felt. The 45th Division, rearmed and vigorously retrained, was a welcome reinforcement to Bulgey Thorne's sparse resources. It was commanded by General Bernard Montgomery. The first indication I had of its quality was the appearance at our sand-table exercises of one of his brigadiers who was not only entertaining in his unorthodox handling of the usually rather boring make-believe of such war games, but, as I was quick to appreciate, in his histrionic gifts as a comedian. It was about this time that I received a letter from G.B.S. suggesting that perhaps by now I realised my folly in deserting him, that I was indispensable to his film making and that I should come to my senses and return to Gabriel Pascal's fold. If he could have witnessed one of Brigadier Horrock's performances, he would reluctantly have had to admit that dramatic action, witty dialogue and audience participation were not the sole prerogative of the theatre.

Rumours reached us of Monty's austerity that included total abstinence from alcohol, zeal (what he perversely called "binge") and vigorous training programmes. His staff were expected to take weekly long-distance runs to keep them up to their physical mark. From what I had seen of some of the senior administrative staff already far gone in the obesity of middle age this would prove to be the death or translation to remote office stools of several of them. My successor at 12 Corps was a retired R.F.C. officer of my own age still handicapped by the effects of wounds he had received in action. I had to warn Monty's B.G.S. that on no account was he to run with the military herd and that his efficiency was not to be in question on this account.

Soon after I joined South Eastern Command General Bulgey Thorne was promoted to G.O.C. Scottish Command. As one time military attaché in Berlin and later commander of a division in France, he accepted his responsibility for defending our Island against an enemy whose potential he appreciated better than any of his contemporaries with incomparable serenity and courage. Like Peter Fleming, he must have found the anticlimax less tolerable. When such crises are past the nation is scarcely aware of the heroes who shielded them from dangers that failed to materialised. His successor at XII Corps was General Bernard Montgomery whose keen eye for military talent marked such men as Horrocks for preferment.

One morning Sir Bernard Paget sent for me to tell me that, alas, he would soon be leaving us. He had been appointed to command our forces in South East Asia from headquarters in Singapore. I commiserated with him in terms of inconceivably false prophecy — namely, that he would be removed from the kind of active service that he preferred. As it turned out a few days later he was appointed G.O.C. Home forces and so, as Sir Arthur Bryant has averred, became the architect of the military structure that would be the instrument of the planners of Overlord.[1] Before he left us, while on an exercise in Kent, he and his staff were eating their pack rations in an abandoned manor house. To them entered General Montgomery and his staff. Monty was now G.O.C. elect to assume the Army Command on Paget's departure. In Shakespearian style Paget introduced his officers to his successor: finally indicating me he said: "And this is Irving who keeps up our morale!" He had in mind, I supposed, the Intelligence room we had set up at Reigate. Monty eyed me sharply, evidently puzzled by my uniform and totally ignored his G.C.O.'s intended jest. Nevertheless, I felt instinctively that our routines of outworn military conventions were in for changes that, however unpalatable to the Establishment, would be for the better.

And so it proved.

At first sight Monty's appearance was not impressive. His bright eyes and sharply defined features reminded me of a ferret with its single minded approach to its exterminating duties. He made no effort to be genial or to engage the affections of his subordinates with affectations of robust heartiness. I was soon to discover that he was distrusted by many of his contemporaries on account of his then suspect professionalism — not a man as they would have put it "to go tiger shooting with". Such facile judgements were rapidly dissipated.

On the day he took over the command our Group Captain went as usual to the General's mess for lunch. He was a little late. Monty sat at the head of the table. Desouer noticed that the assembled staff had foresworn their usual mid-day tipple

---

[1] Codeword for future invasion of France.

and had been served with glasses of water to wash down their meal, in deference no doubt to their General's well known tee-totalism and in hope thereby of winning his favour. Desouer called for the steward and forcefully demanded his usual pint of beer. Monty's eyes lit up with mischievous glee. "That's right, Desouer," he said, "if you want your beer you have it."This immediately established a mutual esteem between them though it may not have enhanced the relationship between the sycophantic abstainers and the irreverent Air Staff. This was of no account, for when Monty was introduced to our Intelligence room he immediately grasped its significance and thereafter hardly a day went by when he did not look in and study the results of our photographic sorties. Moreover during that first week of his appointment as G.O.C. he visited our squadrons at Gatwick and spent some time sitting with our pilots at their dispersal huts, keenly cross-examining them on their experiences and our prospects of developing the techniques that had evidently impressed him.

I attended several of Montys' conferences or rather virtuoso performances of his gifts of oratory. His voice had the sharp bark of a terrier; his delivery was terse and punctuated by reiteration of certain telling phrases that, as he intended, were not forgotten by his listeners. His pronunciation of "r"s as "w"s, an impediment that would be insuperable for an actor, in no way detracted from his utterance.

Though he did not disguise his conceit (if conceit is a man's awareness of his physical or intellectual superiority) his abrupt manner compelled attention. There was something endearing in that he made no effort to court popularity by false bonhomie while at the same time preaching the military gospel that if we accepted and adhered to it with the lightheartedness of schoolboys would triumph over the solemn forces of evil that opposed us. True such humour as he had was sardonic, implying trust rather than affection.

One day a friend of mine met him on the drive outside the hotel which was our mess as a Colonel emerged from it, rubicund after one of those hearty meals that had over the years inflated him with signs of self-indulgence. He saluted the General.

"Ah, Colonel," said Monty breezily, "Had a good lunch?"

"Yes, sir, thank you sir," replied his innocent victim.

"That's good," barked Monty, "because its the last you'll be eating in my headquarters".

Thus he would separate the goats from the sheep he needed to fulfil his mission as the man of destiny he knew himself to be.

Whatever his subject, Monty presented it in such terms that a child would have comprehended it, knowing full well that it was in similar terms that his doctrine and orders must be conveyed to the most simple-minded soldiers if they were to undertake clearly what was expected of them. Those talks appeared to be extemporary. Yet from the window of my office that overlooked the garden of his headquarters, I would see him, preparatory to such an occasion, sitting there, intensely preoccupied as he organised his expressions in an exercise book, now and again licking his pencil and pondering deeply like a schoolboy wrestling with the composition of an essay on a subject that called for the utmost concentration. His act of virtuosity was the result of the painstaking rehearsal that was the cause of the effect it had upon his audience.

Thus, to me Monty's presence was an almost apocalyptic revelation. Here, for the first time, I recognised a commander of stature who, facing the formidable task that lay ahead if we were to prevail in battle, not in the air but on the ground where alone the outcome could be settled, knew that our military amateurism, for all our native courage, would not defeat a ruthless foe perfectly trained in a new concept of warfare and inspired by a leader who demanded absolute obedience from a people prone to fanaticism and submission to tyranny that relieved the individual of moral responsibility.

Monty, I realised, was a man, complementary to Churchill who rallied us at a critical time by emotional exhortations inspired by a deep understanding of our characteristics and basic virtues, who, while not underestimating the enormity of his undertaking had absolute confidence in his ability to transmit them to all who responded to his leadership, and to reject without compunction any of his fellow professionals who resisted it. I became increasingly aware of his unpopularity with the military gentlemen who looked upon him as a professional player. In fact at that time it would be fair to say that he had more antagonists in his own service than in the hierarchy of the Wehrmacht who had as yet not identified the general who before long would, as he would have said, "knock them for six".

The first evidences of the reformation that Monty was

determined to effect was a full scale exercise code named Tiger. Its purpose was to exploit to the full the resources at his disposal for close co-operation of ground and air forces. His Air Staff were party to the planning and umpiring of this exercise. 35 Wing would simulate reconnaissance and close support fighters and bombers for the opposing armies. XII Corps advancing from the Tunbridge Wells area through hostile territory would meet a defence force of comparable strength on a line roughly between Horsham and Guildford. At an early hour of each day of the exercise Monty summoned the Commanders of the contestants and the umpires for a brief conference reviewing the progress of the manoeuvres. At the first of these gatherings, after the soldiers had had their say, he barked at me: "Well, has Air anything to say?" I rose to my feet appalled at my prospective duty.

"Yes, sir. At H hour XII Corps Headquarters moved out from Tunbridge Wells and took the road with all the impedimenta of administrative and domestic vehicles. In spite of low cloud, these were soon spotted by enemy reconnaissance aircraft. Even had this not been so, it could be assumed that their movements were reported to the enemy by agents with radio transmitters. Within an hour that army staff was put out of action by squadrons of bombers and fighters simulated by token pairs of aircraft which easily found their targets of transport."

I could see the stocky and rather pompous B.G.S. of XII Corps, recently under Monty's command, flush with anger and about to utter a vehement protest. Monty relished this confrontation.

"That's right, Irving," he said, "you go on — yes, go on and let's hear the truth of the matter!"

The B.G.S. contained his fury. But, as the exercise proceeded, whenever I had to deliver him a directive or appreciation from the umpires he crumpled it up and threw it unread into the wastepaper basket. Later he rose to eminence at the War Office. Though Monty never needed him in action, he may have found him a useful informant on any back stair plots and stratagems that his forceful egotism might provoke.

Exercise Tiger foreshadowed the decline and ultimate elimination of Army Co-operation Command. In the confused rethinking following the defeat of France by a perfectly co-ordinated German army and air force, this fourth command had been established by the Air Ministry in an attempt to assuage the War Office when a faction headed by my one time military colleagues at Coulommiers was bent on dismantling the Royal Air Force by the creation of the equivalent of the Admiralty's Fleet Air Arm to serve the needs of the Army. It proved an empty gesture, for the Command was given no operational teeth other than the reconnaissance Wings allotted to South Eastern and Southern Commands, and two light bomber squadrons that subsequently were withdrawn for deployment in support of our landings in North Africa. Nevertheless I was glad to hear that the Command's Commander-in-Chief was "Ugly" Barratt, for he was a realist and would, I imagined, have no patience with the military recessionists. At 35 Wing we had to interpret its vague directives as best we could. With mingled mockery and affection we referred to it as the "Chinese Laundry".

Even I had to spend much of my time in trying to make my senior intelligence officers at its H.Q. in Bracknell understand the purposes and techniques we were perfecting at 35 Wing. These officers came and went in tiresomely rapid succession (the professionals, I suppose, appreciating that the post was not one for self-advancement) so that my tactful indoctrination had periodically to be repeated respectfully to new incumbents some of whom naturally bridled at my presumption.

V

By the summer of 1942 our squadrons had been re-equipped with American Mustang aircraft which proved to be the perfect vehicles for oblique cameras, to give their best performance at a low height and to stand a lot of punishment from light anti-aircraft fire. Our pilots were warming to their work and with every mission improving their judgement and skills — to such an extent that one of them Mike Gray, a debonair and apparently careless Stoic, returned with a close up of a disappointingly empty bedroom in a hotel taken through the open window as he hurtled down the main street of Ostend. Now we were able to display the complete cover of

German coast from Calais to Le Treport. Many of the photographs were enlivened by pictures of German troops scuttling for safety; a few taken by the second pilot (all sorties were carried out in pairs) included the victims of his leader who had raked the target as he skimmed along the foreshore at a hundred feet above sea level.

We had adopted a system of recording all information we collected on tracing paper over the sheets of new maps of Northern France which were now in production, and revising it from day to day. Our main sources of intelligence were our own vertical and oblique photographic cover, the weekly top secret bulletins of the Royal Patriotic Society whose members were gallant Belgian and French citizens sending reports of German installations and troop movements, and equally gallant pilots who by night flew over France drawing anti-aircraft fire while their passengers, officers of the Royal Artillery, pinpointed the location of the batteries. For my part, the primary value of this was that in planning our sorties we could ensure that our pilots were able to avoid unnecessary risk in their already hazardous tasks.

We were ready for the test when it came, albeit abruptly and all too secretly. On July 2nd Desouer sent for me and from the safe in his office took a bundle of documents and spread them out on his desk. They were the operational directives for the raid on Dieppe, code named Martian, planned to be executed in 48 hour's time; with them was a small map of its objective overprinted with imprecise details of its defences, strategically indicative but tactically inadequate. The plan had been prepared by Combined Operations under the command of Lord Louis Mountbatten. The troops to make the assault landings were elements of the Canadian Army — high spirited soldiers by now restive from their static defensive role and stale from over-training. Thus South Eastern Command was not privy to this plan, though Monty had collaborated with Lord Louis in its conception. It must have been at his suggestion that our Wing was given the task of visual reconnaissance during the operation. It was evident that the planners were unaware that Dieppe was a few miles beyond the boundary of our allotted front. The responsibility for the provision of photographic and visual surveillance of the port lay with 36 Wing serving Southern Command. At such short notice 35 Wing was called upon to provide continual visual

2

4

6

Group Capt. Anderson, D.S.O., D.F.C., catches his train.

Low level attack on Mezidon railway station.

Cause: Recce for Operation Overlord.
Bridge near Vire.

Effect: Destruction of bridge near Hirson by bombers.

H.Q. 35 Wing. Mobile Unit 1944:

Interior. Group Capt. Donkin planning a sortie.

reconnaissance over roads converging on Dieppe by four squadrons.[1] It would also direct the sorties of two light bomber squadrons of Army Co-operation Command to lay smoke screens as required over German coastal batteries. Naturally I summoned my colleague at 36 Wing to Reigate and asked him to bring me all the photographic cover and intelligence of the defences of Dieppe. To my dismay he came more or less empty handed. His Wing had not responded to the vague directive from Army Co-operation Command, nor had Southern Command Headquarters showed any curiosity about the enemy across the water. Combined Operations, ignorant of all this, had at the last moment ordered, unknown to us, one Spitfire, unarmed and equipped for photographic reconnaissance from a great height, to make a sortie that produced three very low level oblique photographs of the beach in front of the Casino. The pilot, F/Lt. St. John, deservedly was awarded the D.F.C. for his gallant but wholly inappropriate action.

Though I realised that it was too late to remedy this administrative blunder, I went immediately to the Headquarters of Combined Operations to acquaint its intelligence officer of the possible conseqences of this extraordinary muddle. He received me with the courtesy one might expect from the architect of the Curzon Cinema, for Cas Maury like myself was an artistic fish out of Martian waters. He was inclined to regard my protest as irrelevant, and anyhow it was now too late to do anything about it. From there I went to G.H.Q. Home Forces where the responsibility for the ignorance of Combined Operations as to the resources of photographic reconnaissance plainly lay. There the intelligence section, though sympathetic and even apologetic, refused to discuss the matter because I was not in possession of the secret card issued to those privy to Martian. So, on to the Headquarters of 11 Group at Uxbridge where I knew I could establish a *modus operandi* with the senior intelligence officer, Squadron Leader Shallard, from whom for months past I had always received the friendliest trust and co-operation. We agreed that I should set up an intelligence room at Gatwick where radio and telephone communications would provide a link between the Combined Operations command ship H.M.S. *Calpé* and 11 Group to receive reports from our pilots returning from their reconnaissance sorties. Meanwhile,

[1] The two Canadian recce squadrons we had trained would reinforce 35 Wing for this, their first, major operation.

Combined Operations and G.H.Q. Home Forces had become suspicious of a troublesome R.A.F. interloper with a bee in his bonnet and a disregard for security, and had set M.I.5 in hot pursuit of him. But by that time their quarry had safely gone to earth in Uxbridge.

11 Group was no longer under the command of Air Vice Marshall Park, the Nelson of the Battle of Britain, whose cool and inspired handling of his dwindling resources had so perfectly complemented the master mind of Air Marshal Dowding. His appointment to take over Training Command would ensure that in the next phase of the defeat of the Luftwaffe, our fighter pilots would be perfectly instructed in the disciplines and operational principles he communicated to all who experienced his leadership. His successor was Air Vice Marshall Leigh Mallory who, when commanding 12 Group, on which Park relied for critical reinforcements, had not disguised his disapproval of the manner in which the squadrons were deployed. I learned that he welcomed the Dieppe project as an opportunity to bring the fighters of the Luftwaffe to battle. For the massive Wing formations he had sent sweeping over the Pas de Calais had failed to excite much response from our now cautious adversaries. He must have found this galling since his advocacy of deploying Wings rather than squadrons of fighters during the Battle of Britain led to his provoking discussions at a high level that resulted in the discourteous dismissal of Dowding from Fighter Command which Churchill uncharacteristically must have countenanced.

When I returned to Reigate Goronwy Rees told me that earlier in the day he had set out with Monty to visit the Canadian troops already embarked in landing craft assembled in the Solent, in order to give them the kind of informative "pep" talk that thenceforward would win the trust and confidence of all who served under him. The General had been quick to appreciate the intellectual acuity and unintimidated response of his G.2 Intelligence and had made a confidant of an officer who could be relied upon to express his views, critical though they might be, with the discerning frankness of a sharp-witted Celt. Halfway to Southampton Monty became restless. He stopped the car.

"I think I am getting a cold — yes — I'm getting a cold. We will return to Reigate."

Men of destiny have a keen instinct for evaluating the relative importance of their actions. As a young officer in the Warwickshire Regiment Monty had been left for dead in No Man's Land during the first war against the Germans. Later, retrieved by stretcher bearers he recovered slowly in hospital from severe wounds in his chest. This had left him with a damaged lung which made him vulnerable to bronchial infections. Thus he reacted on the road to Southampton to an intuitive warning that his duty was not to risk disablement at such a time in fulfilling a secondary duty of conjectural importance.

His intuition was infallible. During the night Martian was cancelled owing to an adverse weather report. It was, however, only postponed until August 19th, when the moon and the tide would again be propitious. In the account of the raid that was published for propaganda purposes later in 1942, this cancellation and earlier preparation for the raid was not referred to. Understandably those responsible for the affair appreciated the risks of criticism that, in the course of a month, the Germans would almost certainly have been informed of the preparations for the raid and alerted to reinforce the defences of Dieppe. Indeed I was dismayed by what appeared to be a reckless repetition of an operation which thousands of soldiers and sailors had been briefed to undertake. In fact, now that the Ultra secret has been revealed, its operators must have known that the Germans were ignorant of our intentions.

At least I had a breathing space to remedy the flagrant incompetence of the intelligence plans. Two further surprises awaited me. My Group Captain was posted elsewhere and his place was taken by Group Captain Walter Butler, the commander of our 26 Squadron. Butler was a gallant and highly competent professional. He had entered the service as a boy trainee at Uxbridge and had risen from the ranks to command a Lysander squadron in the Air Component in France.

On a Sunday, soon after the postponement, Monty summoned his Staff to a meeting in a Nissen hut adjacent to his headquarters. Without demur he told us that we were there for him to bid us farewell. His actual words so impressed me that I wrote them down when I returned to my office.

"... I am going to be pitted against a Field Marshal. It will be a very interesting experience — a very interesting experience

111

indeed. When I have defeated him — as I shall — I will return and lead you to the final victory."

The Field Marshal was Rommel. Monty was leaving us to take command of the hard pressed 8th Army in Libya.

Many years later Rosalind and I were his fellow house guests of Sir Ashley and Lady Clarke at the Embassy in Rome. Sitting next to him at dinner I reminded him of this incident and repeated his words that I had recorded at the time. Did he remember what he had foretold with such prophetic exactitude? He pondered a moment or two and then said: "Well, you know, if you say these sort of things you've got to carry them out!"

By the time we had sorted out the confusion following the cancellation of Martian, we had three weeks grace to make a thorough reconnaissance of Dieppe and to bring our two Canadian squadrons to a proper state of readiness for the operation. By making two sorties over other sections of our front for every one flown over Dieppe, we were confident that the Germans would not detect any form of attention on our objective.

One of the consequences of Monty's departure was the decision of Combined Operations to abandon the tactics which he regarded as the key to the success of the attack. Dieppe was overlooked by steep chalk cliffs to the east and west of its beaches. It was known that to the westward a battery of six heavy guns near Varengeville commanded the seaward approaches to the harbour. Another battery was mounted on the eastern cliff, but it was suspected that embedded in the cliff itself lighter weapons were mounted to enfilade the foreshore. Monty had insisted that our newly formed parachute troops should be dropped during darkness on these positions and to eliminate, if possible, this threat to our seaborne assault. Though this would be their first experience in action the element of surprise would be much in their favour. In the event a commando led by Lord Lovat, landing below Varengeville, put the western battery out of action; to the east, after initial disaster and premature disclosure of their intention, another commando, including United States Rangers, were able in spite of heavy losses to harrass the enemy gun positions during the critical period of the main assault on the beaches. We believed that the greater danger was concealed in the face of the east cliff. Several sorties produced photographic evidence

112

of what appeared to be camouflaged surfaces superimposed on the natural chalk; Butler and I visited General Roberts at his headquarters near Portsmouth several times to discuss their significance and to plan in detail the range of our low level sorties and distribution of reports on enemy troop movements. At last, by working through the night, we had prepared maps overprinted with all the information we had acquired on the enemy defences and with identification code numbers of the areas allotted to our inland reconnaissance sorties that would ensure the rapid passing of their reports to H.M.S. *Calpé*[1] and to 11 Group. On August 17th photographs confirmed our suspicions of installations on the east cliff. That night we again went to Portsmouth. The General's A.D.C. warned us that our report would be unwelcome and, at that late hour, immaterial to the conduct of the operation which was already under way.

Our orders from 11 Group, where Air Marshal Leigh Mallory would control the air battle, betrayed an ignorance of air reconnaissance in the excessive number of sorties ordered to fulfil our task. Group Captain Butler protested in view of the probable wastage of our limited forces, but his objection was overruled. By the evening of August 18th all our squadrons were at readiness at Gatwick. Marcus Kaye was sent to be our link with the smoke-laying Blenheim squadrons at an airfield near Thruxton.

As darkness fell, in the increasing heat and stuffiness of the blacked-out operations room our army air liaison officers began the all night briefing of the assembled pilots in order of precedence so that those who would make the dawn sorties would be able to snatch a few hours rest, though sleep was unlikely in the prevailing tensions. In the smoky froust the Canadians, like children dressed for a party and deaf to warnings of their nannies not to get over excited, were vociferous, and exhilarated by the prospect of their first major engagement; our pilots quietly concentrated on their briefings but their subdued banter concealed their awareness of their commitment as ground bait for the enemy fighters that 11 Group hoped would rise to the occasion.

---

[1] H.M.S. *Calpé* was the destroyer in which General H. F. Roberts, commanding the assault troops, had his H.Q. and Operations Room. He would be in direct radio contact with Lord Louis Mountbatten, G.O.C. Combined Operations, and with General H. D. C. Crear, G.O.C. Canadian Corps at H.Q.R.A.F. 11 Group at Uxbridge, where Air Marshal Sir Leigh Mallory would direct the confrontation with the Luftwaffe he planned to provoke, and with H.Q. 35 Wing at the R.A.F. Station at Gatwick.

Shortly before dawn our first section took off. Half an hour later our bombers were skimming over the channel below the guard of German radar. Pete Donkin, commanding 239 Squadron, returned at 6 a.m. He had crossed the coast at Dieppe at 5.15 and had seen our Blenheims make a brilliant approach to their target; but he was disturbed by the chatter of the Canadians on their radio sets. As he left, landing craft were grounding on the beach. The Germans apparently had been taken by surprise. His actual words were that, "The Huns had their fingers right up!" If so, they extracted them quickly and the beaches were swept with devastating fire from weapons of every calibre whose gunners on the menacing headlands had held their fire until the assault craft were fatally committed to their forlorn venture. The ensuing shambles is on record. Throughout that morning I was at the telephone passing our pilots' reports to H.M.S. *Calpé* and to 11 Group. Among these was an unrepentant and ecstatic account from Marcus Kaye who had persuaded Squadron Leader Pleasance to allow him, most improperly, a place in the first smoke laying bomber to cross the channel in semi-darkness at sea level, zoom up over the cliffs, and plant its smoke bombs on the eastern coastal battery. In the midst of this traffic, I saw, through the window, a bomber touch down on our runway and, with what appeared to be gathering speed, hurtle beyond the bounds of the airfield. It was not much comfort to recognise it as a Boston aircraft of Bomber Command. Its crew, all but the gunner who had been killed by shrapnel over Dieppe at the same time as its brakes had been shot away, survived the crash.

By noon what remained of the Jubilee fleet was withdrawing from the French coast. An hour later I had my first bitter lesson in the true meaning of discipline or unquestioning obedience to orders as understood by professional fighting men. H.M.S. *Calpé* was halfway home across the channel when 11 Group ordered a close reconnaissance to locate a battery firing from the right flank of the German defences. I protested that, as our forces had long ago withdrawn, such a sortie was not only dangerous but useless. As I was speaking, my Group Captain entered the room and peremptorily ordered me to stop arguing and to obey orders. The pilot I had to brief was Flying Officer Newstead Dawson, a youth bursting with enthusiasm and with an abounding zest for life. A few days earlier he had come to see me at Reigate. Hearing that I had been an artist he sought my advice as to what materials he should use to paint a scale model of a Mustang he had just completed. Having sent him on what he knew as well as I did was a futile mission, I broke a self-imposed habit and walked with him to his aircraft to wish him good luck before he took off. He climbed into his Mustang and, as he adjusted his harness, he shouted gaily: "I painted my model, sir, it looks absolutely wizard!" These were the last words of a victim of inexorable discipline.

That evening Goronwy Rees, who had been a military observer on the destroyer H.M.S. *Garth,* told me that at the time young Dawson must have been over Dieppe the ship's guns were engaging this battery. Indeed the gunnery officer directing the duel beside him on the bridge was killed, leaving Rees to continue the action as best he could. Many lives were lost that day in the confusion and actual breakdown of communications between land, sea, and air forces.

After a long sleep of exhaustion I collected my wits and I tried to assess the consequences of this prodigal expenditure of lives and equipment. 11 Group had, indeed, succeeded in bringing the Luftwaffe to battle and, if it was necessary to do so, had re-established the relative superiority of our fighters. 35 Wing had little to show for the losses it had sustained (7% of sorties, unacceptable in the case of sustained operations) but the detection and harassment of isolated military vehicles on the roads approaching Dieppe, and its undiminished morale, particularly among the Canadians in spite of their losses which were happily beyond their immediate calculation. The cost in terms of men and materials seemed totally unacceptable in the face of the failure to achieve any objective other than the brilliant exploits of Lord Lovat's commandos.

Second thoughts, however, were less dispiriting. These were mainly inspired by a conference called by the Canadian Army and held in a large cinema in Horsham. Never before was there so pertinent a post-mortem. The hall was crowded with officers and other ranks, many of them survivors of the *débâcle* in which more than three fifths of the 5,000 troops engaged had been killed or captured — a testing ordeal for a highly trained professional army. Yet, as I surveyed the scene, I saw no sign of shock, dismay or resentment that such a cruel baptism of fire might have generated. This, I think, was largely due to the admirable conduct of the meeting by Brigadier Church Mann.

He had the bearing of a Canadian aristocrat, if an egalitarian society would permit such distinction. Immaculately dressed as a cavalry officer, the appearance of the landed gentleman with a peacetime passion for race horse breeding might have seemed anachronistic. Calmly and with the assurance of a trained advocate, he explored the planning and execution of Jubilee in detail, neither attempting to disguise its failures or over estimating its values as an exercise, nor wasting time in flattering the survivors whose confidence he took for granted. His performance in its dignity and sincerity was impeccable. No one who attended that meeting had any lingering doubts that the experiment however costly had not served its purpose.

For from its travail was born the conviction that the seaborne invasion of France could not be directed against defended ports or harbours. From that moment the conception of the planners of Overlord shifted its emphasis. The landings would have to be made on open beaches and the scientific and industrial brains of the nation would be concentrated on the design and construction of artificial harbours through which our armies would be nourished with reinforcements, ammunition and food. And, above all, the day had proved that complete co-operation between land, sea and air forces could be achieved to fulfil the strategical orders of a general staff of our combined services and, as it turned out, of allies whose military and naval experiences and prejudices were so rapidly reconciled with our own. Many years later, when Rosalind and I happened to be in Dieppe on the anniversary of the raid, as I stood before the Canadian memorial at the foot of the westward cliff, I knew that no lives so confidently offered on that day had been sacrificed in vain.

For the rest of the year, the Air Staff of 35 Wing, having learned and digested the lessons of participation in the Dieppe affair, strove to impress on higher formations the need to create order out of the prevailing fragmentation of ideas as to how the R.A.F. should reappraise its role in support of the armies now committed to the liberation of Europe.

Group Captain Butler had left us to join the Royal Air Force group working cheek by jowl with General Montgomery in the desert war. He was succeeded by an energetic officer, sympathetic to our heretical purposes and to operations that had now taken on a new dimension. Probably at the instigation of Leigh Mallory, Ugly Barratt had authorised the planning and execution of offensive actions which were welcomed by our pilots who hitherto had been taught that their duty was to take photographs, to bring them back safely, and to this end to avoid engagement with the enemy. The more high spirited of them found this curb on their belligerence frustrating; now they could vent it by attacking with their very effective cannons railway or road transport and electrical installations in France.

On my return from sick leave after Christmas, I had a spell of therapeutic exercise of my proper craft preparing maps[1] of the French railway system, electric generating and transformer stations with the grids of cables distributing their output. Tunnels were of particular interest, for by de-railing trains as they entered them they could be blocked for several days. Our pilots entered into this with their usual zest and by the turn of the year had destroyed about 70 locomotives in addition to taking oblique photographs covering extensive areas of enemy occupied territory.

The planning of these operations to best effect and, as far as possible, to safeguard our pilots, had to be based on accurate information on the targets and their defences. All this was hard to come by. Official channels flowed sluggishly. This was brought home to me when I was asked by the Central Interpretation Unit at Medmenham to congratulate 168 Squadron on photographs of electrical installations at La Vaupaliere. In fact, C.I.U. had asked us to take these photographs three weeks earlier, the sortie had been made at once but the results had only just reached the interpreters. So I decided to by-pass Bracknell and to collect what I needed at source. This resulted in a close and fruitful association with the topographical service at Manchester College, Oxford, manned for the most part by accessible and obliging dons, and by Royal Engineers who were afficionados of the railway system of Europe. So we began to make traces over our maps until before long all the information we needed was readily available. By now I had Shanghaied a W.A.A.F. draughtswoman from a neighbouring airfield where she had no work to do.

Leigh Mallory, his head with his fighter Wings in the cirrostratus clouds, was slow to appreciate the services of our

---

[1] These were designed to display features in N. France clearly identifiable by night — namely sizeable towns, wooded areas, rivers and canals, railway lines and trunk roads. They were admirably reproduced in three colours by the lithographers of the Canadian Army mobile printing unit.

groundling Mustangs. So much so that I had to protest to my friend Shallard against disparaging references to the fighting qualities of our pilots in the 11 Group Intelligence Summary. Tagged on to the end of combat reports by its victorious fighters was a paragraph headed: "Mustang v F.W.190" that criticized the evasive tactics that were reported in our summaries without acknowledging that these were an essential precaution in carrying out photographic sorties. Nor was it made clear that while clear skies were the ideal conditions for fighter engagement, our work had to be done with cloud cover and the lower the better at that. Shallard was, as ever, quick to take my point and thereafter reports of our offensive actions were given due prominence.

My map making task was made easier by the Army's provision of a commodious operations room for its Air Staff where Operations and Intelligence could work side by side with the meteorological officer whose forecasts were vital to our purposes. The latter was a gentle and dedicated ex-schoolmaster who reminded me of Lieutenant Osborne in *Journey's End.* His weather eye became so discerning that we could slip our aircraft across the Channel in a short spell of fair visiblity between south westerly "fronts" coming in from the Atlantic to shield them from attack as they penetrated deeply into France.

Fortunately my transgressions against official procedures coincided with one of the recurring changes of my senior at Bracknell. The latest incumbent was a soldier, who not only condoned my unorthodoxy but proved amenable to suggestions soundly based on experience. I was summoned to a meeting at his headquarters attended by all the senior officers in the Command and by their representative at G.H.Q. Home Forces. The meeting began with much high flown and hypothetical discussion on the doctrine of operational intelligence. I brought this to a halt by pointing out that all these theories and others unknown to the debaters had been put to the test for more than a year past by 35 Wing, had inspired General Montgomery to adopt them in Africa, and had been approved by General Paget when recently he had visited our new operations room at Reigate. This took the wind out of the sails of the theorists and so, while they were becalmed, I pressed on to insist that the low level photographs our pilots were taking day by day were not only serving their immediate purpose of surveillance of the enemy but, when the time came to mount the invasion of France in strength, would provide topographical details of inestimable value to battalion commanders, to navigators of landing craft, and to fighter pilots operating in close support of the army. Apparently this had some effect, for soon afterwards another conference was held at Bracknell attended by higher ranking representatives of the War Office, the Air Ministry and Combined Operations to discuss the regulation of the demand and supply of air intelligence.

At this meeting I met again, since we had served together at Coulommiers, the junior partner in a conspiracy to recreate an old-style army flying corps. He was by now a Brigadier but I could see, as we wrangled amiably on the subject, that he did not take his promotion very seriously. He seemed now to regard the whole affair with an amused detachment; this was as well for he was now General Paget's air-adviser.

During our discussion I caught sight of his fellow conspirator running past the window, ruddy of countenance evidently returning from a game of squash rackets. They made a strange pair — the professional gunner with the appearance and manner of a cardinal of an army/air curia, and his sophisticated amateur colleague like a Jesuit secretary letting his master enjoy frissons of self-importance while discreetly he pulled the strings of backstair politics. I hoped that Ugly Barratt was not conniving at their intrigues. I knew that Paget was far too concerned for the efficiency of the army he was training for the final conflict to tolerate any impediment to reformations he, in his wisdom, knew to be essential to the salvation of Europe if the nation, militarily and industrially, was to perfect the means of making war on equal terms against an enemy that had a head start of twenty years while their victims strove to avoid the bitter consequences of confrontation.

On reflection and as subsequent events proved, above the fog of confusion and in-fighting that shrouded the lowlands of inter-service rivalries through which I was stumbling at that time, at the summit of the Air Ministry the prospect was already bright thanks to the clear thinking of the Chief of Air Staff, Sir Charles Portal, of his brilliant right hand airman Sir Wilfrid Freeman, and of their Permanent Undersecretary, Sir Arthur Street. Already their plans of a Tactical Air Force with operational groups of all arms and with the apparatus of Ground Control as used by Fighter Command mounted on wheels and in tented caravans to support our armies overseas must have been well in hand. Moreover, planners, signal experts, draughtsmen and technicians must have been at work on the design of equipment that in a year or so would astonish us by its perfection when as if by a miracle all present issues had been resolved.

Rightly such foresight and timely decisions were concealed from us. Politically the dismantling of Army Co-operation Command was not feasible. The Secretary of State could not have presented such an action to the House of Commons without apparently having connived at an expedient deception of the War Office and, indirectly, of the electorate. There is nothing more professionally distasteful to civil servants than the dismantling of an Establishment that they have persuaded a Minister to adopt. Contrarily, the continuing existence of Army Co-operation Command on the British Order of Battle on the detailed files of Luftwaffe Intelligence concealed from the Nazis the active preparations that would confound their hopes of continuing sovereignty behind the Atlantic Wall.

VI

Throughout the past two years the predicament of the theatre and of film studios had seldom been out of my mind. I had no second thoughts as to having abandoned my ancillary service to either of them. Second only to directors, stage designers are dispensable to the dramatic arts. As Edith Evans once remarked: "If an actor of genius turns up, he has only to perform in Hyde Park to win audiences and acclaim."

The blitzkreig on London had been the British theatres' finest nights. During those months of incessant bombing, at least forty theatres in London were in inter-action — inter-action because never before in their history had players and audiences faced each other in conditions that called for a mutual display of courage and devotion to an art that transcended terror. In a world of make-believe during the two hours traffic on the stage together they defied the dangers that threatened them from the realities of a world made hideous beyond the imaginations of Aeschylus or Shakespeare or the contrivance of melodramatists. Playing an heroic role to the top of his flamboyant bent, Donald Wolfit set his actor-manager's standard on the stage of the Strand Theatre where bombed but unbowed he nightly took his curtain call to applause that for a few minutes drowned the din of the devastation and of the defence of our throne of Mars.

Wisely our Government had decreed at the outset that the players could serve their country best by providing the relief of entertainment to a population now wholly employed in the conduct of total war. Of the young actors of promise I had worked with, most were enlisted in E.N.S.A., touring provincial cities at no less hazard than our capital.

Ralph Richardson, whose genius for portraying bewildered and impractical sufferers in the human condition concealed a passion for mechanics and speed on wheels, had at the outbreak of the war joined the Fleet Air Arm; once I had met him on an airfield near Southampton engrossed and enchanted by his duties as a pilot. Laurence Olivier, trapped in New York by the first major successes of his career, was advised to stay there as our theatrical legate until the time was ripe for him to assume command of the first truly British film enterprise that the war gave birth to. He, too, served briefly in the Fleet Air Arm; thereby frightening me more than the enemy. For my son, John, wrote that with a party of Wykhamists keen on flying, he was taking the air with Olivier who, if his bravura as a pilot was akin to his performance as a player, made me tremble as to the aerobatics he might perform for his responsive audience. Martin Browne and his wife, Henzie, were maintaining the continuity of religious poetic drama initiated in the Chapter House of Canterbury Cathedral to small industrial communities throughout our island to many of which they gave their first theatrical experience.

My first reassociation with the theatre was sudden and shocking. One morning in April 1941 I heard at the B.G.S.'s conference that in the previous night's air raid a land mine had fallen on the Royal Academy of Dramatic Art.[1] I reached Gower Street an hour or so later. The windows of the ground floor room had been blown out; the front door was in splinters.

[1] For several years past I had served as a member of its Council. The Academy had been the brilliant if somewhat aberrant conception of the actor-manager, Sir Herbert Beerbohm Tree. His intention was to provide a substitute for the vanished provincial stock companies and the touring companies under the then ageing Frank Benson and Ben Greet in which most of the leading players at that time had been apprenticed to their art. In the event what his step brother Max called "Herbert's Gower Street school" thanks to devoted and astute direction of it by the Principal, Kenneth Barnes, was granted a Royal Warrant. Thus it became and so remains the only professional institution that the players can call their own.

I picked my way through the debris to Kenneth Barnes' office. There a strange tableau met my eyes. The windows had been roughly shuttered with boards. Through a chink in them a shaft of sunlight and scintillating dust pierced the gloom and focused on the face of Bernard Shaw huddled in a chair. The cocksure mobile features of the old champion of the R.A.D.A. were pinched and aged; the challenging and mocking eyes were lustreless and evasive in undisguised dejection — the realist, unsparing in his derision of human folly, was for the first time overwhelmed by catastrophe and by the ultimate expression of the barbarity of a totalitarian society that, in other contexts, he had frivolously extolled. Kenneth Barnes was standing. As he faced us both I knew how grievous a blow that night had dealt him. The Malet Street theatre had been totally destroyed and in the neighbouring houses serving as hostels many soldiers had perished. Yet I was conscious that already Kenneth had divested himself of self pity or recrimination. As, at that hour, the forces of Great Britain, having repelled invasion were bracing themselves for the long conflict ahead, so the indomitable Principal was already conceiving a nobler theatre which, by hook or crook, he would build upon the still warm ashes of the first. Perhaps G.B.S., sensing his friend's undismayed reaction to this disaster and calm determination to restore the fabric of the school he had created to bridge the gap in the player's education left by the demise of the old stock companies and the training camps of Frank Benson and Ben Greet vagrant in the provinces, at that moment of truth decided to leave a third of his fortune to ensure the R.A.D.A.'s resurrection and survival.

During the following Christmastide a company of R.A.D.A. students performed a nativity play in a church in Reigate. They had devoted their holiday to touring the units of South Eastern Command. None of the players was over eighteen, but their inexperience was discounted by the grace and sincerity of their performances. Our headquarters staff attended in strength and their appreciation for that youthful mystery was measured by the fervour of their carol singing. I was the more touched by the knowledge that this miracle had been rehearsed and produced by Kenneth Barnes and his staff amid the wreckage of their Academy and under the stress of continuing air raids, staying at their posts and kindling the spark of talent in young people ready to lay aside their theatrical ambitions until they had played their part and for some of them their last, in saving the traditions of the English theatre from extinction.

By February 1943 plans were completed for Exercise Spartan that would determine the fate of Army Co-operation Command and perhaps of 35 Wing. A mock up of a Tactical Air Force, Z Group, was the target on which criticisms of vested army/air interests would be focussed. Leigh Mallory was as determined to prove the redundancy of Army Co-operation Command as, alas, Ugly Barratt seemed inclined to countenance the survival of a makeshift charade conspicuous for the absence of any coherent plot.

In the coming production I was cast for the role of an umpire under the direction of my colleague at General Gort's Headquarters three years ago — now Brigadier Gerald Templar.

My temporary detachment from 35 Wing was tolerable thanks to an appointment that greatly favoured our cause. Pete Donkin, who had commanded 168 Squadron since our inception, was now our Group Captain. No wiser choice could have been made. Devon born, in manner and appearance he reminded me of Gary Cooper, taciturn but with a laconic wit. His chief concern was for the safety and well-being of his pilots but this was so masked by a sardonic humour that many of them failed to appreciate their good fortune in serving under him. When the heat and dust of Exercise Spartan had settled and 35 Wing was incorporated in 84 Group I was asked by its Senior Intelligence Officer to write a confidential letter that I knew was to be the basis of a citation for his D.S.O. I ended it, in support of my assertion that of the three Group Captains I had served under he was outstanding for "his insistence, at all times, on careful planning and flying discipline that made it possible for our squadrons to carry out extensive operations both offensive and photographic with the minimum of loss". As a pilot his leadership was unchallenged in a squadron that had suffered heavy losses at Dieppe; by night he had bagged as many French locomotives as the bad men or redskins Gary Cooper had ever accounted for in a single film. Marcus Kaye, now a Wing Commander, had been posted to Operations Z Group; another of our veteran Squadron Commanders, "Andy" Anderson, had reluctantly been taken off operations to join the planners of the Tactical Air Force to be. So we had friends of like minds in high places eager to keep us informed of the realisation of the policies we favoured.

Before leaving Reigate to join the caravan of Spartan umpires (for the planners of the Exercise were determined on its rigorous conduct) I bade farewell to Nell and Arthur Rank who for so long had given me refuge in times of stress and had made a friend of their "billet" as he had of his generous hosts. For some time past Arthur had become aware of my professional commitment to films and had, I think, found it a relief to confide his problems to one conversant with the perennial crises in the industry but now so far removed from it as to consider them with a measure of detachment. With an eye to the future he had energetically acquired as many cinemas as he could — either in bulk by taking over established chains of them or buying out individual exhibitors dispirited by the risks and anxieties of running them in war conditions. So far his investment in production had been tentative. At that time he had no idea of the part he would have to play as the victim of a Shavian confidence trick, as innocent of its consequences as those who were perpetrating it. During our hand-to-mouth production of *Pygmalion* a few reluctant benefactors threw comparatively small sums into Pascal's begging bowl, Arthur being one of them. All were richly rewarded for their charity. Pascal, having virtually sold his birthright in the film in order to get it financed and exhibited, profited little from its success. This was so phenomenal that when he announced his intention to film *Major Barbara* Arthur had agreed to finance it. The comparative failure of *Major Barbara* did not deter the Yorkshireman, with his love of a gamble, from assuming total responsibility for the cost of producing *Caesar and Cleopatra*. *Major Barbara* had been produced and exhibited during the Blitzkreig. It was not difficult to attribute its lack of success to this rather than to the assumption by Pascal and Shaw of the roles of director and script writer that neither of them were temperamentally or technically fitted to sustain. Arthur, in his modesty, did not pretend to understand the subtleties of Shaw's play that had been presented to him as a vehicle for a de-Millean spectacle. If it could be ready for distribution to a war weary public when in the now foreseeable future hostilities ceased it might attract vast audiences of devotees of de-Mille and Shaw alike.

Wing Commander Maclean D.F.C., explaining tac/r operations to Hilary St. George Saunders, historian of the R.A.F.

Pilots relaxing outside Ops. Room.

Pilot and Army Liaison Officer examining photographs.

Mustang being serviced al fresco.

First photographs of V1 launching site under construction.

German beach defences near Courseulles-sur-Mer at low tide.

5/6 a.m. D-Day. 1st Canadian Army landing near Courseulles.

As he told me of his plans I was reminded that G.B.S. had, by the hand of Ellen Terry, dangled before my grandfather the play that had been deliberately constructed to provide the kind of spectacle that Shaw believed was the chief element in Irving's tenacious hold over theatregoers in Great Britain and in the United States. What he failed to understand was that his dialectical and extravagant wit would have been as unacceptable to those audiences (as my grandfather shrewdly divined) as the recent emendations by the Anglican Church to Cranmer's lyrical Book of Common Prayer had been to churchgoers of riper years resistant to vernacular modification.

G.B.S.'s friend, William Archer, had at the time described the play as an "extravaganza" and expressed the hope that as such it would not be repeated. It is indeed a dramatic mayonnaise of melodrama, Roman tushery, comedy, spectacle and tirades in the "Sardou" style — the latter no doubt attractive bait to my grandfather if he played Caesar. Shaw's biographer, St. John Irvine, bases his admiration for the play on those superb polemics delivered by a disillusioned dictator despairing of mankind's destructive follies. I kept my own council and refrained from warning Arthur that it might not evoke the response from intellectual and "nine-penny" film goers that he had been persuaded would be prodigious.

Oddly enough, Pascal's only rival as a producer of films in a purely British idiom was an Italian solicitor, Filippo del Giudice, who before the war had organised his Two Cities film company to that end. Since 1939 he had been languishing in an internment camp for enemy aliens in the Isle of Man. Now, paradoxically, he had been released to resume command of his company, to reassemble his team of technicians and to produce Shakespeare's *Henry the Fifth* with Laurence Olivier perfectly cast as the monarch and entrusted with the direction of the enterprise. The film met its date line for release shortly after D Day. All concerned had good cause to be thankful that their efforts matched the hour.

Remote from such nostalgic preoccupations, a night or two later I lay wakeful in my "flea-bag" in a large hut resonant with the hubble-bubble of my snoring fellow umpires. In the dim light I watched in the corner an elderly field-officer, perhaps old enough to be my father, sitting up in his valise, puffing at a pipe, sleepless and gazing fixedly at the ceiling as if in a ruminative trance. What years of dull or active service had led to the end of a career begun with such high hopes at Sandhurst or Woolwich and ending with retirement now rudely broken by the call of duty to military service beyond his comprehension. He would have saluted Sir Thomas Erpingham as a fellow old commander and most kind gentleman with sentiments more akin to his own than those of the young philistines lying around him who were purging what he had been taught to regard as the art of war of such remnants of romance as had persisted after the previous holocaust. The sight of him wreathed in tobacco smoke like some phantom conjured from a cauldron for Macbeth banished self-pity and induced contented sleep.

Though I hoped my performance as a supernumerary umpire had been satisfactory — the daily co-ordination of reports and the provision of a nightly summary to our chief umpire Brigadier Templar — my recollections of those decisive days are comparatively frivolous.

During our first night in the field the Luftwaffe added a wholesome touch of realism to our make-believe operations by bombing our headquarters. The trestle tables at which we worked were rocked by explosions and when a Canadian colleague and myself went out for a breath of fresh air we watched a night fighter spouting fiery darts at an unseen intruder, alas without effect. The outcome of this attack was a sharp reminder of the perpetual hazards of security. We learned that a careless signaller had broadcast in clear administrative orders addressed to the headquarters of every military and air formation, and the position of ammunition dumps and of fuel stores locating them by map references. These signals were, of course, intercepted by German signallers in France where the Luftwaffe responded to this welcome invitation. No serious damage was done and to me it seemed significant that only twenty-five bombers had been mustered to make the most of this fool-sent opportunity.

As the battle swung towards Oxford my fellow umpire Goronwy Rees not only invited me to dine with him at All Souls but, having located my son John at New College, who had gone up to Oxford for six months and for training at the University Flying Club prior to joining the R.A.F. and had asked him to join us. His kindly thought was spiced with mischief. For he hoped that the few aged fellows likely to be in residence might imagine that I was my father whom they remembered, as later Max Beerbohm so vividly recalled, as a notable undergraduate. So, indeed, they may have done — all but one, Sir Lionel Curtis, the *doyen* of The Round Table whose dreams of empire must now be dissolving into nightmares. When John and I were introduced to him, with grave regard he murmured: "Brothers, I presume". Goronwy relished this as his guests did a very square meal, mellow wines and far from Spartan conversation.

The cease fire found us in range of Greys Court. I made a brief sortie to my home where I found Rosalind on short rations following the appearance on her doorstep of a famished and exhausted section of Royal Engineers. She invited them in and nourished them as best she could. When, on parting, she commiserated with the starry-eyed young officer on his weariness, he reassured her: "Oh, that's nothing — *we're* winning!" I found this *esprit de corps* more heartening than the sheaves of factual fare I had been digesting day by day.

And memorable was the evening when I sat beside Gerald Templar over one of our meagre and hasty meals. By dead reckoning we concluded that he must have succeeded me as tenant of an attic cubicle in the Blucher dormitory at Wellington College. His reaction to its mores had been similar to my own. But, whereas I found ignoble refuge from it in a nervous breakdown, he was a boy of sterner purpose and had considered seeking a dramatic quietus by hurling himself from the rooftop into the quadrangle below. We dwelt with mutual relish on the scene presented to an appalled house-master summoned by the hall porter to view the mangled corpse of an unworthy *heroum filius* ignored by the unflinching gaze of Generals von Blucher and Lord Anglesey whose terra cotta busts flanked the entrances to their respective penitentiaries. Who can tell whether the Field Marshal to whom that miserable boy was father won his baton in spite of or because of the Iron Duke's legacy of quasi-military education? Yet plainly we continued to share a distaste for boring disciplines that our house-master would have felt it his duty to eradicate in twigs resistant to his stubborn bending.

Soon after I returned to Reigate the most capable staff officers of South Eastern Command began to drift away to organise and train our 2nd Army. Goronwy Rees and Marcus

Kaye left for higher education at their respective staff colleges in the arts of planning and logistics. Archie Chisholm had returned to Persia where, as a political intelligence officer, he became the scourge of those suspected of partiality to the Germans or party to any attempts to sabotage our oil fields.

While Army Co-operation Command was discreetly disbanded, 35 Wing, now assured of its survival and reinforced by a third squadron, moved to the peace-time R.A.F. Station, Odiham, where it enjoyed a few weeks of domestic stability.

Part III
Reconnaissance

In air reconnaissance, our joint venture
enjoyed a great and telling advantage over
the enemy. Without its assistance, no
important operation was undertaken. With
its assistance, much of our work was made
simpler, safer and surer. Whenever we
called on the pilots to help us by
photographing the enemys' defences or
looking behind them, we knew that it
would be done if human beings could do it.
They did not fail.

General H. D. G. Crerar,
C.H., C.B., D.S.O.
G.O.C.-in-C First Canadian Army

I

Our first intimation of the creation of a Tactical Air Force was our appointment as the reconnaissance Wing to 84 Group which, with 83 Group, would operate respectively in close support of Canadian and 2nd Armies constituting 21 Army Group now committed with equivalent American forces to the invasion of France. Incorporated in these Groups was the ground to air control system perfected by Fighter Command but now, mounted on wheels, capable of immediate response to calls from troops in action for attacks by fighter-bomber wings on tactical targets. By now the pilots of 35 Wing were a companionship of Englishmen, Scotsmen, Australians, New Zealanders, a Norwegian, a Czechoslovakian, a German Jewish refugee, and Hindus of the Royal Indian Air Force, whose common denominator was the skill of their performance and pride in their association. As our Sundays were working days like any other we had no church parades or corporative religious services that in such company might have been divisive. Yet if sublime disregard for personal ambition, indomitable cheerfulness and good nature, self-sacrifice and consideration for one another are Christian virtues, they were acceptable novices and might be forgiven for refusing to forgive enemies whose propensity for evil was even more hideous than they imagined. Was it their dedication to this common cause, the recognition of each other's trustworthiness, the absence of a competitive need to earn a livelihood, or to gain promotion at the expense of others that enabled this brotherhood of ethnically and temperamentally disparate young men to live, work and die together in such admirable harmony? The evil of war is, perhaps, that it inspires so deep a sense of fellowship in those who wage it that, when peace comes, they seek it in a society impalpably corrupted by commercial expediency, and all too often, finding it wanting, fail to come to terms with it and nursing their proud grievance endure it in an abiding attitude of resentful adolescence.

As the months went by, Pete Donkin's ability to command and inspire his multi-racial flock of pilots became more apparent to myself than, perhaps, to them; for the merits of his leadership were disguised by his quiet assumption of their competence and obedience to orders on which their survival depended, and by his caustic reprimands to "clots" who fell below the high standard expected of them. Like Monty, he had the measure of the enemy we would be bringing to battle. In this respect, he had a head start on most of his contemporaries. For he and that scarred veteran, Colonel Carton de Wiart had been our official observers of the German invasion of Poland and had witnessed the rout of the gallant but outdated Polish army by carefully co-ordinated armoured divisions and air forces that swept aside the suicidal charges of the finest cavalry in Europe. Thanks to him we had no illusions as to the severity of the ordeal we should soon be facing and at the same time the complete assurance of its successful outcome under the new dispensation.

I was now directly responsible to the Intelligence Officer of 84 Group, Wing Commander Edwin Swale, D.F.C. He was a candid and plain spoken Yorkshireman. From the outset he understood clearly the operational role our Wing would play and how the services I could render him could be used to the best advantage. Our friendship was cemented by nostalgia for past associations and present anxieties. For he, too, had been a fighter pilot in the R.N.A.S. in the previous war, and now his son was at an R.A.F. operational training unit while mine would soon be a flying instructor in Canada thus, for the time being, to my relief, at lesser risk.

My fellow feeling for Swale became more acute when, at Odiham, a young pilot came to share my bedroom in the station quarters. One morning I awoke and through the haze of semi-consciousness saw a slim lad standing with his back to me washing at the hand basin. He was stripped to the waist and for a moment I had the confused impression that he was my son until, hearing me astir, he turned and wished me good morning. In a few days our common interests had bridged the gap of years that separated us and, as always, in the transient life we all were leading our friendship quickly ripened. That afternoon I heard that one of our sections had been bounced by German fighters over Cabourg. The leader, my room-mate, had been shot down in flames; his companion had brought his crippled Mustang to within a mile or two of our coast when it plunged into the sea and he was drowned. My batman and I collected the sparse evidences of my young friend's occupation to be sent to his next of kin. Soon I was glad to leave the room in which his empty bed was a haunting reminder of hopes and fears that were the daily portion of all from whom fortune had exacted such beloved hostages.

The percipient Air Staff had appointed two Air Vice Marshals, both outstanding organisers, to command 83 and 84 Groups on the understanding that, when their task was completed, they would hand over the instruments they had forged to colleagues with operational experience of the purpose for which they were designed. We, in 84 Group, were lucky to find ourselves under the guiding hand of Air Vice Marshal Whitworth Jones. I was delighted to hear that he was the brother of Felix Aylmer, an actor whose performances I had long admired and with whom I had worked on one or two productions. Later Felix and I would become close friends and collaborators when, as Chairman of the Council of the R.A.D.A., he nursed it patiently through a period of difficult transition following the retirement of its creator, Kenneth Barnes. His brother, too, had a measure of histrionic talent that enlivened his conferences that I attended. Once, when we were respectfully urging him to support our revolt against the crass stupidity of some senior jack-in-office, he leaned back in his chair, and with arms outstretched spread his hands upon the table, with a sympathetic twinkle in his eye declaimed:

"Gentlemen, I see the time has come when it behoves us to devise a stratagem!"

Before long I myself had to devise a stratagem that had it failed, would have left me with a self-inflicted wound. The Air Officer commanding the Tactical Air Force in its formative period was John D'Albiac. I had known and liked him well when, as a captain in the Royal Marines, he had been the Intelligence Officer to No. 1 Wing R.N.A.S. at Dunkerque nearly thirty years earlier. His amused approach to life and whimsical urbanity had engaged the affection of all his fellow officers. Clandestinely, Evill had taught him to fly, albeit erratically, so, in due course, he gained a general service commission in the newly formed Royal Air Force. While I was at Reigate he had invited me to lunch with him at his headquarters in Suffolk where he was in command of the light bomber squadrons of No. 2 Group. Our recollections of old friends and the archaic practices of aviation we had enjoyed contrasted grimly with his present responsibilities at a time when his air crews had suffered heavy casualties owing to the deadly personal ambition of his predecessor, and were in need of the humane leadership that he knew to be necessary to the restoration of their morale. In the afternoon, he arranged for me to visit a nearby heavy bomber group for which on several occasions we had taken photographs of targets. I arrived there in time to attend the briefing of Pathfinders for a massive raid on Stuttgart planned for that night. Afterwards, in the spacious mess, I was very conscious of the tense preoccupation of the air crews as in separate little groups they sat in the gathering dusk waiting for darkness and the time of take-off on their long missions. The atmosphere was markedly different to the nervous but alert and volatile bearing of fighter pilots at readiness near their aircraft at their dispersal points, and from the intent but relaxed deportment of our own pilots while they were individually briefed for sorties that called for cool calculation and precise execution. I had very much enjoyed my reunion with D'Albiac whose amiable mannerisms I found unchanged.

Recently Swale had told me that our Senior Intelligence Officer at T.A.F. seemed not only ignorant of the nature of his duties but stubbornly opposed to the adoption of the methods we were agreed upon as to the handling of the results of our reconnaissance operations. Unless we could have his co-operation in implementing the procedures that had stood the test of Exercise Spartan, our plans at this critical juncture would be in disarray. The officer in question was a bigoted and rather vain regular appointed, no doubt, on the principle of "Buggin's turn".

Soon afterwards D'Albiac came to make an official inspection of 35 Wing. Pete Donkin and I explained to him and gave a practical demonstration of the collation and distribution of intelligence we derived from our own and other sources. Inspired by the memory of Nelson's example as to the merits of timely insubordination and risking a well-earned rebuke of presuming on our old acquaintance, I told D'Albiac bluntly of the obstruction we were enduring from his staff and of our conviction that we were right in demanding the adoption of a method that should be common doctrine in the immediate training of the components under his command. Pete let me have all the rope I needed to hang myself; he, as I did, expected a sharp and unfavourable reaction to my presumption. The Air Vice Marshal looked up, eyed me sharply, and tersely remarked; "That will do, Irving!" He left the room to continue his inspection. Yet I was not surprised when a few days later Swale, who was unaware of this stratagem, reported a remarkable change of heart in his troublesome superior and the latter's apparent eagerness to be amenable to our suggestions. New intelligence would not be mishandled for the sake of auld lang syne.

At about this time I met a theatrical obligation that would have far-reaching consequences. Ben Travers, with his abiding tact and good humour was dutifully trying to reconcile the Air Ministry's concern for security with the policies of capricious censors at the Ministry of Information. But, such was his prodigious industry, he had found time to write a farce, *She Follows me Around* which of all his works has the most delightful theme, as ever based on the vagaries of human mischief and perplexity. The first act was set on the coast of Cornwall. Such scene painters as were still available had failed to create to his satisfaction the briny background essential to the comic contrivance on which his plot depended. In desperation he asked if I could help him. Explaining that I could make no scale drawings or a maquette, I sent him a sketch that I knew an experienced scenic artist could interpret without my supervision. Apparently my design met his need; less pleasurable duties prevented me from seeing the production.

Later, much to my surprise, the management sent me a generous cheque in return for what I had regarded as a labour of love. Soon, amidst sterner occupations, I forgot about this welcome distraction. In fact that cheque proved to be an incalculable blessing when, after the war, I was about to continue my career. For it provided evidence that confounded the knavish tricks of ravenous tax-gatherers who after the war asserted in justification of their demand for swingeing tax on the payment of compensation by a film company, when a cold wind of retrenchment in the film industry froze many contracts such as mine, that by rejoining the R.A.F. I had abandoned my profession as a painter.

By September the organisation of the Tactical Air Force was well-advanced. Its purpose was to co-operate with the R.A.F.

134

Home Commands and to administer its Groups' operations in direct support of their respective Armies. In turn, Wings such as ours were to be relieved of all responsibility for accommodation and maintenance by independent airfields organised and equipped to act as hosts to the units temporarily occupying them according to the tactical situation. Ancillary services were provided by Airfield Construction Companies capable of rapidly levelling runways and building bomb-proof dispersal points on predetermined locations in France. During their construction and occupation these airfields would be defended by units of the newly formed R.A.F. regiment.

In the early autumn we left our comfortable quarters at Odiham and took to our caravans that would not rest until they settled down under skies purged of the Luftwaffe on an airfield in occupied Germany.

Shortly before we set out on this victorious pilgrimage Pete Donkin suggested that I should compile and issue a "news sheet" that would record in detail the operations of our squadrons and of individual pilots and keep them well-informed of the day to day progress of the campaign to which they were making their indispensable contribution. At that moment I felt that the mantle of Richard Hakluyt had fallen upon me. Thereafter much of my time was spent gathering newsworthy details of successful sorties from pilots, relating them to the overall military situation, writing brief biographies of eminent characters in our companionship of nearly a hundred young officers, and trying to enliven this factual journal with the kind of humour that might appeal to them. I drew liberally on the style of the *New Yorker* with its exemplary flair for accurate reporting and brevity of wit. Our 35 Wing News Sheet was printed on a portable duplicator and issued once or twice a week according to the intensity of our activities. It was, of course, a secret document circulated only to each squadron and to the staff of 84 Group. Sometimes, for security's sake, the nature or purpose of certain operations were not specified though these were known to those who carried them out. It was published without a break for the last eighteen months of the war. In time to come if a keen historian discovers it he will find a unique record of the occupations and achievements, the prowess and misfortunes, the jests and deeper concerns of a band of brothers, among those who were the last to fight a war in the air that, as time went by, I felt (though never voiced such an opinion) differed very little except in terms of speed and weapons from the one suspended in 1918 and ended for all time with catastrophic sorties over Hiroshima and Nagasaki.

My editorial duties were facilitated by the first practical evidence of our new image — a mobile operations room or rooms, with two large compartments mounted on heavy trucks parked several yards apart and the space between them canopied and walled with canvas, and with tented platforms extended from their outer sides. Thus we had a commodious briefing room, offices for myself and our Army Liaison Officers, and for our wireless operators maintaining communications with 84 Group. This perfectly designed and constructed complex proved impervious to weather conditions and to the strains of constant dismantling and reassembly. Before long its occupants learned to erect it in a couple of hours even in the teeth of a gale.

During the autumn our mobility, operational flexibility and lines of communication were tested severely as we moved from one airfield to another continuing our sorties over France and at the same time participating in two major exercises. The first was an impressively organised deception operation designed to lead the enemy to expect the imminent opening of the 'second front' supposedly under pressure from Stalin and once again to bring the Luftwaffe to battle in order to assess its dwindling strength; the second was to test for the first time integration between 84 Group and 2nd Army in the field. The latter I anticipated with hope rather than with confidence. For Selwyn Lloyd, lately G.2 Operations at South Eastern Command had deservedly been promoted to B.G.S. of the new army. He had not, I think, been favourably impressed by 35 Wing, viewing with disapproval the unconventional and sometimes uncouth behaviour of its staff in general and particularly the bizarre disregard of protocol by Marcus Kaye. In consequence he had been among those able but unenlightened soldiers slow to realise that air superiority was prerequisite to any success they might achieve on the ground. In the event, though Marcus Kaye was by this time Wing Commander Operations, 84 Group, thanks very largely to the tact and professionalism of his Senior Air Staff Officer Theodore McEvoy, the foundations of efficient co-operation were well and truly laid.

This period is illustrated by vignettes engraved upon my

memory — sitting in our mess tent around a coke stove belching smoke as a gale raged around our encampment, striving far into the night to explain to our gallant and most aggressive pilot, a German-Jewish refugee whose parents by then might have been exterminated, the humour of Alice in Wonderland that he found inexplicable — "kid's stuff" he rejected as devoid of intellectual entertainment. His resistance to our persuasion confirmed my belief that disparity in a sense of the ridiculous and of comicality is the greatest obstacle to mutual understanding between nations. So philosophers may in the distant future divine that Chaplin and Walt Disney provided the true catalyst by reducing global audiences to helpless laughter at the same joke.

Then, as briefly we occupied an airfield at Driffield, I realised how rapidly the happy years between the wars were losing their flavour in the sandwich of memory and I recalled that thirty years ago I had patrolled this area in vain pursuit of Zeppelins in fragile contraptions of wood and linen (albeit rapturous to fly) that beside our metal Mustangs, more heavily armed than a battalion of infantry in the first war, would seem as primitive as a coracle alongside a destroyer of the Royal Navy. Yet, in spite of these material contrasts, I found that my present companions were subject to the same hopes and fears, stresses and strains, disciplines and need for relaxations that had governed our lives of active air service so long ago. Undoubtedly the most significant innovation was the resource of the parachute. Whereas we and our aircraft were of one body indivisible in survival or destruction, these young pilots had a life-line inconceivable to us, slender though it might be. During interrogations I tried to gauge the psychological effect of this escape clause on their mental approach to their tasks. It seemed negligible, a saving grace taken for granted which did not mitigate the harsh realities of air warfare far more complex and no less hazardous than that we, who suffered no sense of deprivation from the absence of the inconceivable, had waged in our own fashion.

II

In the late autumn we moved into quarters as bleak as the midwinter which would soon be upon us. Our hosts were 123 Airfield. To our surprise, having concluded our training with

2nd Army, our Group was assigned to Canadian Army and our Wing augmented with a Canadian Air Photographic Interpretation Unit under the command of Major David Morrice. No one could have welcomed this modest and efficient officer more warmly than myself. For I soon discovered that he was a fellow painter from Montreal who had left his easel to apply his skills to service in the army that called for precise observation and a natural concern for the high quality of photographs developed and printed by his unit. He was the nephew of James Wilson Morrice, a painter who had left Canada in 1890 and had been accepted as an impressionist by Manet and his coterie. He made France his home and died in Tunis in 1924. His work best known to British artists is, however, "The Quebec Ferry" that stands comparision with Monet's studies of "Débâcles", — chill grey skies over hills and quayside blanketed with snow and a dark river strewn with ice floes, the bitter cold accentuated by the smudge of smoke from the funnel of the ferry boat generated by its furnaces — the only spark of life in the moribund landscape.

Our accommodation near the airfield at Sawbridgeworth in cement offices and nissen-hutted sleeping quarters seemed damp and penal in contrast to our bracing outdoor life. The camp had been evacuated recently by a detachment of W.A.A.F.'s securely wired in to protect them presumably from predatory males. But the traces of their occupation — mainly cosmetics, hair curlers and a few discarded under garments quenched rather than inflamed the lusts of their successors.

Happily, the addition of a new dimension to our operations rapidly dissipated the gloom of our surroundings. Towards the end of October I was summoned to the Air Ministry by a new section evaluating in understandable secrecy the threat of a German weapon that might imperil the success of our invasion of France. On one of our routine oblique photographs of the Cap Gris Nez area an array of wireless antennae of a new type had excited the interest of specialist interpreters. Following up this clue, vertical cover by our Spitfires had revealed a forbidding structure of vast proportions near Watten in Belgium. Orientated as it was on London, without waiting to determine its purpose, it had been heavily bombed with apparent success. Now I was given nine map references of other mysterious installations that we were ordered to reconnoitre without delay. Nobody was certain as to their nature. I was told that a heavy night bombing raid on Peenamunde had been made at the request of our scientists who had evidence that it was an experimental station using the Baltic as a testing range for guided missiles, two of which had been identified on the ground by interpreters at Medmenham. Now, six months later, it was possible that these weapons, though their development had been delayed by the devastation of Peenamunde, were being deployed behind the fortified coasts of Belgium and France. I returned to Sawbridgeworth, opened a file under the codeword Noball, and gave what details I could to our A.L.O.'s who were to brief their pilots for these urgent sorties. A week later my file was swollen by ninety such map references. Noball proved to be our principal engagement for weeks ahead. Our News Sheet, since its absolute security could not be guaranteed, summarised the situation thus:

> "... it is a battle of great importance and tremendous technical interest. It is a battle between an Air Force that has won domination over a defeated Air Force now forced to poke about in contraptions of cement, launching self-propelled gadgets into a sky in which its air crews no longer care to operate. 35 Wing has an important part to play in this battle. All available information of its progress can be found at your Intelligence Section. There is nothing like a complete knowledge of your subject to put an edge on the execution of your tasks."

Our pilots tackled this exacting commitment with their usual judgement and skill. They identified their targets without difficulty. The importance attached to these installations by the enemy could be gauged by the intensity of anti-aircraft fire that defended them. The constructions our photographs revealed were curious and puzzling. The main feature of each site was a concrete building about 10 feet square and 50 feet long, curved at one end like a hockey stick. For brevity, on this account, they were named "ski-sites". They included a number of smaller buildings and a large circle of cement such as we had on our airfields for adjusting the compasses of our aircraft. The sites were rapidly nearing completion when, in fair weather, American heavy bombers attacked them with good results. But what was their purpose? All were situated close to a small copse or wood, some were evidently completed and yet the key to their operation was missing. At last one of our pilots, Flight Lieut. Raehill, flew at virtually nought feet through a barrage of small-arms fire and discerned through the leafless trees that had screened it from our cameras the long sought launching ramp. We rushed him to Medmenham where, from the details he so accurately described, craftsmen were able to complete models of the sites they had been making from our photographs. Gradually our cover of these targets was completed. It was, I thought, the peak of our squadrons' achievement.

It so happened that our Noball operations coincided with the arrival of a Flying Officer at 268 Squadron who would be a source of anxiety to Pete Donkin and his squadron commander for some time to come. For months past, Jock Colville, the Prime Minister's young private secretary, had been importuning his master to allow him a spell of active service. He had been trained as a pilot in the Auxiliary Air Force but rightly having become indispensable to the conduct of the Cabinet offices and particularly to Churchill to whom his frank and unintimidated responses were invaluable, he was held chafing at his inaction in Whitehall. At last he had been released and had been posted to 35 Wing. It had been conveyed to Pete indirectly but in no uncertain terms that the newcomer having completed a tour of duty must be returned to Downing Street intact. We did not need to be told that, if ill befell him, his loss would grieve one who did not disguise his personal affection for those who served him well. We were equally confident that a young man whose courage matched his intelligence would be quick to detect any attempt to send him on sorties less hazardous than those of his fellow pilots. It was just the luck of the draw that he had joined the Wing in the most stressful period of its existence. He was, of course, unaware of the charge laid upon his Group Captain and of our anxiety as we gathered in the daily reports of operations with their sad epilogues of casualties that meant recurring loss of friends. As it turned out Colville survived his term of perilous leave, proving himself as battleworthy as any of his companions. No doubt his practical experience enhanced his value to the frustrated old warrior he served and enabled him to bear with an easier conscience the burden of his sedentary responsibilities.

DAMAGED BUILDINGS   FIRES

COURSEULLES sur MER

10 a.m. D-Day. Sortie covering British landings flown by Air Commodore Geddes, O.B.E., D.S.O., H.Q. 2nd Tactical Air Force.

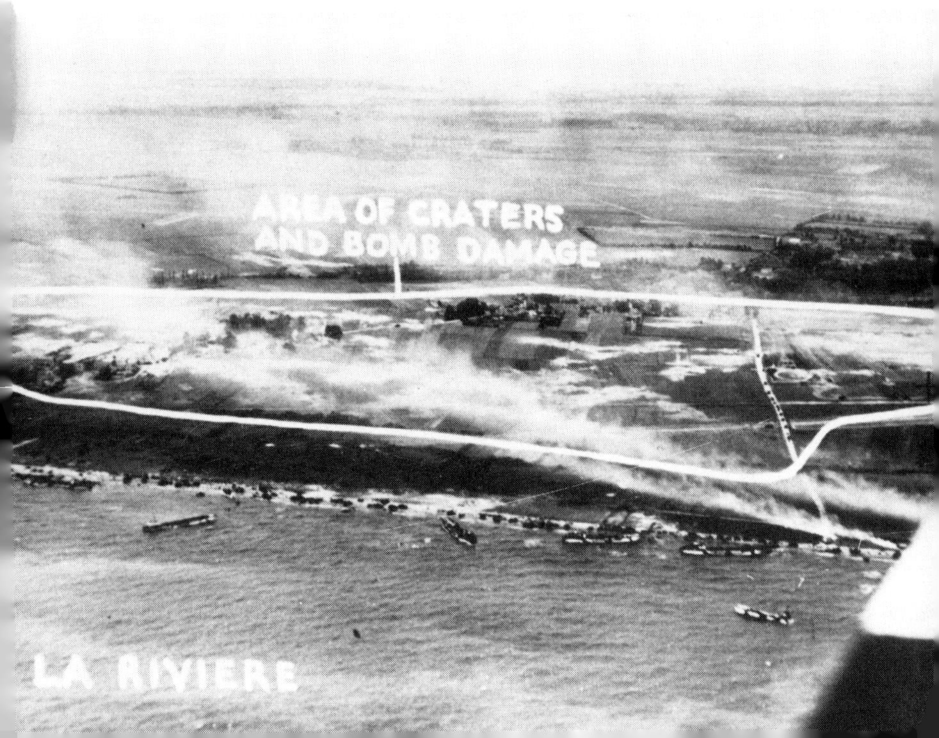

AREA OF CRATERS AND BOMB DAMAGE

LA RIVIERE

FIRE

ST. AUBIN sur MER

10 a.m. D-Day. Sortie covering British landings flown by Air Commodore Geddes,   O.B.E., D.S.O.,
H.Q. 2nd Tactical Air Force.

BUILDINGS

BERNIERS sur MER

Cargo ships sunk to provide shelter off Arromanches shortly after D-Day.

Section of Mulberry Harbour being towed across English Channel.

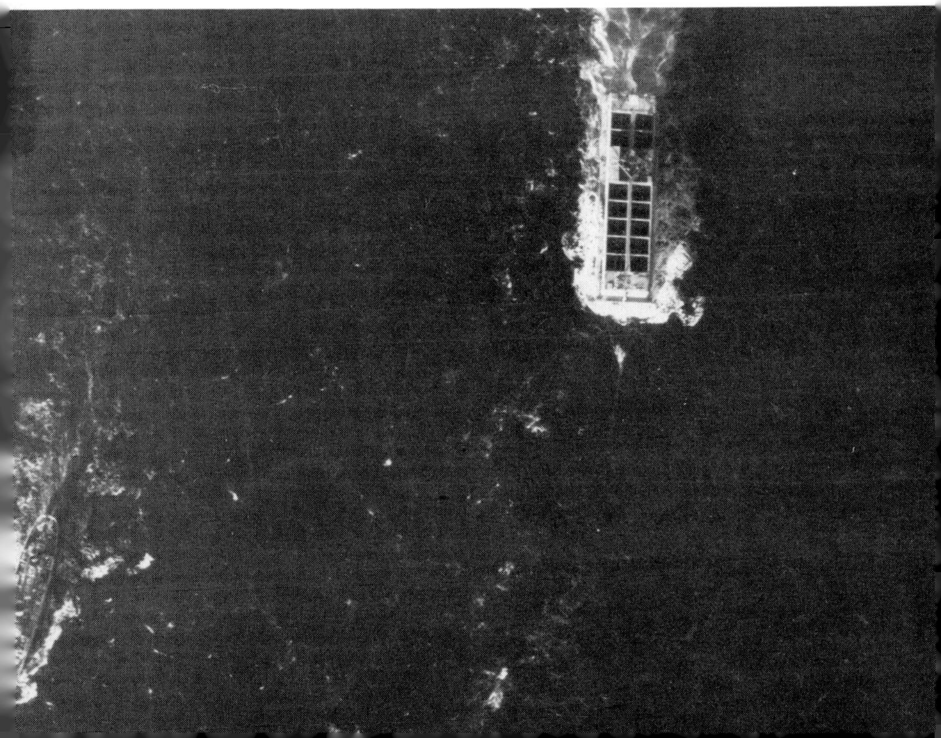

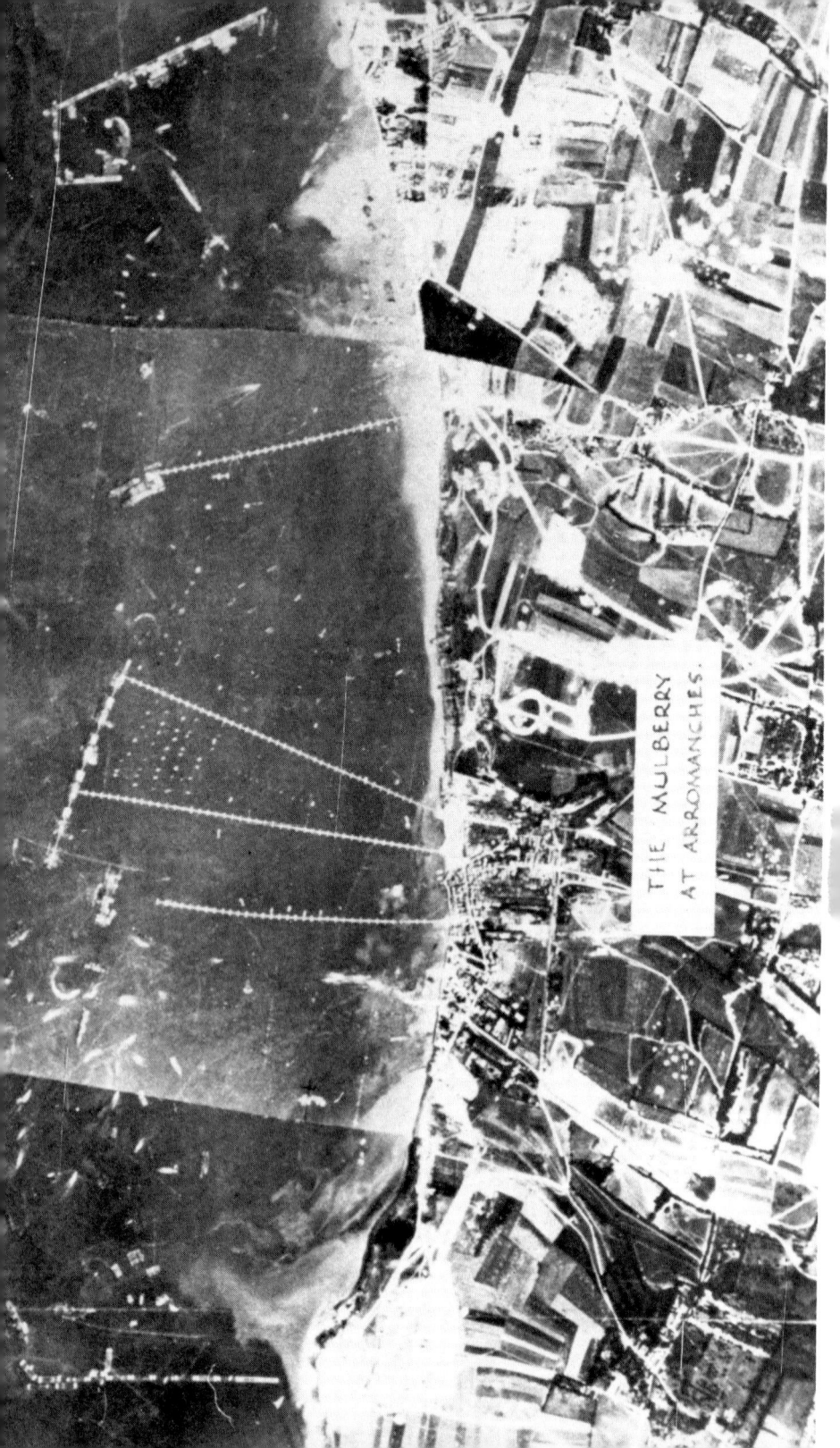

THE MULBERRY AT ARROMANCHES.

One day I was laying feverish and comatose in my hut after being injected with antidotes against all the ills the flesh of British warriors in foreign fields is supposedly heir to, other than those to which their proverbial licentiousness make them most prone. The telephone rang and a voice from our flying control tower told me that a Wing Commander Ingle Finch had landed in a Spitfire and was on his way to see me.

When he arrived he took one look at the dilapidated old buffer in a dressing gown and no doubt reckoned him a sitting target. He had come to ask me for the hand of my daughter in marriage — a courteous formality in such strenuous times when polite conventions had become a casualty of war. Pamela's beauty and good nature had already stirred the hearts of several ardent suitors, none of whom had sought my paternal approval and so, in my view, deserved to be jilted as they had been. Rosalind alone had borne the brunt of these transitory wooings.

Now I was confronted by a tough if rather inarticulate claimant to be my son-in-law. My pertinent interrogation quickly solicited his credentials. He had, I saw, been awarded the Air Force Cross. Having been a fighter pilot in the Battle of Britain (he won my sympathy in that he had taken flight in adolescence as I had done) he had been decorated for the part he had played in testing the Typhoon, an aircraft that, together with Napier's Sabre engine, was the daring concept of designers and engineers that went straight from the drawing board into mass production without a hitch and thus made a decisive contribution to the destruction of the Luftwaffe and the Wehrmacht. It was already coming into service and Michael, as my visitor identified himself in prospectively relative terms, was to command a wing of these formidable fighter-bombers in 83 Group.

I knew that Pam, though she had never told me so, had been one of several A.T.S. officers who volunteered to serve in an underground stay-behind signal organisation operating in support of Auxiliary Units in the event of an invasion. She had been stationed in Northumberland at the time of our recent exercise with 2nd Army and there had met and fallen in love with Michael who now informed me of a *fait accompli*. What could I do but wish him better luck than his predecessors and pronounce a probably incoherant blessing on their union. In the event this proved suprisingly efficacious for in the course of

141

time they became parents of three sons who in turn became successive head boys of their public school. Yet, when having fulfilled his duty Michael bade me genial farewell, I was left with the uneasy feeling that capricious fortune had exacted another hostage to add to my anxieties.

A few minutes later my hut was shaken by the thunderous approach of a missile that reached a crescendo in a rending whine as it hurtled over my already splitting head. Later I was told that the departing Spitfire had done a victory roll over our camp at nought feet.

I was all the more thankful when, soon afterwards, I was relieved of a burden that was not only a constant weight on my mind but a trial of patience that was hard to endure. Earlier the Air Minister had inflicted on me an assistant Flight Lieutenant. He had the appearance and manner of an exiled President of a South American Republic. He was vain, indolent and totally unreliable; his assistance was tolerable only when his sly lackadaisical wit expressed itself in pungent comment on the follies of officialdom. He was relieved by Douglas Goodbody, and so was I. His successor had been serving on the Italian front in close collaboration in an intelligence unit with Thornton Wilder, his counterpart in the American Air Force. Doggo, as he was soon affectionately known to us all, was welcome if only for the news he brought me of his association with a writer I venerated, counting his play *Our Town* with *Journey's End* the two productions (apart from the sequence of verse drama at our Canterbury Cathedral festivals) that had animated my deepest response. He was a barrister-in-law, a member of the Garrick Club, and an amateur of all the arts; his enthusiasm for sports of any kind and active participation in many of them enhanced the image of our Intelligence Section in the eyes of young pilots to whom I could be no more than an avuncular figure incapable of competing with them in games of any kind or even erudite discussion of them.

His congenial company was to mean much to me. His range of interests was wide, his appreciations astute — Wisden and Shakespeare, hockey and the humanities, fly-fishing and philosophy would incline to him to ruminative conjecture that is the making of lively conversation. I felt that to him the war came as a release from the confines of the Law Courts, that he had thoroughly enjoyed his service hitherto, and that he looked forward to the *al fresco* life we should soon be resuming. Above all I knew that we shared the conviction that we had been faced with destruction of all that we believed made life worth living and that we were privileged to play even a supernumerary part in the concluding act that would ensure the preservation of a social order that with all its faults, was the most liberal and humane that mankind had so far achieved.

At the end of March we resumed our nomad life and with a sense of relief and keen expectancy pitched our tents at Gatwick. I heard that Monty had returned to England from his triumphant campaigns in Africa and Italy. He had fulfilled the first of his prophetic utterances when he had taken leave of us at Reigate by defeating the Field Marshal against whom he said he would be pitted. Would he now as C. in C. of 21 Army Group, comprised of 2nd and Canadian Armies fulfil his promise to lead us to the final victory? Our premonitions were expressed in the prologue to the issue of our News Sheet when we resumed operations from our home ground.

III
Into Battle 1944

The traffic of our armies stilly sounds
As the foxed G.S.O.'s by night peruse
The secret minutes of each other's watch.
File answers file, and with their tattered flags
Enclosures pending keep their numbered place.
Ops threatens Int and A belabours Q
Cursing the phones dull ear; and from their tents
The Signallers establishing their lines
With probing pliers, mucking circuits up
Give dreadful note of urgent preparation.

After (a good deal) William Shakespeare.
Henry V. Act IV.

The purpose of our training with Canadian Army was no longer in doubt and its consummation was now to be reckoned by the calendar in calculations of weeks rather than months as hitherto. We were just getting into the swing of a routine that called for closer observation of beach obstacles and obstructions between Le Havre and Cherbourg, when what seemed to be an irreparable misfortune befell us.

On April 13th Pete Donkin and Flying Officer Normoyle (an Australian translated from travelling salesmanship in ladies underwear) took off at noon to take low oblique photographs of the Belgian coast at Ostend. For some time past I had deplored Pete's appetite for action. The weather was calm, the sky overcast, the visibility limited to 1500 yards from coast to coast. As he neared Ostend Pete turned his Mustang almost on its back and dived steeply for the run-in to his target. At 500 feet the section swept past Ostend through heavy flak. At the end of the run Pete climbed away from the coast calling Normoyle to close him as his aircraft had been hit and he would have to bale out. Normoyle saw his leader jettison his hood and heard him send out the usual Mayday signal; his own transmitter was unserviceable. For two minutes Pete flew northwards with smoke streaming from his aircraft; then turning it on its back he fell clear, his parachute opened, and as he landed in the sea he was seen to pull himself into his inflatable dinghy. He waved to Normoyle circling overhead who, satisfied that he was unhurt, returned to base. At noon intensive search and rescue operations were set in motion by our own squadrons reinforced by others of 11 Group. I was appalled by the prospect of Pete's loss for, perhaps, I had a keener understanding than most of the Wing's dependence on his wise and stern control of its activities. Moreover he would be known to the enemy as one of an elite of operational commanders and might, if he was taken prisoner, receive rough treatment at the hands of interrogators who would suspect that he had access to information that could be critical as the day of reckoning approached.

Squadron after squadron searched the area unavailingly except to rescue another pilot in a dinghy off the North Foreland. As dusk fell I left Gatwick with a heavy heart to break the news of his loss to his wife, Betty, at their home in Rudgwick, daunted by the knowledge that she was expecting imminently the birth of their second child. I knew that he would be contemptuous of any attempt on my part to wrap up the cruel facts in sentimental reassurances or to raise false hopes unjustified by the day's fruitless search. I knew that her courage and plain spokenness matched his own. Yet I still remember with gratitude the quiet composure and dignity with which she eased the stress of the harshest duty that the war, so far, had imposed upon me.

Next day fog hampered the continuing search and as the third day drew to a close so our hopes of Pete's survival finally waned. "Andy" Anderson was sent from TAF to take command of the Wing. His ebullient spirits and legendary prowess in action quickly restored the morale of our pilots, depressed not only by the loss of their leader but their failure to rescue him. Indeed they responded recklessly to Andy's expert command, accepting risks cheerfully taken by himself and a consequently higher rate of casualties than Pete would have tolerated.

Six days and five nights later the duty officer wakened me at 3.30 a.m. with the incredible news that Pete had been found alive in his dinghy by naval craft minesweeping in the Downs. He had been admitted to hospital in Dover an hour earlier.

Andy and I set off at once and arrived at the hospital to find him, all things considered, astonishingly well. Sitting up in bed and relishing his breakfast he looked like a famished eagle — his beak-like and sun scorched nose projecting from his pale and emaciated face below a pair of dark sockets from which his eyes blazed fiercely. The only serious injury he had suffered was to his feet swollen by continual immersion in the sea.

He greeted us sardonically and came straight to the point. He did not think he had been hit by flak. His first intimation of trouble was the smell of escaping glycol and the reflection in his mirror of the trail of vapour behind him at the end of his run. He had made a rough landing in the sea about 15 miles off Ostend slightly injuring his hand and thigh and losing the smoke flares that were part of the dinghy's equipment and perhaps for lack of them his life. For although many aircraft flew over him he was unable to signal to them.

The first night adrift had been the hardest to endure; thereafter his mental approach became purely objective, his will to survive sustained by persistent optimism. Once he fell out of his dinghy, managed to clamber back into it and realised that it would be fatal to do so again. One heavy fall of rain saved him from dying of thirst. Though I knew his capacity for self-discipline, I was astounded to hear that when he was picked up four of the dozen or so concentrated chocolate and condensed milk tablets in his survival kits were still in reserve.

His most anxious time had been when wind and tide carried him towards the French coast near Gravelines. He planned, in the event of being cast ashore, to find a boat and make a bid for home — unaware that his crippled feet rendered him immobile. He caught a seagull and, in the tradition of maritime adventure, killed it and tried to swallow its blood only to be instantly seasick.

As I listened to his terse account of his miraculous survival my diagnosis of his psychological endurance was that he had been sustained by his smouldering rage that the 'clots' of his Wing had failed to find him.

When we returned to Gatwick Andy summoned all our pilots to an 'indaba' outside our operations room. He expounded the lessons to be learned from the near loss of their Group Captain, insisting on the need for intense dinghy drill, assessing the flaws in the conduct of air sea rescue operations which should be studied and rehearsed by every squadron. He coated the bitter pill of justifiable criticism by telling them of the esteem in which 35 Wing was held in high places, Army and R.A.F., where great value was set on the increasing importance of their photographs.

When I returned to Rudgwick with the glad news of Pete's survival I was not prepared for the effect on Betty whose pent up grief so bravely borne found instant relief in floods of tears and signs of emotional stress that made me, in my ignorance, more fearful for her unborn child than I had been after my previous experience of her composure. But all was well, and as in such fabulous stories, their second daughter arrived safely and lived happily ever afterwards.

A week or two later a refreshing breeze of Elizabethan chivalry stirred the air of our headquarters. To Andy, deeply distressed as he was by the assumed loss of an old companion in arms whose temper and humour perfectly complemented his own, the appointment to command the Wing, in which he had served since its inception with such distinction, on the eve of great events that he had helped to plan must have fulfilled his heart's desire. Pete was soon on his swollen feet again and in May resumed his post. Though this was a relief that could but inspire Andys' thanks, the prospect of returning to his office desk must have galled him. I was deeply moved as I witnessed the public hail and farewell exchanged between two young gentlemen whose urbanity proved as invincible as their courage. Behind the banter and ribaldry of this most unceremonious ceremony both concealed a deep emotion that this quirk of fate must have stirred in them — the one taking possession of a new lease of life, mortgaged to the hilt and so nearly forfeited; the other surrendering the fortuitous and brief fulfilment of his consuming but selfless ambition. Both would have mocked at my admiration of their dignity and generosity on an occasion long remembered in a changing world when the resumption of competition for personal fame or power would erode a chivalry that can illumine the grim visage of war and too often fades behind the smiling mask of peace.

In the middle of May, David Morrice arranged an exhibition of the Wings' photographs, and of the interpretation and distribution of intelligence derived from them. His gifts as an artist were apparent in its attractive layout and in the clarity of presentation designed to inform all our customers of the services we had rendered them and of our capacity to meet any demands they might make on us during their impending campaign.

By chance, our first visitor was Hilary Saunders. I was delighted to welcome my exhilarating old friend now wearing the uniform of a Press Officer. I had last seen him when he was writing the pamphlet published soon after the end of the Battle of Britain had been determined and could be celebrated. His vivid narrative, though necessarily based on our own combat and intelligence reports and subject to the restraints of security, remains unique in the dramatic emphasis of its relation by a writer still under the spell of emotions prevailing at that time. Recently he had been engaged by the Air Ministry to write articles on the work of all its units in operation. For some reason or other the existence of reconnaissance squadrons had been concealed from him. The exhibition was such a surprise to him that he spent the rest of the day interviewing the staff and our pilots whose attention he held by his flow of good stories related with histrionic flamboyance of the conditions prevailing in occupied France; the most memorable was of the *graffiti* scrawled by the Maquis on walls in public and very private places that ran: "PICK YOUR BOSCHE NOW — THERE WON'T BE ENOUGH TO GO ROUND".

David's exhibition drew the attendances he aimed at including General Crerar, G.O.C. Canadian Army and many of his staff and division commanders. Another visitor who thoroughly commended it was Air Marshal Sir Arthur Coningham who had succeeded Sir Arthur Tedder, now Deputy to General Eisenhower, in command of the Tactical Air Force in Africa and Italy and had resumed his old relationship with Monty by taking over our 2nd Tactical Air Force. It was twenty years since I had last seen him when, as a debonair young R.A.F. officer stationed at Manston, he had been admitted to the theatrical coterie resident in Birchington which took its hilarious cue from its bear-leaders Gerald du Maurier and Freddie Lonsdale.

A week later Hilary returned as impresario of a performance that would have had no parallel in any other theatre of war. His articles on 35 Wing had appeared in a Sunday newspaper; perhaps for self-defence he had brought with him Sir Edward Fellows, Clerk of the Private Bills Office of the House of Commons, and Orlo Williams, Clerk of the Journals, whom he, as Librarian of the House, had had no difficulty in recruiting. The weather was perfect. Throughout the day these courteous gentlemen sat in the sunshine outside our operations room expounding to fluctuating but attentive and enquiring groups of pilots returning from their sorties the intricacies of parliamentary procedure. I wondered if the lecturers and their multi-racial audience appreciated the incongruity of their participation in so significant a curtain raiser to the coming drama.

IV

The quickening tempo of our operations and an increasing note of urgency in our communications with Canadian Army reached a climax when Pete Donkin and I were ordered to attend a conference in Uxbridge, now TAF headquarters, to be held by Coningham on Saturday June 3rd. Malcolm Barclay, our Senior Air Liaison Officer, had received a similar summons from General Crerar.

We arrived at Uxbridge in good time. We were met by a friend, once the security officer at Army Co-operation

Command, who was outraged to find that the cinema in which the conference was to be held was open to any intruder and that the R.A.F. policemen responsible for guarding it were asleep in the stalls. He had reported this to the Provost Marshal and was angered by the latter's reluctance to charge his defaulters with dereliction of such a paramount duty.

For all my life-long exposure to theatrical occasions never before had I felt such pressure of intense expectancy as the capacity audience waited for the curtains at the end of the large hall to part. At last they did so to reveal Coningham standing stage centre supported by a chorus of high-ranking officers of our own and American services. With an arresting glance that commanded our attention and a smile that anticipated our response the Air Marshal with quiet assurance announced:

"Gentlemen, we are now at D — 2!"

We forebore to cheer. The murmur of deep satisfaction expressing the relief of tensions generated for months past was hushed as he turned towards the back cloth of large scale maps covering the English Channel and the coast of France between Le Havre and Cherbourg. The sea space was hatched with lines indicating the course of convoys heading from almost every English port to the invasion fleet's point of departure south of the Isle of Wight and thence to beaches between Ouistreham and Port-en-Bassin ringed with bands of colour and bearing the legends SWORD, JUNO and GOLD that would be engraved on the tablets of our naval and military history as deeply as Trafalgar and Waterloo. I knew that this was the most profound revelation I should ever experience as the plan of the vast operation already under way disclosed the majestic conception of the planners and the magnitude of the sea, land and air forces committed to its execution. No wonder Overlord was the proud and confident code word for such a mightly enterprise.

As we drove back to Gatwick discussing the roles allotted to our Wing, I decided not to tell Pete of personal strains I had been subjected to during the past few weeks and of which, thank God, I was now relieved. I had called at Norfolk House, St. James Square, the headquarters of the planners of Overlord, to discuss with a military colleague of long standing some matter relating to our current operations, when he arose from his chair and, turning towards the map of northern France on the wall behind him muttered:

"Of course, you have been bigoted ..."

Before I grasped what he meant he had spread his hand over the Bay of Arromanches, assuming that I knew this to be the focus of our assault on Normandy. I realised immediately that BIGOT was the code name known only to those closely involved in the planning of it. I had the presence of mind not to declare my ignorance of it and decided that for both our sakes I must let him retain his illusion. At the time I had considered whether or not I should confide my secret to Pete. Later, when it seemed possible that he might have been captured by the enemy off Ostend, I knew that providence had prompted my reticence. Immediately we reached Gatwick orders were given to sever all but official communications with the outside world. All hands were confined to the airfield. Sunday dawned deceptively brightly but by noon a gale was buffeting the canvas walls and rain drumming on the roof of our operations room. By then we had received a signal postponing the operation for twenty four hours.

This gave us time to go over the plans more thoroughly with our ALO's and squadron intelligence officers before the briefing of our pilots at 7.0 p.m. on June 5th. Though the storm showed no signs of abating Pete assured them that the chances of being given the go-ahead were 9 — 1. At first light on the morrow, 2 and 268 Squadrons would take off for the Royal Naval Air Station, Lee-on-Solent to direct the bombardment of enemy coastal defences by the cruisers *Mountcalm, Belfast, Kempenfelt* and *Hawkins.* Thereafter the whole Wing would concentrate on the close surveillance of the approaches to Sword beach from which Canadian Army would make their bid for the capture of Caen. It was of vital importance that any signs of an expected attempt by a Panzer division known to be in the area to drive a wedge between Canadian Army and 2nd Army on its right flank should be instantly reported to 84 Group so that their fighter bombers could bring it to a halt.

Before we dispersed Pete's optimistic forecast was confirmed. Through the short night I lay sleepless on my camp bed praying, as best I knew how to, that the hopes of all those now committed to this stupendous adventure and upon whose courage, tenacity and endurance the liberation of Europe depended would be fulfilled.

By midnight the sky was a sounding board for the pulsating drone of hundreds of aircraft heading south — tugs towing gliders carrying the first assault troops of the 6th Airborne Division, transports bearing paratroopers to their dropping zones and the "heavies" of Bomber Command heading for the Atlantic Wall to shatter its emplacements and stun their occupants.

The sun did not rise like thunder on this momentous day. As I walked from my tent to our ops room night was changing imperceptibly into a grey and cheerless dawn. The wind had moderated. Through gaps in the low scudding clouds I could see the intermittent flashes of navigation lights. Our well-planned operations were set in motion with quiet despatch. An ambience of an almost reverent calm alone distinguished the occasion from any other working day.

The first eye-witness of our soldiers gaining a foothold in France was Bob Weighill, a rugger player of renown, who, at the request of H.M.S. *Glasgow*, flew low along the shore to report the progress of the invasion fleet. Missiles from rocket carrying craft about a mile off shore smothered the fortifications with smoke and flames. Under this cover soldiers were wading ashore and, followed by tanks, were advancing up roads and tracks behind the beaches. Pete Donkin was close behind him and saw a salvo of shells from a shore battery obliterate one of our cruisers in clouds of black smoke. Though the saturation of the defences by our bombers had kept the heads of the enemy down, it was the accurate gunnery of our ships, directed at target after target as our pilots reported their destruction, that enabled our troops to overrun these beaches with minimal losses.

Having completed this task successfully, for the rest of the day our squadrons quartered inland approaches for signs of any movement of Panzer units towards the coast. Results were negative and interference by enemy fighters negligible. Here, at least, we had achieved the miraculous advantage of surprise. By nightfall we had flown 74 of the 1,050 sorties ordered by 84 Group and had lost but one of its eight aircraft missing in the course of finding and destroying a score of tanks and many other vehicles.

It was heartening that during this day of triumph Pete Donkin received letters from the headquarters of General Eisenhower expressing gratitude "for the magnificent way our demands for photography of all descriptions had been met both in the past five weeks and in the long months of planning that now lie behind us". Our persistent struggle for the recognition of the value of reconnaissance and of our pilot's prowess had availed.

The afternoon had been sufficiently relaxed to enable a B.B.C. reporter to record a vivid description of our day's work by our Wing Commander Operations, Maclean, who had directed our operations from Lee-on-Solent, and by Bob Weighill.

"Mac", as he was know to us all, had served in the Wing since it was formed. He was a good deal older than most of his fellow pilots, certainly wiser, and had won the D.F.C. for his conspicuous and sustained gallantry and leadership, particularly during the Dieppe episode. Though I knew that he was overdue for a rest, he had been reluctant to leave his Squadron. Perhaps he knew that to be Pete Donkin's deputy would require reserves of patience and tact — qualities with which, in fact, he was richly endowed. As a Squadron Commander he had been aware of Pete's tendency to deal directly with his pilots if he judged it to be expedient to dispense with a go-between. I had by now learned that, as a rule, a punctilious and efficient staff officer lacks the attributes of leadership, that a born leader of men does not take kindly to administration, and that staff duties as we conceived them in our Wing did not conform to the orthodoxy of the colleges which taught them. Macs' opinions and decisions were expressed concisely and with a Scotsman's contempt of equivocation. In fact, though temperamentally disparate, he and Pete were equally forthright in expressing their opinions and this may have prevented their relationship as staff officers from being as congenial as their capable conduct of affairs should have made it. Mac was a trusted and respected member of our companionship. I, for one, found him a philosophical friend in need at times when a true understanding of our pilots' idiosyncracies and limitations were essential to the proper performance of my own duties.

After D Day, the work of the Wing seemed a resumption of our usual routines, spiced with a sense of immediate purpose.

On June 10th Raehill and Lewis of 268 Squadron made 35 Wing history by landing on the first airstrip in the beach-head to refuel before and after a long sortie beyond Paris. They were four hours overdue when, to our great relief, they came into circuit and so safely home. Out of the truck bringing them to the ops room jumped Lewis wearing a German infantry cap. They told us that the runway in Normandy had been bulldozed over a sandy clay soil that, according to the weather, was liable to become unserviceable from dust or mud. Raehill narrowly avoided a bomb crater before ground crews emerged from slit-trenches with yellow flags to guide him to a dispersal point. The airfield was under intermittent shell-fire by day and bombing by night. He was told that the local population were hostile to their liberators. Snipers were a constant menace, many of them women married to or collaborating intimately with the Germans. The R.A.F. Regiment were dealing with this nuisance. Two women carrying rifles had been shot near the airstrip; another *franc-tireuse* was posted on the roof of a church tower that had to be demolished to bury her in its ruins. Further inland the mood of civilians was very welcoming. It seemed as though the Germans only admitted to the defence areas men and women they believed to be reconciled to their lasting subjugation. Two or three of our ground staff had been killed by booby traps.

Since D Day our communications with 84 Group had been perfectly maintained. McEvoy was sympathetic to an anxiety that began to beset us after two weeks of intensive operations. Our losses, 7% of sorties, were unacceptable and we were heading for a crisis as our pilots were beginning to tire. It had become clear that the Army, unaware of the inadequate allotment of recce squadrons, was calling for sorties on a scale that, though we had been able to meet them under pressure for the last ten days, were now beyond our resources. The climax was reached when one evening forty sorties were called for, some of them penetrating deeply behind the front. Pete brought the matter to an issue by vetoing those that he considered superfluous.

We had, I feared, become the victims of old inter-command jealousies. The complacency of TAF, which was primarily responsible for this shortage of trained recce pilots was, in a measure, due to time-servers on its staff, such as Pete's predecessor, who knew the truth of this but failed to speak out for fear, no doubt, of prejudicing his chances of preferment. Pete had protested when four recce squadrons had been disbanded a year ago at the insistence of Fighter Command.

Sometimes I despaired of the obduracy of high-ranking officers who opposed each other as fiercely as their juniors assailed our enemies. Thereafter Canadian Army moderated its demands and left Pete to use his discretion as to priorities. Had the Luftwaffe fighters disputed our air superiority effectively, 21 Army Group might have found itself losing the sight of its tactical eyes. It was galling to know that no heads would fall among those guilty of this folly and incompetence; the culprits would hang together like the statutory medals that in due course would decorate their bosoms and assuage their consciences.

When I visited Coningham's headquarters I was struck by its mood of aloofness in contrast to the prevailing sense of urgency and contact with the battle at our own where we were evidently better informed as to the hour to hour progress of the campaign. When I lunched with a friend a fortnight or so later at Eisenhower's headquarters he told me that the only place that had up-to-the-minute information was the War Room, but that nobody as a rule but Ike and his staff were admitted to it. He said he would ask the G.2 Intelligence in charge of it if he would make an exception in my case. This officer turned out to be Major Bill Bennet, a cheerful and obliging Green Jacket who had been my mess-mate at Bulgey Thorne's 12 Corps headquarters. Enjoying our reunion as I did, he took me at once to his forbidden sanctuary. It was a surprisingly small room but my glimpse of it never to be forgotten as the setting in which Ike, Spatz, Tedder, Harris and Leigh Mallory had made their fateful decision before D Day. As we entered I saw the left hand wall papered with maps and graphs admirably displayed and lit; down the right wall ran a partition with sliding glazed panels behind which worked staff officers, their conversation and telephoning muted when necessary by closing them. Here Ike held his morning conferences. I noticed that the dispositions on the map for that day were 36 hours behind our own — a time lag, as Bill explained, due partially to the departure of TAF headquarters to Normandy and to the fact that General Patton had jumped into his jeep a day or two previously saying that he would capture Brest in three days and would not be heard of until he had done so. Bill himself was very well informed, particularly as to the tactical dispositions of the enemy. While we were talking Air Marshal Sir Sholto Douglas rang up from Fighter Command for news of the situation at Brest which was scheduled for an attack that night. Bill could give him none and later the operation was cancelled.

He bore eye-witness to the historic conference on D — 2. Leigh Mallory was harrassed by his colleagues who considered his plan for fighter cover inadequate. For two hours he remained adamant and finally won his point. The next morning Bill congratulated him on sticking to his guns. "If I hadn't won, I would not be here this morning", he replied. The failure of our armies to meet the optimistic date that the planners had forecast for the capture of Caen and its nearby airfield made it clear that our fighter-bombers would have first call on the few available airstrips. There would be no room for 35 Wing until D + 21 at the earliest. This was just as well, for the present arrangements for the reception, processing and distribution of our photographs was facilitated by operating from England; moreover, since one of our squadrons had been re-equipped with Typhoons (an administrative blunder for they were not really adaptable to our purpose) we were forearmed against troubles suffered by those of 83 Group that first operated from the beach head. In the course of the penetrating researches by the scientists and geologists during the planning of Overlord, one obscure factor had been overlooked with unforeseen results. One after another the Sabre engines had developed inexplicable faults. These were diagnosed by Napiers as due to abrasion of sleeve valves from dust sucked in by their air scoops. Nobody had discovered that Calvados provided the crushed grit used for the manufacture of emery paper. Thus those engines had literally ground to a halt. As usual, our engineers rapidly produced a modification that eliminated this hazard.

At Gatwick the drama of our operations was relieved by an administrative sub-plot worthy of Gogol's comic invention and ridicule of bureaucrats. Doggo had received a peremptory demand from the department of Secret and Confidential Publications for the return of two maps, numbered and duplicated copies, depicting restricted areas for flying over England — Secret Documents 300. By now the skies over England were so thronged with aircraft that any restrictions must have gone by the board. Reporting that he had already returned them, he was charged with having sent only two copies of one document. He had joined us at the height of the Noball season. I vaguely remembered that his predecessor, who was responsible to me for the safe keeping of secret papers, had mentioned that one had been mislaid. Evidently, when handing over to his successor he had tricked him into signing for two separate documents by a skilful act of prestidigitation. Now the wrath of the Department fell on the head of Doggo that was already awhirl with epoch making events. I could do little to help him but to dismiss the affair as of no account — wrongly as it turned out, for this was just the storm in a tea cup to rock the bureaucratic boat, stirring its crew into frantic activity and causing deep concern to professional officers. Even Pete Donkin, normally indifferent to protocol, took a grave view of Doggo's alleged carelessness and refused to believe that he had been the victim of a confidence trick. The receipt he had signed was irrefutable evidence of his guilt. So, for weeks he was harrassed by everyone but myself (for I refused to take this persecution seriously) determined to ferret out the documents now lost beyond recall. I remembered how joyfully my colleagues at Coulommiers had made a bonfire of accumulated and then meaningless bumph before our retreat to Troyes. Would it not have been most appropriate to celebrate our imminent conquest of the enemy by a similar incineration. Short of this, as I would be the ultimate victim of S. and C. Pubs., the sooner we reached Normandy the better where its writ would move at a snail's pace and I would be unlikely to suffer the utmost rigours of King's Regulations and Air Ministry Instructions.

The frantic quest for secret documents was checked by the materialisation of Hitler's Secret Weapon. In the early hours of June 16th I was roused from sleep by the sound of a giant gargling with crude oil. It was still dark but I was out of my tent in time to see a flying object with flames spouting from its tail streaking northwards about 200 feet over my head; before I could identify it, the gargling ceased and, after a few seconds of ominous silence, the flash and shock of an explosion ended the flight of this strange missile. I realised at once that the threat of Noball, totally forgotten in the stirring times we had been through for weeks past, was now fulfilled. At the ops rooms signals were being received that several flying bombs had crossed the coast between Kent and Dorset. Silhouettes of them, we were advised, could be seen in tomorrow's *Daily*

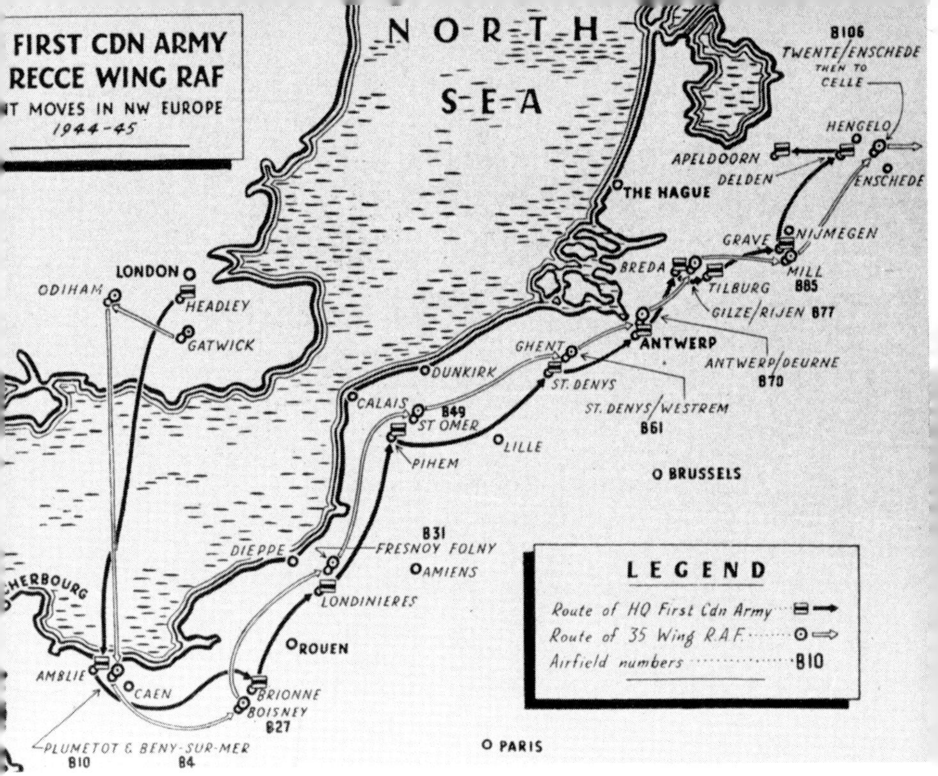

FIRST CDN ARMY
RECCE WING RAF

...T MOVES IN NW EUROPE
1944-45

NORTH SEA

B106
TWENTE/ENSCHEDE
THEN TO
CELLE

HENGELO
APELDOORN
DELDEN
ENSCHEDE

THE HAGUE

GRAVE — NIJMEGEN

BREDA

TILBURG   MILL
GILZE/RIJEN B77   B85

ANTWERP
ANTWERP/DEURNE
B70

GHENT

ST. DENYS
ST. DENYS/WESTREM
B61

DUNKIRK

LONDON
ODIHAM   HEADLEY
GATWICK

CALAIS
B49
ST OMER
PIHEM

LILLE

O BRUSSELS

B31
FRESNOY FOLNY
AMIENS

DIEPPE

CHERBOURG   LONDINIERES

O ROUEN

AMBLIE   CAEN
BRIONNE
BOISNEY
B27

PLUMETOT & BENY-SUR-MER
B10   B4

O PARIS

LEGEND
Route of HQ First Cdn Army
Route of 35 Wing R.A.F.
Airfield numbers B10

H.Q. 1st Canadian Army and 35 Wing joint moves into N.W. Europe.

H.Q. 168 Squadron. 35 Wing on air strip near Amblie sheltered by "Maclean's Folly".

R.A.F. Intelligence Officer briefing pilots.

H.Q. 35 Wing. Operations and Army Liaison Staff Officers.

Gliders of 6th Airborne Division holding left flank of 21 Army Group to E. of River Orne.

Mirror — a triumph of Fleet Street over Intelligence. Next morning I found the crater. Considering the force of the explosion it was surprisingly shallow. The trees around the small field where it had fallen showed little sign of blast — though in a confined space this would be considerable. I was impressed, not to say shocked, by the pieces of the contraption I managed to collect — scrapes of thin steel crudely welded and assembled reminding me of the shoddy tin toys made in Germany that, as a child, I had despised. The remains of the propelling apparatus — for to call it an engine would be a solecism — were even more disturbing. It appeared to have no moving parts other than a device that, misshapen as it was , looked to me like a fuel injector to provide some sort of jet propulsion. Clearly this flying bomb could be produced by unskilled labour in great numbers and at little cost. I realised how much the planners of Overlord owed to the R.A.F. and to the American bombers who one way and another had delayed for six months or so the deployment and discharge of these sinister weapons that might have hampered seriously the preparations for D Day.

Gatwick must have been in the flight path of one of the undamaged launching sites for the "grumblebugs" as our airmen called them, gargled over us at regular intervals. I saw two destroyed on the perimeter of the airfield, one by anti-aircraft fire of the R.A.F. regiment, another expertly flicked off balance by the wing tip of a pursuing fighter — a daring tactic that cost the lives of several pilots when their quarry exploded on contact. Soon we were ordered to pitch our tents over slit trenches. At night, as I lay in my premature grave, I could hear the waves of gunfire and explosions breaking like surf on our southern strand sounding nearer and nearer as the missiles were launched in succession from east to west across the Channel. Thanks to the brilliant improvisations of our ground and air defences comparatively few reached London but enough to test the endurance of the population just recovering after the end of night bombing by the Luftwaffe, and now subject to bombardment by pilotless aircraft all around the clock. I noticed that these weapons were referred to as "they" for, to most people, the idea of a pilot-less aircraft was inconceivable.

A side effect of the sufferings of Londoners was the intrusion of another serio-comic sub-plot to the drama in which we of 35

Wing, as members of the cast, were moving swiftly to the beginning of its last act.

Pete, when lying in a Canadian hospital recovering from his near-fatal exposure, was horrified to see early one morning three of his most dependable pilots from his old squadron being wheeled on stretchers past the door of his cubicle. He was told that, after a party in Reigate the previous night, they were on their way back to the airfield in an army truck driven by an A.L.O. who, having no headlights, ran into the back of a stationary convoy of vehicles that had no rear lights. The truck was badly damaged and several of its occupants more or less disabled, though not as seriously as at first was thought. Nevertheless, even the brief absence of these injured officers put a heavier strain on their companions when pre-D Day operations were at their height.

I was fascinated to watch the military old-boy network in action. The truck was hidden in a hangar, spare sparts were wheedled out of willing conspirators eager to keep their chums out of trouble, and gradually it was reconditioned and returned to duty. The soldiers had not reported the accident thereby avoiding a court of enquiry and disciplinary retribution which should deservedly have fallen on the driver. As an amateur I felt a sneaking admiration for the organised discretion, however discreditable, with which the affair had been handled.

Now, thanks to the V Bombs, I witnessed a contrasting episode that must have set my grandfather churning in his urn in Westminster Abbey.

The Adjutant of the Airfield was a one-time actor — probably no more than a small part player in touring companies, but for all that a dedicated theatrical. Later I learned that he was not very efficient but did his best under chaotic conditions that might have daunted a professional officer. His wife was an actress then appearing in a London production under stress of this new bombardment. Her husband, going on 24 hours leave, found her suffering from the effects of playing under such nerve-wracking conditions and to comfort her spent another bomb riven night with her and thus was absent without leave for a further 24 hours.

Alas, no old-boy network caught him as he fell from grace; no age old caste system came to his rescue. He was immediately placed under close arrest (itself a breach of King's Regulations) while the sledge hammer of punitive proceedings was poised to smite this nut of explicable delinquency. I found him utterly bewildered by the reaction of his colleagues to what impenitently he regarded as the fulfilment of a compassionate duty when his absence from Gatwick would be of little account. I begged Pete to intervene or at least to mitigate the humiliation the prisoner was suffering. But I soon discerned that, in the eyes of authority, the fact that he was an actor aggravated his misdemeanour and that, as such, he must be taught what discipline meant. A summary enquiry was held and the prisoner was dismissed from his post. The discrepancy between the consequences of these two breaches of discipline depressed me — the second so trival in comparison to the first that might have been catastrophic for the Wing. I remembered Dizzy Desouer predicting that the Royal Air Force would take a long time to rid itself of a suburban mentality.

Thus, when later I met accidentally the defendant in this judicial farce in Normandy, I was relieved and delighted to hear that, unembittered by his experience, he had found himself another job playing a useful part in the confines of the beach-head and determined to see the campaign through to the end.

At the end of June we moved to Odiham, a more commodious base from which to organise our impending departure for Normandy. Unlike fighter wings our movements were hampered by impedimenta essential to our purpose. Though our squadrons were self-contained and mobile the value of their operations depended on their proximity to the photographic unit for the speedy distribution of their results to our customers who, in addition to Canadian Army Headquarters now included light bomber squadrons operating from England and needing cover of their targets. The complexity of our tasks was illustrated perfectly by an incident that occurred after I had reached Normandy with an advanced party of our headquarters. Canadian Army, prior to its final advance to Falaise, had asked for a mosaic covering its whole front. Two Spitfires with their magazines of film fully loaded took off immediately from Odiham and returned at 14.15 hours having completed their sorties. Arrangements had been made to fly the 6,000 prints to General Crerar in Normandy as soon as they were ready. When, however, at 21.10 hours they were delivered to the squadron A.L.O., Ian Duffus, the weather in France had closed in making a night landing impossible. Duffus then flew to Gosport and an hour later was heading for Cherbourg in a fast coastal motor boat of the Royal Navy; three hours later he handed over the prints to the Canadian Intelligence Staff. Thus this massive demand, thanks to the flexibility of our system and to the initiative of our A.L.O. had been met within twenty four hours.

Though we were no longer bombarded by grumblebugs, I found this period of suspension depressing. Situated as we were between the realities of the battle and our traffic with 2nd TAF and HQ. 21 Army Group we were plagued with rumours and gossip indicating prevailing dissensions in high places. Air Vice Marshal Broadhurst, A.O.C., 83 Group,[1] naturally exploiting his réclame as the pioneer of army air support, had claimed priority to use the few available airstrips in the beach-head. Now we heard that it was his intention to reorganise 2nd TAF and to disband 84 Group on the grounds that there was no room or indeed need for more than one Group headquarters and ground control system. We were given to understand by knowledgeable busybodies that the dissolution of 35 Wing was under consideration. Senior air staff officers who should have known better, hungry for more airfield space, did not disguise their impatience with Monty for his apparently sluggish advances in spite of the prodigious air support they were giving him. It began to look as though the harmony we had striven to compose between the army and the R.A.F. was, owing to the indiscreet trumpeting of top brass instrumentalists, about to end in strident discord. It may well be that the integrity of the 2nd TAF was preserved by the wisdom and patience of Air Vice Marshal L. O. Brown, commanding 84 Group, a self-effacing and modest officer who, with McEvoy at his side, directed our operations with a firm hand and, like Air Vice Marshal Park, was indifferent to the kind of personal publicity that some of his contemporaries regarded as spoils of war. There was even talk of Ike's inclination to remove Monty from his command, though when it reached us we were unaware that Churchill, scenting this intrigue, had intervened and averted a crisis that might have had disastrous consequences. Though my faith in Monty was

[1] Group Captain Harry Broadhurst D.S.O., D.F.C., A.F.C. As Senior Air Staff Officer to Air Vice Marshal Coningham, A.O.C. Desert Air Force, he had studied and developed the principles of army/air co-operation. Throughout the campaign the R.A.F. had effectively harassed the enemy ground forces, but without the understanding or co-operation of remote Army H.Q. Staff officers. When Monty took command of 8th Army he insisted on H.Q. Desert Air Force being adjacent to his own.

unshaken, I was infected by the general malaise of my superiors provoked by the apparently static limits of the beach-head.

It was, therefore, a great relief when on July 22nd Mac, while Pete was on leave, told me that 2 Squadron and a skeleton Wing staff under his command would be leaving for Normandy forthwith. Provision had been made for one Flight Lieut. Intelligence Officer. I telephoned to Swale who gave me to understand that I, though a Squadron Leader, could if I wished fill this post. It was, alas, typical of our rather casual approach to logistics that we had received no movement order. Thus Mac and I had to make what for me was a difficult decision. As it happened 2 Squadron was blessed with the most efficient and popular R.A.F. Intelligence Officer in the Wing — Jock Atkinson who, moreover, was on the friendliest terms with his A.L.O. Tug Wilson, a colleague of his own calibre. Jock had been a traveller for Heinz and his character was a synthesis of 57 varieties of the qualities his job called for, including tact, patience, alertness of mind and a natural geniality that won the trust and friendship of all his young flock. Finally Mac agreed that the squadron should be left intact, while I stayed with Pete until I could join him later. In the event, a few days later I was put in charge of a small convoy consisting of my jeep, our mobile ops room vehicles, Pete's caravan and my own more Spartan Intelligence trailer to board a tank landing craft at Gosport, accompanied by my faithful Corporal Hickman who for nearly a year past had deciphered my scribbled texts for the News Sheet and published them stylishly on our Roneo machine.

All my misgivings as to whether or not I should have gone with Mac were dissipated when I realised that I should return to France as I had left it, by sea. The choice, either way, had been purely sentimental. But I knew in my heart that only by landing on a beach in Normandy would my years of acquittance come full circle.

During my brief pre-embarkation leave, Rosalind told me that Michael had been awarded the D.F.C.; knowing that Typhoon squadrons were suffering the heaviest casualties I would rather have heard that he had finished his tour of operational duty. Pam and Michael had been married shortly before D Day. As I stood at her side in the Chapel Royal, Savoy, close to the lectern that was the memorial to her great-uncle Laurence raised by his fellow players, I wondered how he would be regarding us. For, though Pam was in becoming mufti (if a wedding dress can be so described) the three of us were fellow combatants in a struggle that he, as a disciple of Tolstoy responsive in his life to the claims of the ideal, could not have envisaged. Nevertheless, I felt we were assured of Laurence's blessing. For had he not perished in the Gulf of St. Lawrence in 1912, I think that he might as bravely met his end serving with a field ambulance on the Russian front, true to his principles and to a people whom he regarded with more compassion than most of his western contemporaries.

We were grieved to hear from a dear friend that her eldest son had been killed while serving in 6th Airborne Division. He was the young sapper officer who four years ago had listened so attentively to my diffident remarks during the prophetic discussion promoted by the Independent Guards Brigade on the feasibility of an invasion of the Cherbourg peninsular with air support. As I watched my sister's four boys playing cricket on their lawn, I could now dare to hope that we would finish the war before they reached military age. Rosalind, I felt, found a measure of relief from her anxiety by serving, with Celia Fleming, as a telephonist and car driver at Henley police station. I left Greys, capsulated in its beauty and serenity from the embattled tumult of the counties south of the Thames that were now virtually the base area of our British and American armies, confident at last that the continuity of our national traditions was assured, now priceless in terms of young lives spent so readily for their preservation.

V

On the following afternoon I set out from Odiham with my convoy. The driver of my jeep, Jackson, had been a Morecambe Bay fisherman and was glad to swap yarns with an amateur Whitstable shell-back. All my drivers were skilled and reliable; Corporal Hickman was perfectly instructed in the workings of the conveyer belt of transportation to which we were about to surrender ourselves with blithe irresponsibility. Mac and 2 Squadron commanded by Mike Gray, the famous *voyeur* of Ostend, with 6 Dakotas carrying ground crews and a small ancillary staff had flown to and were now operating from an airstrip at Plumetot about half way between the old German redoubt at Douvres la Deliverance and the vital bridge across the Orne captured by our glider troops on D day. Pete, who had flown over several times, told me that the strip was in open country devoid of cover and under observation by the enemy from high ground on our eastern flank and likely to be shelled as soon as aircraft were seen to be using it. It was, however, surrounded by fields of corn, potatoes, beans and onions which were to be had for the picking. Before I left, Bill Urmston, a planner at Norfolk House and now happily at rather a loose end, had told me that one of our pilots had been captured with a map showing the locations of all our landing grounds. Evidently the Luftwaffe were powerless to molest them. Since then Jock Atkinson had written to tell me that all was well, the squadron not too hard pressed and in good spirits, shelling only sporadic and ineffective but for two holes in Mike Gray's tent.

Travelling at a steady 20 m.p.h. we crossed Salisbury Plain and halted a mile or two from the first reception area in order to make our rendezvous exactly on time. A motor cyclist led us to hard standing where, during the night, our vehicles would be inspected, refuelled and, if necessary, waterproofed. After my men had been checked in and their gear overhauled, before being conducted to their quarters, I staggered, bowed down by my load of personal luggage, to the officer's transit camp where I was allotted a tent, a straw palliasse and a bolster. The mess tent had a well equipped bar and, as usual in such monastic establishments, a gallery of photographs of nude females guaranteed to excite the libido of young crusaders but interspersed with salutary posters warning them of the perils of fornication overseas. The camp included two cinemas and a theatre. Now it was only half occupied — so tidy and peaceful that it was hard to believe that hundreds of thousands of soldiers had passed through it before and since D Day, for many of them the final point of departure from homes to which they would never return.

At six o'clock the next morning I breakfasted with the officers of a signals unit on its way to Ike's headquarters at Granville, south of Cherbourg. Although they had been travelling all night and were eating the previous evening's supper they were as chatty and banterful as a carriage load of commuters on their way to work in the city. Their colonel would have delighted the cartoonist David Low for, verging on blimp-dom, he was florid and irascible. Whenever I caught sight of him in the course of our coming journey, he was venting paroxysms of rage upon our shepherds as the only foes whom, with quixotic illusion, he was likely to encounter.

A bus took us to be briefed at a nearby air station by a marshal with the precision and courtesy of the conductor of an Hellenic cruise. Owing to frequent traffic jams, our journey to the marshalling area was tedious and our reception vexatious because of the antics of a pompous little officer in a van with a loud speaker who herded us and barked orders at us like an ill-tempered sheep dog. When he ordered all other ranks but our drivers to fall in at some distance from their parked vehicles I thought it ridiculous that Corporal Hickman should be parted from us. I told him to stay where he was while I explained the situation to the Camp Commandant who amiably conceded my point. On my return I had to put the hectoring marshal in his place. There was something disagreeably symbolic about a nonentity who, armed with a loud speaker, was able to assume the role of Stentor, inflating his self-importance and reducing his audience to sheep as Hitler had done and so brought us to this pass. This camp bore unfavourable comparison to the previous one. It seemed designed to confuse its visitors and reeked of stale cooking and urinals, so that by the end of a stifling day, dizzy with hunger and headache I fell exhausted on my palliasse and slept through the night undisturbed by the perpetual blaring of Tannoys that orchestrated my dreams. Waking early I groped my way through thick mist to a cavernous Nissen hut equipped with basins and hot water where, as its sole occupant, I washed and shaved feeling like Pinocchio in the belly of the whale.

Rejoining my convoy on the Farnham road I found my chaps buoyant in spirits but lacking the statutory "life-belts and vomit bags" that were prerequisite to their voyaging. Having remedied this, after an early ration lunch, until the time came for us to move on I sat on the grass verge reading a book of E. V. Lucas's essays that by a happy chance I had found in the officers' bar. He had died while I was in Hollywood working on *The Doctor's Dilemma*. He had been, after my father's too early death, my avuncular mentor. As I

read his urbane reflections on an English scene that had been
struck forever by the stage hands of the European theatre of
war, I was thankful that he had not lived to see his adopted
nephew dissipating the most productive years of an artist's life
combating, for a second time, the Teutonic menace that he had
recognised with sorrow and disgust.

Our last halt was in a street in Gosport — a cul-de-sac
leading to the shore of Portsmouth harbour where newly built
concrete ramps ran down from the hard to the water's edge. On
our way we had been greeted by V signs and blessings from
kindly old folk which made me feel rather a fraud. The street
was flanked with rows of workmens' houses, its pavement on
the near side crushed to powder by hundreds of tanks that had
preceded us. Children swarmed around us. A six year old girl
and her younger brother, both pale and grubby, invited
conversation;

I: "What's your father doing?"
Little Girl: "Aint got no farver".
I: (not very bright) "What d'you mean?"
Little Girl: "'Itler killed 'im".
I murmer sympathetically.
Little Girl: (to cheer me up) "We've got annuver now!"
I: "Another father?"
Little Girl: "Yes".
I: "Well, what's he doing?"
Little Girl: "Oh, 'e works in a factory (pause and then with
rapture) but 'e makes lovely toffee balls at 'ome!"

Thus, the step-father was winning the hearts of his wifes'
children while the memory of their father was fading as they
sucked the succulent sweets of his successor.

In the early evening we moved onto the hard; to the east lay the
upper reaches of the estuary, and the castle the hills beyond it
scarred with chalk diggings; to the west, *Victory* unscarred
graced the harbour teeming with naval craft of all kinds.
Nearly a decade earlier, Rosalind and I had anchored
Dorothea[1] there to be entertained by the C-in-C, Sir John D.
Kelly, and to enjoy his indiscreet confidences. I wondered if the

[1] A 32ft cutter designed by Dr. Harrison Butler and built for us in Whitstable. When war seemed
inevitable regretfully I sold her. In 1961 she was bought by a Norwegian amateur mast mariner
who, from Chichester Harbour sailed her around the World (see *Sea Gipsy* by Peter Tanguald.
Kimber 1966). At the outset of his second circumnavigation while on passage from Cayennt to
Fort Lauderdale she hit a submerged object and now lies full fathom thousand on the sea bed of the
Atlantic.

nation, at this time of triumph, realised its indebtedness to the old "salt horse" who had steered the Royal Navy through its mutinous crisis at Invergordon and had revived the spirits of officers and sailors demoralised by the antics of a vacillating government in time to fulfil the greatest task ever to be undertaken in the Royal Navy's history.

A square-cut landing-ship-tank lay with her bow ramp resting on the hard. Dwarfed by her gaping maw a movement control petty officer guided a procession of tanks into her belly until, satiated, she withdrew the tongue of her ramp and closed the jaws of her bow doors with a clang that led one to anticipate the sound of a gargantuan gulp. Up the river came our *LST 366*. Nosing into the shore she opened her bows and dropped her ramp like the drawbridge of a rusty iron castle. Jackson and I were the first aboard, charging through two feet of water and up an incline steeper than I had expected. In the darkness of the hold we were guided to a lift which bore us into the sunlight on the upper deck. I had realised that our trucks would not make the grade with Pete's heavy caravan in tow. They were at the tail end of the queue to be embarked so I had time to persuade the traffic controller to have a recovery vehicle handy to winch them aboard.

Looking around I found that this starkly functional vessel had a beauty of her own. She had been built in the United States and was powered by two diesel-electric locomotive engines that in happier times might have pulled great freight trains from coast to coast. Running around the lift shafts between the decks were steel bunks for some 200 men with showers, wash rooms and lavatories to match. Under the bridge was comfortable accommodation for her officers and crew. Her First Lieutenant welcomed me to his mess and allotted me a cabin. Above us swayed two jaunty balloons tethered fore and aft to discourage enemy dive bombers.

Before we sailed at dusk I had seen that our vehicles were properly secured in the hold and that Corporal Hickman and his mates were settled into their quarters. Chatting with some of the ship's company I learned that *H.M.L.S.T. 366* was a veteran. She had crossed the Atlantic four times. She had landed her cargoes of soldiers and weapons in North Africa, Sicily, Salerno, Anzio and on D Day under fire of coast defences. Her Captain, although he was now Commodore of convoys, was a Lieutenant Commander R.N.R. I thought with shame of my comparable stripes and of all the land lubberly officers, many of them amateurs like myself, jockeying for desk-bound jobs and promotion to acting ranks above their station while this master Mariner was content to keep the seas and to accept incomparable responsibilities for the meagre rewards of comparatively humble rank.

I was on deck at first light and delighted to receive an invitation from the Captain to join him on the bridge. Dawn was luminous with sea and sky mingled in light mist. Out of the haze loomed majestic processions of ships meeting or overhauling us without naval escorts, proof of our domination of the narrow seas. Only the mine-sweepers busily at work ahead of us, suggested that the enemy still had a sting in his tail. The Captain told me of a new type of mine being dropped by the Luftwaffe to which craft such as his were particularly vulnerable. They were activated by the displacement pressure of ships passing over them — thus the bows set off a fuse that did not explode the mine until it was under the ship's stern where in an L.S.T. all her vital organs were situated. As cautiously we approached our destination, so slowly that astern we left an almost imperceptible wake, I was sharply reminded that, threatened by magnetic mines dropped by German bombers, the ship that had borne me away from France four long years ago had crept as slowly through the narrow entrance of the harbour at Brest.

Though the mist thickened as the sun rose the increasing traffic of vessels, the sighting of several at anchor and the flotsam of a tidal stream meant that we were nearing land. Then, suddenly, to port and starboard of us I saw the gigantic portals of the artificial harbour at Arromanches — as massive as the entrances to Dover Harbour. Though I had studied photographs of the concrete caissons that were being towed into position and sunk to make solid breakwaters enclosing an area as great as any harbour I had seen, the grandeur and boldness of conception of this project on which the success of our invasion depended was beyond all my imaginings. One of 366's engines had broken down so the Captain had called for a tug to meet her at the entrance to the harbour at noon. I had plenty of time to take in that amazing scene. What once had been an unbroken sandy coast was now the foreshore of a busy port. Every caisson bristled with batteries of anti-aircraft guns; the calm water was furrowed with bow waves of tugs, pinnaces and picket boats (most of them old assault craft); merchant ships at anchor were unloading cargoes into lighters while French trawlers pottered about on their lawful occasions. And over this panorama of maritime activity presided the guardship, H.M.S. *Adventure,* sparkling with bright paintwork, guns at the ready and festooned with wireless aerials and radar antennae.

Entering the harbour we were nudged alongside the end of a floating articulated pier about half a mile long that rose and fell with the tide. The pier-head was so designed that ships like 366 could discharge their cargoes on and below deck simultaneously. I and my jeep were the first to disembark. After a brief discussion with the pier-master, the rest of my convoy was unloaded without mishap. I led them proudly as they rattled over the floating steel causeway to the shore.

We were directed to a track leading through the dunes to an assembly area a short distance inland. As I walked from my parked convoy to the movement-control office, hitherto entirely preoccupied with the business of disembarkation, I was suddenly overwhelmed by the realisation that I was walking on French grass across a French field, that this was the moment of fulfilment of our years of alternating despair and hope — if not the end of a journey begun at Coulommiers in 1940 at least the beginning of the last lap. During the voyage I had begun an air mail letter to John in Canada. Now I finished it and, conscious of Goronwy Rees's ribald scorn had he been aware of my emotional gesture but utterly careless of it, before sealing the envelope I poured into it a few grains of French soil.

Our progress to Plumetot was slow, heavy traffic on the secondary roads through Crepin, Revieres and Douvres continually forcing us to halt on the verges. It was some time before I realised that the landscape had a strange but familiar aspect. It was devoid of colour, a grey monochrome like movie sets before the introduction of panchromatic film. The whole countryside was thickly powdered with dust and above the horizon we were enclosed by a pall of it merging into the blue sky. No wonder, for the area we passed through was a vast stores park, every field crammed with equipment, stores, fuel and ammunition so that night and day, as trucks collected and delivered their loads to the battle line, from the unmetalled roads and tracks rose a perpetual miasma of powdered earth.

We reached the airfield in the late afternoon. It was indeed bleakly situated and earlier must have been in range of enemy artillery beyond the river Orne. To the westward the ground sloped away and there Mac, very wisely, had used bull-dozers to scoop out a large pit, such as gipsies camp in by the road sides in the chalk downs of Sussex, where our ops room, trailers and tents could be snugly protected from anything but bombs. We shared the airfield with a Polish fighter wing commanded by Group Captain Gabrilov whose volatile temperament and rapid transition from geniality to intransigence reminded me of Gaby Pascal. Henceforward, when we broke out of the beach-head, my Group Captain and I would race him to the next airfield hoping to stake a prior claim to its amenities; this led to dramatic confrontations and often heated disputes that ended in fraternal reconciliations with honours easy.

My reunion with our squadron was saddened by the news of the loss of Jack Haselden. His No. 2 had seen the wing of his Mustang hit by flak and explode before the aircraft plunged to earth. Jack was another of our elder pilots, a debonair but forceful character loved and esteemed by all his fellows; he had recently been awarded the D.F.C. Mike Gray was deeply distressed by the loss of his closest friend and most valued section leader. I, too, had cause to mourn his loss. For the bond between us had been his father, W. K. Haselden, who for years had been the dramatic cartoonist for *Punch*. At the beginning of the first war he had drawn a brilliant caricature of my father who had bought the original drawing and given it to me in the hope, perhaps, that the stern parental posture it wittily depicted would curb my foolish impulses. Maybe it did and, as now I view it daily, still does.

There was, however, little time for melancholy reflection. For on the day after my arrival we moved to another airfield further south. During the previous evening Pete and I had visited our Group Headquarters. It was situated in a motif of the Barbizon School with a nuance of Poussin as I glimpsed some of the staff disporting naked in the nearby stream. On our way back we were pleased to find our new camp pleasantly shaded by leafy orchards some distance from the dusty airstrip.

Throughout the next morning four of us, stripped to the waist, wrestled with the heavy canvas of the ops tent until caked with mingled dirt and sweat and short winded, we finished the job. We cast baleful glances at the idle young Nazis basking in the sun behind the wire of a prisoner of war cage and cursed the Hague convention. The squadron flew in at tea time. By now we knew that we would be in at the death of the German armies that for weeks past Monty had forced to expend themselves against his persistent probing towards Falaise. Jock Atkinson had brought me a photograph taken from a prisoner. Outside a dummy haystack open at one end lay the bodies of eight young men and girls of the resistance movement. Four S.S. soldiers regarded their victims dispassionately as they cleaned and reloaded their rifles. A French informer carrying a shotgun accompanied by a female fellow-traitor faced the camera of an incorrigible Nazi snap-shooter characteristically recording such brutalities. I handed it over to the Field Security Police at Canadian Army, confident that the informer would be identified and would meet the fate he deserved.

Thus our hearts were hardened to witness without pity or compunction the havoc about to be wreaked upon all ranks of the Wehrmacht which, for all its arrogant professional bombast and cant of military honour and oaths of allegiance, was no more than a host of exterminators clearing the ground they conquered to make it fit for ruthless oppression by Hitler's S.S. assassins and Himmler's malevolent Gestapo.

Part IV
Retribution

The Rivers, or Diminishing Returns.

Von Kluge's Army, having sworn
To hold the British on the Orne,
Was driven back and forced to leave
Its rearguards rotting in the Dives.

The SS gallantly forsook
Their comrades fighting on the Touques
And, anxious only to conceal
Their badges, slunk across the Risle

The Wehrmacht withered; few remain
To brave the crossing of the Seine,
While all that lived to reach the Somme
Were *huit chevaux et quarante hommes.*

35 Wing News Sheet, No. 48

I

Five days later 35 Wing was itself again. Our four squadrons were in action from the airfield; the rest of our staff arrived by air, including my affable understudy Doggo now safely beyond the reach of the long arm of S and C Pubs. With him he brought two welcome guests — William Dring and Frank Wootton, accomplished painters commissioned by the Air Ministry to record the operations and maintenance of 2nd TAF in Normandy. Dring, seven years my junior, had already made his name as a portrait painter and before the year ended would be elected an Associate of the Royal Academy. Wootton, who looked younger than many of our pilots, had begun to earn his living before the war as an illustrator. He was first in the field as a keen observer of industrial *motifs,* discerning in them, particularly in relation to the production and intrinsic beauty of aircraft, aesthetic values, that he interpreted with a mastery of draughtsmanship and a facility for *alla prima* painting far beyond his years. Dring handled crayons as boldly and vigorously as Kennington who portrayed the heroic and almost superhuman aspects of his sitters,[1] seeming to hew their features out of a more substantial material; in contrast, he discerned the personalities of our pilots (which, by now, I had learned to gauge) with a tender perception, delineating the synthesis of courage and sensitivity requisite to the performance of their varied and technically demanding tasks. His masterpiece was a drawing of Squadron Leader Karun Krishna Majumdar whose proud spirit and contemplative reticence he perfectly portrayed.

Majumdar was, by common consent, one of the elect among his companions. He visited me often in my trailer. Gradually I pieced together the details of his brief but remarkable career. Born in 1913, he was the son of a Bengal landowner; his mother had been educated in England; while at Newnham College, Cambridge, she had become a Christian and later brought up her son in that faith. At St. Paul's School, Darjeeling, he gained the Cambridge Higher School Certificate and with it entry to the Royal Air Force College, Cranwell. Returning to India he joined and soon commanded No. 1 Squadron of the Indian Air Force at Karachi. When the Japanese overran Malaya he won the D.F.C. for gallantry while covering our

[1] Representative of the thousand or so young fighter pilots whose valour and endurance that won the Battle of Britain had alone assured the ultimate liberation of Europe.

Gliders of 6th Airborne Division holding left flank of 21 Army Group to E. of River Orne.

First sightings of German tanks and armoured vehicles retreating eastward in daylight.

German column ablaze after rocket attack by Typhoons of 84 Group, R.A.F.

The closure of the "Falaise Pocket" containing the bulk of the German 7th Army.

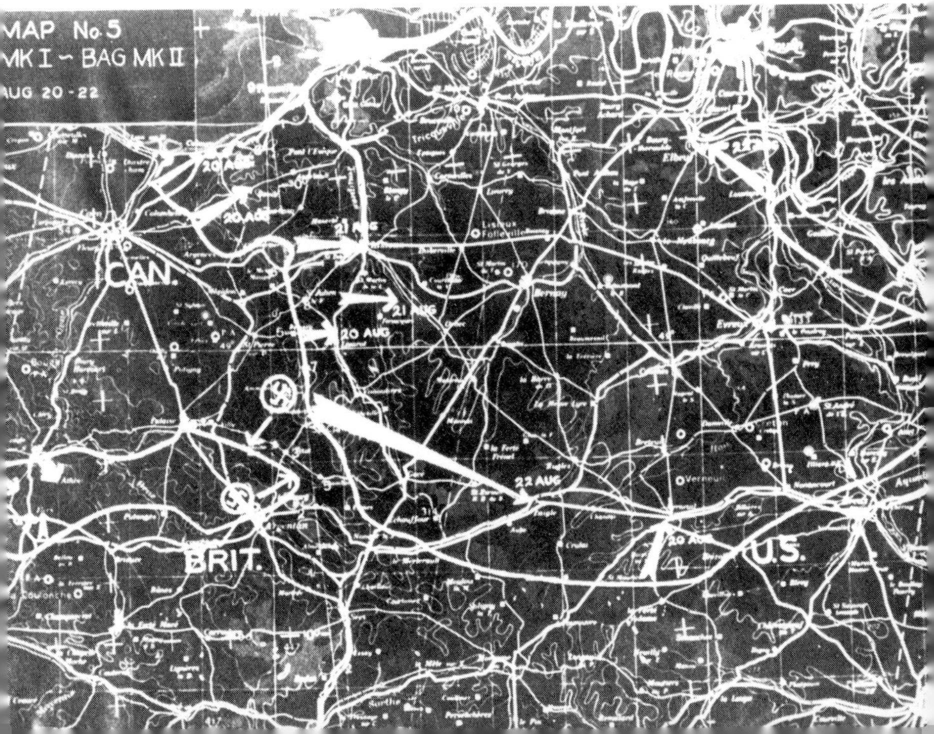

German units that escaped from the Falaise Pocket approaching Rouen.

The last bridge across the Seine at Rouen destroyed by R.A.F. bombers.

retreat from Rangoon. A spell of service as Wing Commander on the staff at Delhi persuaded him that in India, as elsewhere, too many of his contemporaries were preoccupied with promotion rather than experience. At his own request he reverted to the rank of Squadron Leader, was posted to England and ultimately to 268 Squadron which he was delighted to find was commanded by Squadron Leader Mann with whom he had served in Burma.

Though his service with 35 Wing soon won him a bar to his D.F.C. his whole desire was that the Indian Air Force should attain the standards of efficiency to which his prowess in action testified, conceiving his Service to be symbolic of the unity of the British Empire — perfectly trained, speaking a common language, transcending the distinctions of caste or faith, and capable of co-operating anywhere with any of its armed forces. All too soon he left us to fulfil this ambition. Three months later, in the course of this self-imposed duty, he was killed during an air display at Lahore. If it is within the competence of a painter to convey the character, achievement and sensibilities of such a man, Dring has faithfully recorded for posterity the appearance and disposition of one whose friendship touched me deeply.

Airmen, like horsemen and seamen, are stern critics of painters illustrating their particular vocation; such works will be judged by their technical accuracy and no aesthetic flourishes will extenuate their verdict. Frank Wootton soon excited the curiosity and admiration of our pilots as he worked up canvas after canvas accurately depicting their aircraft in action and the work of servicing and rearming them in the field. They invited him to share the Spartan hospitality of their tents and accepted him as one of themselves, appreciating his response to their environment. The skill with which he recorded action in Normandy and later in the Far East is incomparable; the few canvasses that are not in our museums are eagerly sought by private collectors.

The Admiralty and the Air Ministry understood the purpose of employing artists better than the arbiters of contemporary taste who selected "official" painters for such work. The task of battle painters from Paolo Uccello to Detaille and Philippoteaux had been to observe and to depict the facts of war and not to make it an opportunity to display their virtuosity or technical eccentricities. Muirhead Bone,

Kennington and Orpen had fulfilled this duty faithfully in the first German war; historians seeking evidence of the life of the private soldiers at that time will find it clearly defined in the mural paintings by Stanley Spencer on the walls of the chapel at Highclere. Conversely, those who commissioned Paul Nash to record the Battle of Britain were at fault in leading a painter who had changed his style repeatedly to keep abreast of critical trends, to suppose that he could apply his dogmatic perception or technique to the composition of a graphic record comprehensible to posterity of that unprecedented and decisive conflict.

The intervening days had been climactic. The pattern of our grand strategy was coming into focus. American armoured divisions, led by General Patton, were sweeping down the west coast of the Cherbourg peninsular and fanning out westward towards Le Mans and eastwards towards Brest. Thanks to Hitler's order that his panzer divisions must dam the stream of enemy armour by a thrust from Mortain, three of his armies were now threatened by encirclement as the Canadians and Guards' Armoured Division stubbornly advanced on Falaise while elements of Pattons' forces swept up like a scythe towards Argentan at a speed exceeding that of any previous German blitzkrieg.

Soon after we had settled into our new camp, Marcus Kaye joined us for supper. With 83 Group Advanced Headquarters he had landed at Arromanches on D Day. Having braced himself for the ordeal by battle on a beach swept by the fire of guns of every calibre, he stepped ashore on one no longer defended by the enemy and controlled by efficient beachmasters who courteously sent him on his way — an anti-climax that left him on the verge of a nervous breakdown. The following evening I dined with him at 83 Group's headquarters, pleasantly situated at the Norman castle at Creuilly where William the Conqueror had planned his combined operation against England in 1066. He had invited Michael to join us. My son-in-law, at our third meeting, looked very fit; far less tired than I expected him to be and immaculate in a tailor-made battledress embroidered with his well earned ribbons. After dinner I drove with him to his air strip where from the dark recesses of his entrenched tent he produced two bottles of wine to celebrate our reunion. When later I visited him at the end of a long days' operations I found him organising a game of cricket for his officers and men on a pitch sporadically under shell fire, though he was evidently under strain and no wonder, for on the previous day his Wing had fired 43,000 rounds of cannon shell and rockets at enemy columns now forced to move in daylight. He had lost his second in command whom he had seen make a belly-landing in the now vast no-man's land created by the rapidly shifting boundaries of the battlefield. The commander of his airfield proved to be Tim Maurice, whom I had last seen at Rheims where he was in charge of the R.A.F. Press Officers and journalists whom he had found as intractable as I had done. Like myself he was savouring the present revenge for the humiliations we had suffered in 1940.

My nights were now sleepless for at irregular intervals shells from some heavy gun burst over the beach not far to the north of us near Courcelles. At dawn I would wander about peeping enviously into the tents of my companions lying fast asleep like puppies blissfully unconscious and deaf to anything short of the crack of doom. Soon a pair of them, at my instigation, located the source of this nuisance that murdered my sleep near Pont L'Eveque — a long range gun that emerged from a railway tunnel at night, fired at random its quota of shells, and retreated into its lair at daybreak. Within a few hours Typhoons bottled it up successfully with rockets.

As the demands increased for close reconnaissance of the area on which the Canadians and Americans were converging, our pilots were heartened by the miraculous news that Jack Haselden had been seen by another prisoner of war who, in the confusion, had made his way through the lines and thought that Jack would probably do the same.

On August 11th three German armies had been almost surrounded in an enclave equivalent to that enclosed by Notting Hill Gate, Piccadilly Circus, Battersea Bridge and Putney Bridge. Around Trun their vanguard was fighting desperately to keep open a narrow line of retreat by night, for by day they were under heavy attack by fighter bombers and artillery. Our pilots were returning goggle-eyed, having for the first time in this campaign sighted and photographed roads crammed with vehicles bumper to bumper and in places spewed out into adjoining fields. Our main task was to determine whether or not the enemy still held Trun. Athwart this bottle neck, Polish parachutists were making a gallant stand on high ground, hoping for reinforcements to enable it to be corked up. In the prevailing melée they were attacked by Typhoons; providentially the pilots were their own countrymen and they accepted this misfortune with commendable resignation.

Historians have criticised our armies for their failure to close this gap. As it happened it lay exactly on the boundary of the axis of advance of our own and American forces predetermined by the planners of Overlord. Though Ike had agreed that this should be disregarded, the situation was fraught with tactical risks that inclined the Canadians to be cautious in avoiding a collision with their allies. Moreover it was far more important that Patton's divisions should not be deflected from their race to gain a bridge-head across the Seine. In fact comparatively few German troops, notably nearly all their generals and the S.S. elite, made their escape and none of their equipment crossed the Seine. Historians, too, have failed to remark that this crushing defeat was inflicted by free British and American men, who had left their homes and occupations to learn to be soldiers the hard way in unpremeditated action against German armies trained for twenty years past by a general staff clandestinely kept in being by Von Seeckt (at the outset in Bolshevik Russia of all places) and ready to serve any political leader who would give them an opportunity to exercise their bloody genius. The prisoner of war cage near our camp was constantly replenished with young Nazi soldiers who, though dishevelled or exhausted, maintained their arrogance, evidently judging this débâcle to be no more than a temporary set-back to their Führer's ultimate triumph. Conscripted Europeans of lesser tribes subjected by the herrenvolk sat dejectedly apart from and evidently fearful of their fellow prisoners. If an officer arrived, the young Nazis would discard their overcoats and make a bivouac for him that he accepted as his due. One of our guards who daily escorted truckloads of prisoners to the coast to be sent to England in returning tank landing craft, told me that their morale was unimpaired until, cresting the dunes, the spectacle of the Mulberry Harbour at Arromanches stunned and demoralised them. For most of them this was the moment of truth that finally quenched their hopes of victory.

All this coincided with the first anniversary of our News Sheet that inspired many kindly and appreciative signals from unexpected quarters. It was now enlivened by reports of our pilots taking time off to make forays into the "pocket" and returning with booty varying from helmets and accoutrements to reparable staff cars and huge Nazi flags. These excursions nearly cost us Tug Wilson, his batman and two pilots who, losing their way, spent five hours in hiding surrounded by the enemy.

Jock Atkinson and I set out for the front firmer of purpose. We approached Caen by way of Troarn in the wake of our armoured divisions. Almost every farmhouse was in ruins and the unreaped fields strewn with disabled and burnt out tanks. This was the erupting landscape that the eyes of Rex Whistler last surveyed before the blast of a shell forever eclipsed his fanciful vision. I had learned with sorrow that he had been killed with the Guards Armoured Division fighting its way towards Falaise. Yet I felt a kind of pride in that a fellow artist whose elegance of expression I had long admired, had not sought refuge in the deceptive craft of camouflage. He had wholly, and with a courage that in a man naturally gentle and fastidious cannot be measured, committed himself to active service in the defence of the country that had been his lasting inspiration. Sometimes we had worked together in Alick Johnstone's studios, back to back as we supervised the Japanese artists at work upon our giant canvases. Fascinated, I would watch him begin a *trompe l'oeil* moulding or decorative motif on an architectural setting, trusting those craftsmen, Iko and Kono, to reproduce exactly his technical mastery of scenic illusion. His unassuming way of life, his quiet concentration on any task he undertook, his style undeviating from the English tradition of romantic illustration, suggested a premonition that, like Bonnington, the time for the flowering of his genius would be brief. He died as he had lived, true to his occupation. His memorial, I think, is the painstaking drawing that he made to show his guardsmen how their kit must be laid out for inspection as customary in the Brigade. His epitaph, surely, is inscribed in the last lines of his brother Laurence's valedictory poem.[1] Shortly before D Day he painted a portrait of a fellow officer in their camp. Both were killed before the oil on that canvas was dry.

[1] A Portrait in the Guards. *Audible Silence.* Laurence Whistler. Hart-Davis. 1961.

It could be, while a cigarette
Hung grey, each recognised the other
As valid utterly and brother.
It should be so. Because of all
Who in that mess tent shortly met
These would be the first to fall.

In Caen we passed a building with its façade stripped away leaving its rooms open and furnished like a doll's house. A boy with a satchel over his shoulder was climbing perilously from floor to floor towards the wreckage of his little bedroom in an attic where his writing table was teetering on the floor's edge. The golden angel of peace surmounting the memorial to the last war rose pock-marked but undamaged above the surrounding rubble. The area around the new Montgomery bailey bridge looked as though an angry giant had stamped upon it and with his heel ground the ruins into the earth. Our first objective was Mezidon, a railway junction that had often been photographed by our pilots and had been Andy's happy hunting ground for locomotives. More recently it had been the target for the "heavies" and was now unrecognisable, its railway lines grotesquely intertwined, rolling stock tumbled and burnt out, and the station a shambles of broken furniture and carpeted with tickets, labels and forms. The buffet, odorous with the smell of dead Germans in the cellar, a surrealist composition of splintered mirrors, bottles, glasses, nickel plated fittings churned into a saturated *collage* under the gaping roof. An undaunted sapper officer assured us that he would have one line running in ten days. On the remains of the platform we were greeted by the station master. Without rancour, he told us that some twenty of his staff had been killed or wounded. Proudly with one hand he caressed the empty sleeve that hung from his other shoulder. Among the wreckage we found the black and red German sign-board bearing the station's name. Reverently we disinterred it and put it in the back of our truck.

So on towards Lisieux hoping to find No. 652 A.O.P. (army artillery spotting) Squadron in action — one of several such equipped with light Auster aircraft and manned by gunner officer pilots and observers; two years ago we had helped to set them up for training on an airfield near Penshurst. Soon immaculately turned out army traffic controllers warned us that we were close on the heels of the Highland Division making their final assault on Lisieux which had changed hands several times in the last few hours, and that the roads had not yet been cleared of mines. As we drove cautiously along a deeply sunken lane we were deafened by a shattering explosion immediately overhead; another such blast a few yards further on led us to suppose that we were under the muzzles of a 5″ howitzer battery in the field above us firing on the town. Beyond an open gate stood a tank recovery vehicle. Carefully following its tracks we left our truck beside it and set off across country to find the squadron we knew to be nearby. By now, its men were masters of self-concealment. Looking around in a large field we discerned the little aircraft hidden under the surrounding hedges; we made for a group of farm buildings at the far end of it. There on the lee side of enemy missiles, we were welcomed by Major Cobley who invited us to join his "mess" — a number of officers lying on the turf and basking in the sunshine. They plied us with great mugs of tea while they told us of their adventures. Since D + 2 they had flown 1300 sorties directing 500 artillery shoots. They had lost 7 Austers and five officers shot down by small arms fire or hitting trees while taking evasive action from enemy fighters. Beyond us on the high ground above Lisieux the white wedding-cake Cathedral of St. Teresa stood unscathed above the burning town. A canopy of shells whined over our heads as our own and the enemy's heavy guns duelled at fairly short range. Now and again, they burst uncomfortably close to us but the *sang-froid* of our hosts compelled me to affect a spurious composure. I was, moreover, engrossed in watching from a point of vantage the end of the last engagement in the battle of Normandy, for news was brought to us that the war-weary Highlanders had ended it triumphantly once and for all.

Returning to our truck we were conducted over a very recent battle ground by the driver of the tank recovery vehicle. The little fields surrounded by ditches and high hawthorn hedges were typical of the *"bocage"* — each, when held by resolute troops, a strongpoint that our armies had to capture piecemeal. Along the easterly ditch of this one lay the arms and equipment of its dead defenders and here and there, like large molehills, the shallow graves in which they lay. I picked up a sniper's rifle; Jock reluctantly forebore to add to his trophies a helmet pierced by a bullet and lined with coagulated blood and brains. Our guide invited us to see his little bivouac tent. It was cobbled with bundles of franc notes of every denomination. These he had picked from the pockets of dead enemies. The Canadian Government, he told us, had undertaken to redeem this currency at pre-war rates of exchange. If he survived he would be rewarded with a new and well-heeled lease of life.

It was late in the afternoon when we reached our third goal — the little church at Ranville where lay many of the dead of the 6th Airborne Division. The countryside around it was strewn with wrecked gliders striped black and white — the recognition markings borne by all our aircraft engaged in Overlord. A party of sappers directed us to the cemetery; they had served with the young officer whose grave I sought and spoke proudly of his courage and devotion to duty. Most of the crosses were painted white, but his was of oak and his name skilfully carved upon it — perhaps the last tribute of a thoughtful comrade-in-arms, While I made as faithful a drawing as I could of the lad's last resting place to send to his mother, I remembered the words written by John Buchan that his father had quoted when he told us of his death:

> "Life to them is given to be safeguarded but lived; not hoarded but spent, but in no headlong and unthinking rush into danger. Every risk is mapped, analysed, duly considered and, as far as possible guarded against. If Death comes they have long looked him in the face; to them possibly death is the supreme adventure, the highest mountain scaled, the widest sea crossed."

So, indeed, was life spent by all the pilots of 35 Wing. While I was so engaged Jock had, sympathetically, gathered a beautiful sheaf of wild flowers. When I laid them upon that grave, those around it looked strangely desolate.

We returned to our camp to find, by happy chance, that Andy was discussing with Pete his impending command of the Wing before we made our next advance. With hilarious ceremony we presented him with the name-board of the station and conferred on him the title and honours of Duc de Mezidon.

Figures 1 to 8: Destruction of an Army. Wreckage between Villedieu les Bailleul and Lambert-sur- Dives.

3

6

7

Spoils of War. R.A.F. pilots retrieve German General's Buick staff car.

Liberation of Abbeville. Note crowds outside the "Mairie".

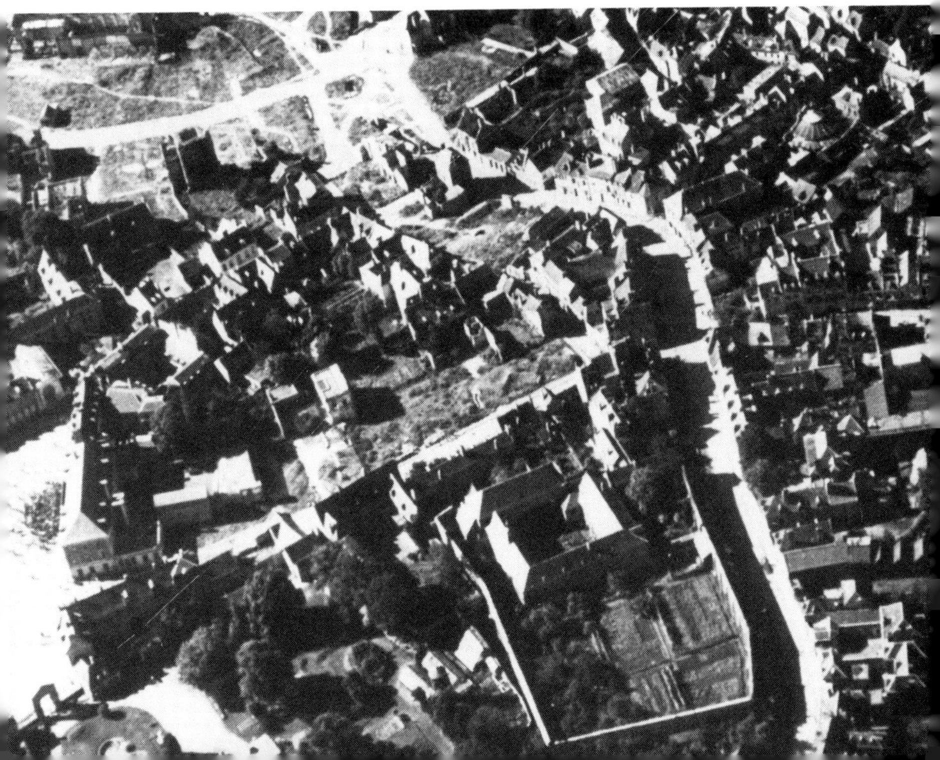

Ferry crossings at Rouen after attacks by R.A.F. bombers.

German installation near Wizernts for firing volleys of powerful rockets at London, put out of action shortly before completion by British and U.S. Air Force bombers.

II

It was not my duty to view the carnage in the Falaise "pocket"; our imminent advance to an airstrip near Dieppe made it unlikely that I could do so. Since childhood the sight of the havoc death can make of man's physical perfection has repelled me. But Nemesis arrived in the cherubic form of Hilary Saunders, his chubby face well tanned and framed with a halo of golden curls that concealed nature's tonsure. He had come from Ike's headquarters bringing with him an American staff officer, Cusick, who had been active during the first two years of the war in urging his countrymen to come to our aid. We soon found that we had a mutual friend in Frank Morley[1] (whose brother, Christopher, had been a stubborn isolationist) with whom our son John, when he was at a flying school in Saskatchewan, had often spent his leave in Connecticut. Both were eager to see the charnel battlefield.

So I agreed reluctantly to be their Virgil and to guide them through a place, terrible though not eternal, where no cries could be heard from the departed souls of thousands of poor wretches whose torments dire were over. When towards midnight we turned in, the western horizon was aglow with fires that our day's work had kindled in Rouen. Our pilots had located the last pontoons and bridges and ferries across the Seine that within a few hours Typhoons had destroyed or sunk. On the left bank they had detected all that remained of German tanks and transport that had escaped through the gap at Vimoutiers packed in woods and warehouses in readiness for crossing the river by night but now the target for our heavy bombers. Hilary reported that Patton's armoured divisions had crossed the Seine near Mantes, and, having established a bridgehead some were sweeping northwards to clear the enemy from the right bank, thus enabling our armies to make their crossing unopposed.

We made an early start. Hilary was in my jeep with a reliable driver; Cusick followed us in his own. I took them through the northern suburbs of Caen where bomb craters overlapped each other in a moonscape. In the centre of the town civilians were to be seen making tentative efforts to create some sort of

---

[1] In 1924 Frank Morley then a Rhodes Scholar, and I were commissioned by E. V. Lucas to collaborate in writing and illustrating a book on the River Thames. Morley's observation of Sweet Thames from its source to its briny dilution at the Nore and recollection of the literary utterances it has inspired as yet has not been excelled. (*River Thames.* F. V. Morley Methuen. 1926).

181

order out of the prevailing chaos. As we picked our way slowly through the rubble, Hilary rallied the little groups of old and young women with expressions of sympathy and hopeful exhortations in fluent French which drew no response from his dazed audiences. Falaise was in ruins but above them stood the Norman castle apparently unscathed. The road to Argentan was flanked by wreckage bulldozed onto the verges. About two miles beyond the blasted forest of Couffeur we came to the small and more or less unscarred village of Villedieu Le Baileul. On the right hand side of the road through it was an innocent looking turning leading into a narrow lane. It was, in fact, the entrance to an inferno beyond Dante's imagining. A few days ago it had been a winding track, barely wide enough for farm carts to pass each other, linking the main roads from Argentan to Chamboise and Trun. It served the farmsteads of Tournai-sur-Dives and Lambert-sur-Dives. As in Devonshire in places it ran between high banks crowned with saplings and wild flowers, and through corn fields and orchards, and over ancient stone bridges spanning rivers and little streams.

Along this track a German column had attempted to make a cross-country dash from the "pocket" by night to escape from the holocaust on the main roads. As dawn broke Typhoons attacked and made havoc of the vanguard before it reached the Trun — Chamboise road, and of the rearguard in the outskirts of the village. Throughout the day fighter-bombers and artillery had systematically destroyed the immobilised mass of men, vehicles and, most pitifully, horses.

For a few hundred yards the track ran between high banks against which, like bas-reliefs, corpses of soldiers were transfixed in attitudes sculptured by the hand of death — some clawing at the embankment for protection, some with arms and hands shielding their heads, some squatting like broken puppets staring at us with protruding eyes and teeth rigorously bared. Here and there groups of three or four were pressed against a bank of wild flowers stricken in poses of panic flight. Emerging into open country we reviewed the retribution of the Wehrmacht whose troops four years ago, healthy and exuberant, had blasted their way through France driving terrified civilians before them. Now sprawled amid the wreckage of their arms and equipment, bloated and irridescent with a green sheen lacquered by the heat of the sun and heavy rainfall, they seemed to be grinning apologetically for their pretensions to being a master race. I felt more compassion for their horses, prone and swollen, their eyes protuberant in appealing wonder, their lips contracted from their incorruptible jaws, giving them a mask of unnatural ferocity.

At the first stone bridge a cascade of horses and men tumbled into the ravine, hanging in their harness from gun-carriages and vehicles jammed between the parapet and surrounding trees. We wove our way along this *via dolorosa* between burnt out tanks, trucks and wagons; the fields around us were littered with others whose drivers had sought escape from the rocket swept road. On some tanks dead soldiers slumped in the turrets or lay along their tracks; on the lips of bomb craters others, fully equipped, lay head downwards, their boots buried in the earth behind them. In the front of a horse-drawn wagon the driver, reins in hand, sat rigid, held upright by the backboard of its seat; over its tailboard drooped, like a prettily dressed doll, the slim body of a girl, her long dark hair decently veiling her face.

I was more appalled by the shattered farmsteads. Three days ago they had been isolated from the war in remote serenity. The farmers and their families had been preparing to gather in their harvest. Only the distant thunder of guns and the curious lacing of the blue sky by threads of strange white cloud heralded their liberation. Then, in the night, the clangour of traffic and shouts of men shattered the silence of their countryside. They woke to find themselves surrounded by a teeming mass of strange intruders and appalled by the unnatural uproar. Before they had time to understand what had befallen them, from the twilight sky aircraft came hurtling down spouting trails of smoke from missiles that enveloped them in a hell of explosions. From burnt out homes blackened chimney stacks stood out starkly against the yellow pall of dust on the horizon. Bewildered women and children, still dazed and uncomprehending, wandered aimlessly among the wreckage and carnage, as though seeking for the broken threads of their lives. So far no signs of anyone to aid them, no chlorate of lime to save them from the contagion of the pervading corruption. In a field a noble percheron mare stood motionless by the swollen body of her foal.

And, as we drove slowly through this grisly litter of military rubbish it might, I thought, have been a sketch drawn by the hand of Goya on a sheet of paper; for everywhere the ground was carpeted with the scattered waste of administrative files and documents blown into the air by the tornado of bombs and rockets to fall like snow upon the fields where men and women should have been gathering their hard won harvest to produce the means of life.

As at a fun fair we had entered this dreadful exhibition through a narrow tunnel and gazed on either hand upon a succession of horrid *tableaux morts,* so we emerged at last through the shambles at the head of the column heaped into an alley of scrap iron on to the main road from Chamboise to Trun. We made for the high ground to the north. Before we reached it we were stifled by a malodorous blast as from a gas shell when we passed a roadside quarry into which heaps of dead horses had been bull-dozed and left to decompose. Beyond the ruins of Trun I stopped on a wooded hill. Though we had left the nether hell far behind us the sickly sweet scent of corruption still tainted the air. Hilary, with his journalist's eye had missed nothing; grave but voluble he recalled dispassionately the grimmest details of our pilgrimage. I walked back to Cusicks's jeep to see, for the first time in my life, a man literally struck dumb. The American sat stunned and speechless. I realised then that, while Hilary and I had throughout our adult lives become inured to the prospect of mankind's propensity for inflicting such havoc on himself, Cusick had no such conditioned reflex to protect him against the shock of this revelation. Now I understood what baptism of fire meant to his fellow countrymen, dedicated to the cause of peace and remote from the civil strife of Europe. This was the measure of their courage and achievement in coming to our aid in the very nick of time when unbowed but near exhaustion we stood alone against an aggressor whom, though we did not admit it, we knew in our hearts we had no hope of defeating single handed.

As their Virgil I might have bid them "wait awhile that thus our senses may grow used to this foul scent and after that it will not trouble us". For here our appetites, such as we had, were stayed by American "Breakfast and Dinner Units" offered us by Cusick — elegant packs of ham, eggs, coffee, sugar, cigarettes and jam compressed and packed in a container no bigger than a hard back novel. These tasty and titillating provisions were balm to sweet-toothed G.I.'s mindful of their national fare, but fugitive as fuel for human energy compared to the British pack ration, functional and sufficient in calories, more or less tasteless but sustaining.

We passed through Lisieux on or way to Ranville where Hilary, who was to write the history of our airborne divisions, could view the field of their first historic action. There was hardly a sign of life as we made our devious way through streets unobstructed by debris, where only a few hours ago I had watched the fierce rear-guard fighting as the Highlanders drove the Germans from the town behind the screen of an artillery barrage. Here Cusick left us. On the outskirts of the town a young Frenchman waved us to a halt. He asked for a lift to Vimont. Sitting in the back of the jeep with Hilary, he told us that in July he had been hiding a Canadian pilot whose Spitfire had crash-landed on his farm. He had been able to pass him over to the escape organisation but he feared that on his way to Mezidon he had run into trouble. At his direction, we turned off the main road and along a deeply sunken lane for a mile or two before we saw the nose and bent propeller of a Spitfire overhanging us. His small farm house stood in open country. In a field nearby lay several triangular hen-coops, each about six foot long and eighteen inches wide. When the Germans arrived to search the area, in one of these the pilot lay hidden. Later the farmer had fitted his guest out with civilian clothes. Now he wished to give us the uniform he had left behind and the films from his camera-gun that recorded the combat in which he had been shot down. In due course I sent this gear to the pilot's squadron and recommended that his rescuer should be honoured for his courage and resource.

After Hilary had surveyed the battlefield, glider-strewn and slotted with fox-holes still bearing traces of their occupation, I took him to what was now and what forever would be known as Pegasus Bridge.[1] Nearby he interrogated the crew of a battery of Oerlikon anti-aircraft guns that had defended it since D Day. Twice daily they had been attacked by ME 109's determined to put the hydraulic drawbridge out of action and had shot down 38 of them. At the inn at the western end of the bridge Hilary was in his element. Monsieur Gondré and his handsome Alsatian wife, recognising Hilary at once as a guest of honour, produced the finest vin blanc in their cellar and after voluble exchanges of toasts and pleasantries, vividly described their experiences during the occupation and on the night of their liberation. They were abed in the early hours of D

[1] Pegasus rampant was the badge of the 6th Airborne Division.

Day when, hearing a rustle in the garden below, Gondré went to the window and saw a shadowy figure standing in the moonlight who, raising his finger to his lips, whispered in English, "All right .... all right". Gondré told his wife that he had recognised an English soldier. "Mais nous pleurons ... nous pleurons, vous savez!" and as he recalled the scene tears of joy again ran down his cheeks.

Madame Gondré told us that when war seemed inevitable she had laid in sacks of sugar and stored them in her attic. Long after the Germans had overrun Calvados she found to her dismay that mice had been relishing her sugar for months past and what was left of it was permeated with their excretions. The hated enemy had not yet discovered the wine cellars below the inn. When she realised that her stock of hard liquor was running out and at her wits end to know how she could conceal this, she was inspired to distill with patriotic malice a raw liqueur from her mouse-tainted sugar that her boorish customers lapped up with relish.

Hilary's visit had been thoroughly productive. He had time to watch Frank Wootton at work and with particular satisfaction for it was he and Bill Urmston who had found Frank employed as a technical draughtsman at Training Command and, immediately recognising his precocious abilities as a painter, had persuaded Leigh Mallory to give him a commission worthy of them. Now the exultant francophile was off to be in the van of the armoured division poised to liberate Paris. His cup of happiness would then be brimming over and he would quaff it with boisterous ecstasy. I asked him to raise a glass to our old association should he lunch, if less sumptuously than heretofore, at Le Pavilion Bleu.

Hilary was only one of the many war correspondents who had visited us in the field. I was glad to see the wonders that had been wrought in the relationship between the press and the services since the days of their mutual antagonisms at the start of the war. Now our trusted journalists, from whom almost no secrets were hidden, thanks to their pre-D Day briefing were as well trained as the troops with whom, in many cases, they had gone into action. Typical of them was Richard Dimbleby who often spent an hour or two with me in my trailer hearing all I could tell him of our operations in exchange for his experiences on our other fronts. I was sharply reminded of the stress that the prospect of defeat had put on my, perhaps, inept handling of the refractory and irresponsible press corps in 1940. The prospect of victory deflated the pressures of security just as hundreds of inflatable rubber replicas of tanks and aircraft designed to deceive the enemy as we fought our way to Germany, remained, as far as I know, flaccid in the beach head. The foundation of the confidence with which, in this hour of victory, the war correspondents could fulfil their obligations to their readers throughout the Empire had been laid by Lionel Heald; valiant for truth, he had persisted in allaying the suspicions of the combatants towards those reporting their achievements and in persuading the latter to eschew bombast and sensationalism that enemies could quote to their advantage. Now both realised at last that the pen, if not mightier than the sword, could bring home to civilians the measure of the debt they owed to those who wielded it.[1]

II

A ceiling of low cloud hung over the day when Pete took off in a Typhoon and was soon lost to the sight of all of us who had served under him so long in 35 Wing. It was hard to believe that our long association had ended. I should miss his mocking response to my emotional expressions. He had told me, with characteristic nonchalance, that he had been appointed Air Commodore commanding the newly formed R.A.F. School of Army Co-operation at Old Sarum. It was a welcome sign of the times that the Air Ministry had chosen a comparatively young officer to co-ordinate all the lessons he had learned in action and to direct the study of a syllabus ensuring the continuity of theories now demonstrably proven in practical action. I wondered how he would adjust himself to the role of academic authority. No doubt his Gary Cooper image of laconic toughness (the six-shooter symbolised by the swagger cane with which, quick on the draw, he would slap the ops map when a sortie had been planned to his satisfaction) would dissolve into that of an uncompromising director of studies, impatient of pedantry and with the *savoir faire* to handle his staff and pupils with tact but with no glad sufferance of

---

[1] On one occasion Lionel had faced Churchill alone in his Downing Street den when he knew that claims, easily refuted, by Bomber Command were to be the subject of an imminent prime-ministerial broadcast. The old lion roared his protest. But Lionel's dauntless opposition led his formidable master to see reason and to heed his sound advice not to voice those claims.

opinionated fools. Over our last meal together he told me that before he was confined to sedentary duties he was making a flying visit to all our fronts — a decision I could hardly applaud for his predecessor had been killed in the course of a similar farewell to active service.

That same day we made the first of our rapid advances in pursuit of Canadian Army. Our airfield commander reported that the strip at Bernay, between Lisieux and Evreux was completed. The area was not yet cleared of enemy stragglers and his car had been fired on by snipers. A patrol had picked up an S.S. trooper wearing a Canadian uniform and had despatched him to a limbo where no such disguise, if divine justice was to be done, would be of any avail. For the last time we dismantled our cumbersome ops room. Four days later we moved on to Fresnay Folnay, 15 miles south of Dieppe, having abandoned our tentage and, for the sake of greater mobility in future working in our vehicles and trailers. In the absence of a Wing Commander Ops I took over his caravan where I was able to indulge a mild attack of influenza without resource to our medical officer whose hands were full with patients succumbing to the Normandy Evil, a form of dysentry apparently epidemic among the Germans when we landed there — an effective if not secret weapon, for at one time or another many of our pilots were out of action, suffering the discomfort and indignity of dashing from their tents to the latrines in all weathers. I proved to be immune to this infection but lack of sleep was aggravating my long suffering lower intestine which, periodically revolted against maltreatment by the nervous system that wags the tail of Brother Ass.

While on the road to Fresnay Folnay I was waiting with our convoy to cross the Seine over a pontoon bridge at Quillebeuf, when it dawned on me that our armies had reached the river line on D + 80, almost exactly at the time estimated by Sir Bernard Paget and the planners of Overlord. Thus criticisms of the conduct of the campaign were utterly refuted. I remembered how, when making the film *Moonlight Sonata,* M. Paderewski had recorded several times each of the pieces he played. In every case the overall length of his performance was exact to a second; but within this uniformity the variation of emphasis and tempo were so disparate that no one sound track would be cut into another. So it was that the major objective of Overlord was punctually achieved and that Monty's unwavering determination to let the tempo of the operation respond to each phase of the battle, maintaining the initiative while forcing the enemy to a wasting strategy of containment, had been justified. Moreover, although it must remain a matter of conjecture, in the fighting from the beaches to the Seine our casualties had, owing to his tactics, been fewer than the planners had expected.

At Fresnay Folnay the mood of our companionship perceptably began to change, due in part to Andy's light hearted but no less combative conduct of our operations but mainly, perhaps, to our pilots' exhilarating task of hunting and harrying their routed enemies. Our chief concern was our failure to track down the remnants of two S.S. Panzer divisions; though their tanks and transport littered the roadside on the lines of our advance, many of their officers and men were known to have slipped through the "gap" and across the Seine. As will be seen their success in evading us would have serious consequences.

Though we made only a brief halt at this airstrip, I managed to spend a day at Dieppe. My purpose was to confirm that our estimate of its defences prior to the raid had been realistic. I made straight for the top of the East Cliff. I had with me tracings of our recce maps made at that time. While I was inspecting the remains of the heavy battery a few hundred yards from the coast, a Canadian sergeant took me to the well concealed entrance of a dug out on the brow of the cliff. A flight of narrow steps led to a subterranean fortress beyond our most pessimistic assumptions. In semi-darkness we stumbled through tunnels hewn out of the chalk until light ahead guided us to embrasures overlooking the harbour two hundred feet below us. Branching out from the tunnels were spacious galleries providing accommodation for at least a battalion of troops, a field hospital and magazines of ammunition. As our photographs had indicated, almost the whole cliff facing westwards was now refaced with cement, expertly camouflaged, and pierced with loop holes for guns of various calibres that would have deceived the eyes of our 20″ oblique cameras. I reflected bitterly that had Monty's plan been followed through, a small party of paratroopers could have taken the entrance to this maze of fortifications by surprise and by lobbing grenades down the shafts and galleries ahead of them, might have put these defences out of action.

Dieppe was badly knocked about but the harbour, vital to our communications as our armies surged eastward, would soon be partially serviceable. I went on to Le Treport that had been the limit of our operational area. As I sat in an *estaminet* I watched men of the resistance parading through the streets a girl with her head shorn — punishment I presumed, for her collaboration with the enemy. It was then that I began to suspect, as later proved to be all too true, that the genuine men and women of the Resistance had by now been reinforced by many who, lying discreetly low during the occupation, were emerging as patriots and joining them, using their rough justice to settle old personal scores and thus embittering the lives of ordinary folk all over France for years to come. I remembered, ruefully, the courage of the prostitutes of La Maison Blanche near Dieppe who had so bravely fed and tended our soldiers while for several hours they held their brothel as a strong post during the raid. Were they, too, being shaved and publicly humiliated?

I returned to Fresnay Folnay to find an invitation from one of our pilots — Alan Mogg, to join him and his tent-mate for supper in the farmhouse where they were billetted — that is to say where enough room had been found for them to lay their flea-bags on the parlour floor. The farmer's wife, Madame Lerniégre, had discovered that it was Alan's name-day and had insisted on celebrations to which Andy and I were summoned. There had been alluring promises of a tomato omelette which after weeks of bully beef and camembert cheese (the caterers of Overlord had overlooked the good fortune that the battle would prevent the export of this delicacy from Normandy and so provide us with an abundant supplementary ration) would be relished by all of us. Dusk had fallen when we foregathered. Flickering candlelight left the recesses of the spacious room in darkness but revealed a mass of furniture and bric-a-brac heaped in the centre of it, like those left in the middle of a movie set by property men for the set dressers to arrange to the art director's satisfaction. We were being introduced to our hosts on the circumference of this pile, when the farmyard reverberated to the roar of an engine with an open exhaust and the clatter of a ramshackle vehicle brought to an abrupt halt. There burst in upon us a huge, voluble and elated man,

M. Lerniégre's brother, who had left all his worldly goods in the latter's safe keeping before the invaders ejected him from his own farm. Now, liberated in every sense, he had come to collect them. There followed a scene of exuberant chaos that only the Marx Brothers could have contrived as we were all enlisted to load his goods into a battered *camion* which, weighted down to the springs, rattled off into the night to our valedictory shouts of "Vive le France!" and "Bonne Chance!"

There was now plenty of room to admire the table laid for the birthday party by the children. In the centre of it illuminated by the glimmer of electric bulbs captured from a derelict Volkswagen, was a gargantuan omelette. The company sat down and set to as Madame served out lavish helpings. *Vin du pays* flowed freely, toasts were drunk to the guest of honour entering the dotage of his thirtieth year, and to the heroic past and victorious future of *L'Aisle Trente Cinque.* Pushing back our chairs, replete and reaching for captured cigars, we were astounded when Madame re-entered bearing a great platter of viands — roast saddle of pig garnished with *haricots blancs.* Having with difficulty done justice to this delicious and unexpected entrée, realising that the honour of British gourmandise was at stake, we made a brave show of greeting, with cheers disguising our dismay, a child bearing a large apple flan followed by another with cheeses of the neighbourhood. By now we were in danger of the fate of the too-rapid nourishment of starving men as we washed down the cheeses with the last of the wine, when our host left us to return with a bottle of champagne and another of cognac. Thus inspired M. Lerniégre proved a gifted raconteur, entertaining his dazed guests with tales of life under the heels of the Bosches, of his secret watch kept upon the nearby V1 site and of the perils of its operators, of nocturnal visits by British agents, of his arrest by the Gestapo, and of his release to hear that his faith in the ultimate liberation was to be fulfilled. His saga, with pauses for further fervent toasts continued until dawn. The generosity and kindness of this courageous Norman family, together with the inevitable after-effects of the birthday banquet, banished our recollection of the tales we had heard of their less stalwart and all too human fellow-countrymen who in the course of years had succumbed to the subtle temptations and ruthless oppression of the master race.

Two days later we made a longer hop to Fort Rouge near St. Omer, the first German airfield familiar to me as one on which daily I had kept an eye on the comings and goings of Kampfgeschwaden operating from it. Andy invited me to drive there with him. I suggested that we made a detour and had a picnic lunch on the field of the battle of Crecy. Half way through the forest of Crecy we realised that there were no signs of our armies having passed that way. For all we knew the dense woods walling in the road were sheltering S.S. refugees waiting for nightfall. We were certainly an inviting target for trigger happy snipers and our car virtually safe-conduct for its captors through the confusion of the fluid front line. We were glad to see the light at the end of the leafy tunnel, to reach open country and our goal, a flat stretch of turfy ground bordering a stream with here and there hillocks which might mark the graves of long dead French and English soldiers. We were dozing in the sunlight after our meal when a shepherd boy cautiously approached us, regarding our uniforms with justifiable suspicion.

"Is this where the battle was fought?" I asked him in Churchillian French.

"Quelle battaille?" he asked, as well he might since his boyhood had been spent overshadowed by the continuing ravishments of war.

We arrived at Fort Rouge on the heels of the Luftwaffe. Four days ago German pilots had been operating from it as best they could, continually under attack and short of fuel and ammunition. The runway was cratered by bombs; our airfield construction company would soon make it serviceable. The enemy officers had left their quarters in a hurry. The Wehrmacht had abandoned the area, leaving garrisons to defend Le Havre, Calais and Dunkerque to the death. In the Luftwaffe headquarters half eaten meals lay on the mess room tables. As usual the offices were strewn with paper. Pilots had been comfortably accommodated. The Gruppenfuhrer, exercising privileges denied our own Group Captains, had evidently shared his quarters with his mistress; her name was Martha and her flight so urgent that she had left behind her an empty dressing case and one silk stocking. The bedrooms of his subordinates were still redolent with the scent of eau-de-cologne. Perhaps, ever since Blucher had greeted Wellington at Waterloo after a long hot summer's day in the saddle with the words: "Ich stinke eis wenig!" his military heirs have been sensitive to body odours. Here, too, we found all the culinary equipment that our field kitchen lacked — aluminium pots and pans, crockery, glass, coffee percolators and even mechanical bread and meat slicers enough to set up all our messes in the style they deserved.

In the afternoon I crossed the frontier to Belgium, determined if possible to hear the time honoured sounding of the Last Post that I had learned was to be blown by a bugler of the Royal Marine Commandos for the first time since 1940 at the Menin Gate — the memorial to the thousands of our soldiers who for years had held the enemy at bay before Ypres. In the city I was astonished by the signs of energetic recovery. In all the shattered French towns and villages we had passed through, I had seen but one Frenchwoman in red-cross uniform among the apathetic civilians wandering about aimlessly or standing in little groups disputing individual claims to authority. Here, round and about the Cloth Hall, civic and para-military organisations were busily and cheerfully restoring order, dishing out meals from mobile canteens and setting up first aid and information centres. I could recognise the *consoeurs* of our Women's Institutes, Women's Voluntary Services, Volunteer Aid Detachments and District Nurses going into remedial action for which they had been trained clandestinely and had waited for so eagerly. It seemed strange that a line drawn upon a map could so sharply divide the spirit and resilience of neighbour peoples who, though for centuries together they had endured invasion and rapine, were so characteristically diverse in their reaction to adversity.

As the sun went down I found myself almost alone as I waited for the restoration of an immemorial ritual. The eastern face of the noble entrance to the city was pock-marked by shell fire. It was here that in 1940 the Chaplain to the B.E.F., Alfred Naylor, had collected a small force of soldiers who had lost their units or had been serving on our lines of communication and with them had, for a short time, halted the onrush of the *blitzkrieg* to Boulogne. For this practical witness to his church militancy he had been awarded the D.S.O. — a worthy fellow Christian of Archbishop Baldwin who, during the Crusades, had led an attack on the camp of the Saladin, his vanguard bearing aloft the banner of his predecessor, Thomas Becket.

Naylor had told me of his martial enterprise while, as Chaplain General of South Eastern Army, he was driving me from Reigate to attend the enthronement of William Temple as Archbishop of Canterbury.

The sun set behind the Menin Gate. The bugler of the Royal Marines suddenly materialised in the deepening shadows. The evening air was still. The clear notes of the most moving and evocative of all trumpet calls were, in some strange way, muted as though this symbolic reassurance might prove illusory. I drove away in a mood sadly at variance with the romantic inspiration that had sent me speeding to meet an appointment with hope. Why had the cadences of the Last Post sounded irrelevant to our present triumph and to the defeat of enemies who for so long had seemed unconquerable. Must our bugles forever blow over our own rich dead, the endless procession of our young islanders doomed to fertilise foreign fields? Is the soil of their homeland less fertile for lack of the dust of thousands of Europeans who might have fallen in battles for our liberation? Would the grazing lands of Romney marsh nourish greater flocks of sheep if beneath its turf lay the corpses of thousands of German invaders trapped in a hell of their own contrivance? Must this pattern of self-sacrifice, intricate in its gardens of rememberance, in its massive monuments on far-flung battlefields and in its less accessible hospitals where the maimed live out the empty hours of life-long convalescence, forever be repeated? Does custom stale the richness of our dead as the causes for which they died evaporate into the expediencies of international politics. Indefinably, the clarity of convictions that had sustained me and my companions for so long, were already being sullied by the pale cast of suspicions that if Hitler perished, the havoc he wrought by the moral corruption of the peoples he had subjugated would mock the brave bugle call that had aroused my sombre reflections.

Remembering that one of the first V1 sites we had reconnoitred was near Fort Rouge I went in search of it, accompanied by Edwin Swale who was on a visit from 84 Group. Ringed with bomb craters its installations were dispersed in now leafless orchards. The launching platform, about 100 feet long and inclined to 30°, lay more or less undamaged in a copse of blasted trees. The concrete pill box from which the launching of the missiles was controlled, was several feet thick pierced only by a narrow slit through which the operators observed the result of their discharge. The owner of the nearby farm told me that several bombs toppled over the end of the ramp and the blast of the explosions had put the launching crews to flight with blood streaming from their noses and ears. On one occasion a Spitfire attacked a "grumblebug" soon after it was airborne, causing it to gyrate madly in ever decreasing circuits over the site before it crashed and blew the barrack huts to pieces. A French lad who had joined us gleefully remarked: "Le Chef etait tué!"

One of our bombs had fallen near the foot of the ramp where several V1s now lay bent and battered; from one of them oozed gouts of some lethal looking fluid. I viewed the scene with some alarm for the air reeked of chemicals and their seepage looked dangerously volatile. Edwin, however, was undaunted, romping among the wreckage like a boy on a choir-school outing, picking up chunks of metal and suspicious looking lumps of explosive and chucking them aside with careless abandon. I was relieved when his curiosity was satisfied and I got him safely back to Fort Rouge.

I was, however, like a biddable dog forced to return to Hitler's vomit. The following day we were paraded on the airfield for inspection by our C. in C., Air Marshal Leigh Mallory. Before the formalities ended, Andy called for Squadron Leader Irving who, stepping as smartly as he could from the ranks, saluted the Air Marshal with a steady hand that within seconds was atremble on receiving orders to conduct him over the V1 site. With fearful apprehensions that I hope I disguised, I gave a running commentary as I guided my illustrious charge over the shambles, lingering reluctantly while his pilot, a New Zealander and keen photographer, took innumerable snapshots of ourselves and details of the bomb damage. At last they, too, were safely returned to their aircraft. My fears for their safety were, as it turned out, all too briefly premature. A fortnight later Leigh Mallory was appointed to command our air forces in East Asia. He bade Frank Wootton, whose work in Normandy had deeply impressed him not only by its quality but by its quantity, to accompany him and his wife in his private aircraft to Ceylon. But forty eight hour's notice would not give Frank time to put the work he had done in order and in the safe keeping of the Air Ministry or to collect the materials he needed that would be unobtainable in the Far East. He was, therefore, told to take the first available flight when he was fully equipped for his new commission. Leigh Mallory's aircraft ran into bad weather in Southern France and crashed into a mountain. All on board were instantly killed. Frank's guardian angel had other plans for him that in due course have been richly fulfilled.

My chemical intuitions proved well founded. The next day three of our pilots asked me the way to the site. With some misgivings I told them, and off they went in a jeep. Half an hour later my trailer was rocked by a distant explosion. I looked out and saw a mushroom cloud of black smoke hanging over what I knew to be their destination. Anxiously I awaited the return of the party. All were in a state of shock. One of the bombs had spontaneously combusted. Blinded by smoke the pilots staggered away to find that they had come unscathed through the flying debris of cement and steel. Only one of them had come to grief. He was examining the bomb that was about to explode when he saw the earth in which it was buried beginning to erupt. He flung himself to the ground and so saved his life, suffering no more than a burst ear drum and the loss of his trouser legs. I hoped this would put a damper on my companions' dangerous enthusiasm for sight seeing. David Morrice had already lost two of his best men killed by a mine on an uncleared roadway.

We did not linger long at Fort Rouge. Our next airfield, at St. Denis Westrem near Ghent, provided the first opportunities for social recreation we had enjoyed for months. Our mess was in a pseudo-gothic mansion once the pride of some Belgian tycoon. By now I had surrendered my comfortable caravan to our new Wing Commander Ops, an old friend of Andy's who added to the gaiety of our companionship. I set up my camp bed in an office under the roof of a small transformer station; only after a day or two were my fears allayed that I might be sleeping over an obvious resting place for a delayed action booby trap.

I was disappointed to hear than Bruges was out of bounds. A recollection of the days when Rosalind and I had been entranced by our first visit to the town and the sight of its incomparable Flemish masterpieces would have been a much needed spiritual tonic. But the area was still inhabited by pro-

Bombing of sea wall and flooding of Walcheren island.

H.Q. 35 Wing on parade at Antwerp/Deurne. Andy, Monty and their Merry Monarch.

Group Capt. A. F. Anderson,
D.S.O., D.F.C.

Wing Commander K. K. Majumdar,
D.F.C. & Bar.

*Squadron Leader
Albert Sydney Mann, D.F.C.,
O.C. 268 Squadron.*

*Fl. Lieut. Owen Raymond Chapman,
D.F.C., R.N.Z.A.F.*

Fl. Lieut. Trevor Mitchell, D.F.C.

The Author

German partisans not only inclined to sniping but continuously cutting our field telephone lines.

Of the many tales of 35 Wing our *Fête Gandoise* was noteworthy. Partly to do justice to the elegance of our Mess and partly to repay the hospitality we had received from the people of Ghent, the suggestion that we should return it by inviting them to a dinner-dance was acted upon speedily and with enthusiasm. A voluntary fast for three days provided our cooks with enough materials to exercise their art on a grand scale. Liquor was, of course, abundant. Ardent scouts, who had done a good deal of pathfinding in the neighbourhood, had found matrons aplenty sighing for a party, the first they had been invited to for years, and ready to chaperone some thirty girls of varying age, beauty and virtue, all of them vouched for as non-collaborators by our guests of honour the Mayors of Ghent and St. Denis Westrem and the local leader of the White Army whose Catholic good faith and record of persistent resistance was impeccable. I alone found that the problems of security precluded a carefree evening. By assuming the dual role of a Yeoman of the Guard and a house detective at Harrods I did my duty as security officer discreetly. I had been warned that among our guests was the one time mistress of an agent of the Gestapo. By tactfully shepherding her and the lady who threatened to denounce her into different rooms I managed to prevent a dramatic confrontation. The buffet displaying the transformation of our unappetising rations into inviting delicacies was admired by the drooling company until, at a given signal, hosts and guests fell upon them and in a trice consumed them. I was reminded of a similar party attended by the Iron Duke at Brussels when, hearing that ops were imminent, officers were ordered to leave it unobtrusively. No less deftly one or two of our lighter headed pilots were quietly spirited away, some for the same reason while others with no thought for the morrow and obdurate in their pot-valiancy had to be forcibly removed.

All things considered this impromptu gala was an unqualified success and was a significant landmark in the nomad existence of 35 Wing. We spent two weeks as comfortable cuckoos in this nest of our enemies — memorable for two incidents which curbed any hopes we may have had that at home or in the field the worst was over and the days of endurance were numbered.

On September 17th one of our sections during a routine sortie to keep an eye on the movements of shipping in the estuaries of the Schelde, saw two vapour trails rise vertically from the island of Schouwen. The leader, covered by his No. 2, made straight for the base of the trail about 10 miles away and was able to give its map reference over his radio before, now short of fuel, he was forced to return. They had been the first to see the launching of two of Hitler's second secret weapons, the V2 — long range rockets fired into the stratosphere and then by radio control tilted automatically into a trajectory aimed at a distant target. The velocity of these sinister weapons (for their approach was inaudible and undetectable by radar) was so swift as to create the accoustic phenomenon of the ear-splitting roar of its descent following the thunder of its explosion, not unlike a high speed train hurtling through a railway station, its whistle screeching to a diminuendo followed by the clatter of its carriages rattling over the points. Fortunately the weight of the rocket and its propelling fuel was so great that the size of the war-head was limited — but enough to devastate a larger urban area than its predecessor that our rapid overrunning of its launching sites had virtually put out of action. The scientists had been divided in their estimate as to the feasibility of such a weapon and its potential danger. Now Londoners had to brace themselves for another bombardment by a weapon immune to weather conditions and to our defences.

As soon as we received our pilot's report vertical photographs were taken of the launching pad and within a few hours they were being studied by interpreters at Medmenham. Only one more trail was sighted soon afterwards. But the Cabinet was now fully aware of the new threat to London to which no effective retaliatory action seemed possible.

Early the next morning another section reconnoitering the Dutch coast south of Rotterdam crossed the van of an airborne armada heading eastward. Fortunately the leader, one of our most reliable pilots, kept radio silence, and did not report this amazing sight until he returned to base. Immediately we reported this to 84 Group. They, like ourselves, had received no warning whatever of what was evidently a major operation now in progress in the operational area for which our Group was responsible both for air reconnaissance and close support of the army. Had the pilot reported his encounter over the r/t the armada, whatever its objective, would have lost the advantage of surprise. Edwin Swale was as mystified and angry as myself. Canadian Army, he told me, had no idea as to what was afoot; nor, as it turned out, had the reconnaissance wing of 83 Group serving 2nd Army. After long delay the latter gave me a rather incoherent account of the purpose of an airborne assault to capture the bridges at Arnhem and Nijmegen, though there was little news of its outcome. Soon many Dakotas were landing on our airfield. For the most part their crews were Americans. I interrogated a laconic Texan pilot who described what he had seen of the first stages of the dropping of paratroops on the outskirts of Arnhem, surely too far from the bridge if that was indeed their objective. The confusion of communication between all concerned was very disturbing. Arnhem was supposed to be under the surveillance of 35 Wing. We had not been called upon to make any close cover of the area preliminary to the planning of this attack. As it turned out the survivors of the S.S. Panzer Divisions that we had lost track of before crossing the Seine had recently re-assembled near Arnhem, rapidly re-organised themselves, and were being partially re-equipped in time to be a formidable obstacle to the success of this *coup-de-main*. Whether or not we could have detected signs of its presence in the neighbourhood was a matter of conjecture. Nevertheless we were appalled by the apparent lack of co-ordination by the planners of what proved to be an over-ambitious project, conceived by Monty to be carried out by the 1st Airborne Division and 2nd Army for which no close reconnaissance had been made comparable to that which had contributed so much to the success of the 6th Airborne Division on D Day. In no subsequent account of this affair have I read any reference to this contributory factor to the costly failure of a bold enterprise. From previous experience, we were confident that we could have provided data from which a decision could have been reached as to whether or not gliders could have been landed near enough to the bridge by night and so taken the defenders by surprise.

Major General Urquart, commanding the 1st Airborne Division, in his report attributed its failure to capture and hold the bridge until the armoured divisions of 2nd Army came to its relief in part to intelligence reports exaggerating the anti-aircraft defences in the town and to inadequate fighter support. 35 and 34 Wings had been continually operating in the area and could have reported accurately on the opposition they had to be contend with from the ground, which was not all abnormal, and 84 Group could have provided adequate air cover had it been called upon to do so. In retrospect it appears that this operation was doomed to defeat for the now all too familiar failure of the staff officers of our army and air forces to realise that if they did not adhere to the principles of co-operation that had taken so long to perfect their best laid schemes must fall apart and the lives of many brave men must be the price of their obduracy.

Soon we moved to the larger airfield at Antwerp-Deurne situated in the suburbs of the city. Apparently no British forces were deployed between the airfield and the enemy who had abandoned the southern archipelago of islands beyond the Dutch frontier, leaving only a small but determined force to hold the right bank of the Schelde on the island of Walcheren in order to obstruct our use of the port which surprisingly had fallen into our hands intact and without opposition. But until Walcheren was cleared of the enemy this logistic advantage could not be fully exploited. It was therefore my melancholy duty to plan close photographic cover of the dykes that for centuries had kept the waters of the Schelde at bay and protected the islanders from natural innundations, in order that they could be demolished by Bomber Command prior to an assault by Marine Commandos launched from the opposite shore. For all I knew I was aiding and abetting the submersion of the polderland on which the towns of Middleburg and Vere had been planted in all their architectural loveliness where Rosalind and I and Albert[1] had begun the first of our summer voyages through a land where every *motif* pleased and men and women were uniformly kind and hospitable and their children angelic to behold if healthily mischievous.

IV

It was with regret that on October 7th we left the pleasance of St. Denis Westrem where we had enjoyed the first relaxation of our monastic order and the comforts, if not of home, of a roof over our heads and concrete pathways underfoot and the prospect of the ancient spires of Ghent rising above the mists

[1] Albert Stroud our nautical guide, philosopher and friend who trained us as seafarers voyaging to and throughout Holland in our one time oyster-dredging craft converted to the seaworthy and commodious yacht, *Pamela Mary*. See *Windmills and Waterways* (Heinemann 1927) if still extant.

of a golden Indian summer. In heavy rain and with heavy hearts we of the advance party surveyed the dismal contrast of the airfield at Antwerp. We had approached it by a roundabout route leading to a long and gloomy tunnel where Canadian sappers were still searching for delayed action demolition devices which the enemy, even in their hasty retreat, had the time and tactical duty to instal. The extensive damage to the hangars and installations and the closely packed housing estate that bordered them and the squalid relics of our predecessors gave our new and probably more permanent base a purgatorial aspect. Nevertheless it was cheering to see on the opposite side of the airfield a row of Typhoons, glinting under the downpour. We were, it seemed, to share the airfield with 126 Wing for which for some time past we had been providing close-ups of their targets and evidence of their devastating attacks on them.

The urban surroundings and the dispersal of our pilots in billets seemed to reduce the zest of our previous campaigning, as we had moved from one staging post to the next for months past united in our communal relationships and in the inspiration of our objective. Our mess was in a draughty pavilion in a nearby park. Douglas Goodbody and I shared the ground floor of a villa adjoining it, a functional glass house in the Bauhaus style, its flooded cellars permeating our quarters with their clammy effluence. My intelligence trailer stood on the bleak perimeter alongside the remains of the German air control hut that, incongruously, was lined with Delft tiles so beautiful and out of key with their setting that for the first time I was tempted to join the elevated ranks of R.A.F. looters. For by now tales were reaching us of Dakotas returning to England loaded with *objets d'art* retrieved from abandoned chateaux by our seniors at 2nd TAF. Nor was this the only symptom of the corrupting effect of war upon victorious crusaders firmly convinced of the nobility of their cause. For, soon after Brussels became the mecca of our airmen on short leave, one of our most trusted N.C.O.'s was arrested by the military police for trafficking illegally in tobacco.

A week after our arrival, all these doubts and disillusions were forgotten when daily orders informed us that on Friday October 13th, His Majesty King George VI accompanied by General Sir Bernard Montgomery would inspect 35 Wing. The pomp of this occasion was mitigated by the circumstances of its fulfilment. Though we were paraded as smartly as conditions permitted, the ceremony suggested that the General's purpose was to introduce his Monarch to his one-time subaltern in the Warwickshire Regiment, an honour that Andy accepted with a joviality that immediately transformed the customary formalities into a merry meeting in which all the principals joyfully participated. The proceedings seemed at once to crown the Wing's achievement and to epitomise the eccentricity of the part it had played in stubbornly emphasising the importance of the contribution it had to make and had superbly achieved, relying on the individual achievements of each pilot in the performance of duties that varied in terms of technical skill and danger from day to day. Thus the mood engendered by our Sovereign's visit and patently enjoyed by him and his conducting General, was best conveyed, not in the operational reports in our News Sheet but in its supplement "On and off the Perimeter" that invited ribald contributions usually in verse.

Among the ranks of our pilots stood Alan Mogg whose recent birthday celebrations have been recorded. He had never disguised his love of a good gamble, indeed he boasted of the gains and losses of a mis-spent but thoroughly enjoyable youth unfortunately and prematurely interrupted by the present game he was playing for the ultimate in chances and stakes. Indeed he had been one of a party of friends who, hearing that the Germans had been driven out of Deauville, at the earliest opportunity drove to that resort expecting, no doubt, to find the casinos in operation and the roulette wheels spinning as in days gone by. In the event, they came on men of the resistance burying their dead at one end of the plage and at the other, having driven past the drab deserted hotels and gaming resorts along the front, groups of spivs offering them tempting wads of French franc notes in exchange for post-dated cheques. Thus Mogg excited the curiosity of his King and inspired the Muse that smiled upon our New Sheet.

GREY MATTER

Our dauntless pilots were arrayed
Upon the fields of Antwerp/Deurne:
Their Sovereign, taking the parade,
Shook hands and spoke with each in turn,
Asking what ops they each had done
Or where their medals had been won

202

And so the royal dialogue
Ran smoothly till at last he came
To shake the hand of Alan Mogg:
When, having heard our Hero's name,
Still finding Alan hard to gauge,
His Majesty enquired his age.

On hearing it, the King retired
And from his Marshal standing by
In awe, he eagerly enquired:
"Can such a man as this still fly
With hair so grey, more grey than mine,
And yet be only twenty-nine?"

What caused this grizzled mien? What sight
Or fearful hazard bleached these locks?
Was it a single horrid fright
Or sequence of alarms and shocks
Incurred while doing Tac/R low
That flecked this sable head with snow?

Thus each surmised. None knew the truth
That these grey hairs so premature
Were symbols of a mis-spent youth
In Paris and the Cote d'Azur;
Indeed in all such places where
They sing and play chemin de fer.

The King departs. He'll never hear
The dazzling tale of Alan's past,
Nor why so quickly year by year
The grey hairs grow so thick and fast
Among the strong and vigorous locks
Of Mogg, the modern Charles James Fox.

The only peremptory order I was ever given by Andy I
obeyed with alacrity. A Dakota was leaving for the R.A.F.
Station Northolt within the hour and I was to take four days
leave at home. Apparently he and Doggo had decided I needed
a rest. Happy though I was to be with Rosalind and Pam (who
had been released from the A.T.S.) this break did not prove to
be recuperative. The release from operational tensions and
from the pressure of recording the Wings' operations from day
to day and providing the intelligence on which, to some extent,
the lives of our pilots depended, made me all too aware that my

physical resources were running down. For weeks past I had reason to suspect that a mouse was gnawing at my vitals.

So as I flew back to Belgium my spirits were at a low ebb, having to face the fact that I was expendable. Nevertheless I was glad to hear from our pilot that he would have to land at Eindhoven before returning to Antwerp. Thus I had the satisfaction of walking for a few minutes on the liberated soil of Holland. Moreover, as we flew low above the corridor, a main road bordered by dykes, along which our armoured divisions had made their gallant but unsuccessful attempt to relieve our airborne troops desperately defending their scattered strongholds at Arnhem, I realised the enormity of the odds against the success of such a venture. By now the road was clear. Such German troops as were left in Zealand had been driven out of range of this single highway. Now and again shell bursts on the horizon to the right and left of us were the only signs of far distant holding actions while both our own and the enemys' armies were making preparation for the winter campaign that Monty had striven to avoid by penetrating deeply into Northern Germany. As I viewed the ground below, I marvelled that even the bridge at Nijmegen was now in our hands, for to advance along what was virtually a causeway on which there could be no turning back, under fire from artillery on both flanks, and to be continually halted while tanks put out of action were cleared from the embankment must have called for prodigies of valour and the ruthless surmounting of successive obstacles.

I returned to find that the Wing, though constantly in action, had no longer the clear and critical objectives that had sustained us with the sense of urgency for months past. Canadian Army had lost its coherence and our services to them had become diffuse. Its divisions were still clearing up enemy strong points left behind along the coast. Smaller forces were probing towards Bergen-op-Zoom and eliminating the Germans isolated in Walcheren following the successful breach of their defences by the Royal Marines. I had been depressed by the discovery of what was a miniature Belsen (though that ultimate infamy was as yet unsuspected) in Brendonck, one of the old fortresses designed by Vauban for the defence of Antwerp. It appeared that the Germans had corrupted and recruited dissident Belgians to perpetrate the cruelties and exterminations committed in casemates and dungeons immune from interference by the commanders of the occupying armies whose behaviour was said on the whole to have been "correct".

This was the first intimation I had of the depths to which Hitler and his minions had sunk in their lunatic assertions of the supremacy of their race. The crimes for which the prisoners at Nuremberg were justly condemned set in motion an infectious degradation of human values for which, as I write, no antidote has yet been found to extirpate the deadly fever of fanatical violence that still plagues mankind. At about the same time I heard of what one newspaper described as Rommel's "untimely end". I was sickened and disgusted by the sentimental obituarists paying tribute to his "prowess, dash and élan". Indeed I hoped, though I was unable to prove it, that one of our pilots had hastened his overdue end, for the aircraft that had blasted his staff car off a road and put him out of action had been a Mustang. I vented my feelings in an intemperate letter to the *Daily Telegraph* which to its credit and my surprise, it printed.

"Rommel", I wrote ... "whatever his rank and calling condoned the crimes of his employers and countenanced the bestialities of his subordinates ... He was a criminal who perished whilst trying to escape from the police... There is a real danger to mankind in this tendency to relieve the professional sailor, soldier or airman of the normal dictates of conscience or of the proper exercise of free will. Loyalty and discipline cannot be made an excuse for the violation of human principles. The Allied armies are not fellow-professionals enjoying a trial of strength with the Wehrmacht or the Luftwaffe; they are the instruments of the judicial punishment to which a criminal class has been condemned by the verdict of world opinion. In 1938 the leaders of the Luftwaffe were entertained in London, and their hands, red with the blood of Guernica, were shaken on grounds of expediency. Tolerance of such expediency nearly brought England to her knees and certainly deceived these gangsters into believing in her helpless decadence. It has taken five years to prove that we have still a clear conception of right and wrong and are prepared to make any sacrifice in defence of the right.

Let the Germans bury their dead hooligans with all the false pomp and circumstances they choose; that is all in the gangster tradition. Let us close Rommel's file in the criminal records and leave it at that. As an officer I have censored and franked this letter myself. The subject is not a military but a criminological one."

At about the same time the Germans began their continuous bombardment of Antwerp with V2's in the hope, I supposed, of making the port untenable. I found these weapons a good deal more nerve-racking than the V1's. They fell without warning at hourly intervals in the neighbourhood of our airfield. My trailer would rock when they exploded, for ten minutes or so I would try to locate the damage, if any, they had done us, then back to my desk for half an hour before intuitively I began to brace myself for the next "incident". Once, when one fell upon a servicing dispersal point killing many of our men, I found myself standing some distance away but reluctant to view the carnage where already ambulances and rescue teams were at work. Rooted to the spot, I was ashamed of my cowardice until I realised that someone was close by me and turned to recognise one of our squadron commanders who had won the D.S.O. and D.F.C. We faced each other and tacitly confessed that neither of us had the cold courage to offer to do what we could, however ineptly, to cope with such a bloody situation. In contrast, when another rocket fell upon a house adjoining the airfield, I arrived on the scene to see one of our gentlest and most sensitive A.L.O.'s, Jimmy Palmer, emerging from the ruins with a grievously wounded child in his arms, his uniform soaked in blood. Now, when an occasional "grumblebug" gargled over us, it would be greeted almost as an old friend who at least had the grace to give warning of its approach.

By the end of November the mouse in my vitals had attained the stature and appetite of a rat. I lay awake in our dank quarters restless in the silence broken only by the continuing barrage of V2's and my room-mate's sussurations as he slept in his flea-bag dreaming of giant trout rising to his flies on some well-loved stream. As I gazed into the night through our uncurtained wall of glass, I imagined that if one rocket had our names on it we would be sliced to mincemeat, dying the death of a thousand cuts with, I hope, the resignation of Chinese noblemen.

I have only a confused recollection of finding myself in a

hospital in Brussels recently evacuated by the Germans and now in the skilled hands of British doctors and nurses. Radiologists patiently watching my digestion of a barium meal diagnosed a condition that, when after a day or two I had gained an inkling of the pangs of childbirth, necessitated my removal to England in a field ambulance Dakota. Alongside me lay a sergeant of the Grenadier Guards who had been wounded during the previous night near Aachen; so perfectly ordered were our medical services that he would be safely bestowed in a hospital at home by the following afternoon.

Ben Travers would have been as delighted as I was to know that, as together we had laughed ourselves to sleep on the floor of our office at the Air Minisry where so incongruously we were keeping the night watch at Christmas five long years ago, so my military service, conventional and often bizarre though it may have been, ended on a note of comedy.

The medical officer on duty at the reception desk of the hospital to which I and my companion were delivered was a psychoanalyst. Unimpressed by the record of my physical disabilities, he laid it aside, leaned across his desk and, with tender regard, earnestly asked me if I was troubled by domestic anxieties. Yes, indeed, I was. His eyes lit up in anticipation of emotional confidences and of psychopathic diagnosis, only to be averted as I added:

"My daughter is married to the commander of a fighter bomber wing continuously in action, my son is about to fly as captain of a Liberator from Canada to South East Asia, and my deepest concern is how soon my wife can come and take me home for a spell of peace and quiet before the remedies for my ailments can be decided upon".

As I had watched the Sussex coast sliding under the starboard wing of our Dakota I had not realised that the Great Interruption, as far as I was concerned, was ended. At times the prospect of arriving at this conclusion had seemed no more than a tenet of faith as irrational as man's intuitive belief in his survival after death.

Appendix A

Draft for an address given by Air Marshal Sir Arthur Barratt at his H.Q. British Air Forces in France at Coulommiers to war correspondents accredited to G.H.Q. British Expeditionary Force at Arras prior to their visits to units of the Advanced Air Striking Force.
April 5th, 1940.

Though there is no doubt that, in the last resort, our ultimate victory in the struggle upon which we are engaged can only be assured by the success of our arms, the spirit of those at home upon whom we rely for moral and material support depends very largely upon the fluency of your pens.

War, for most of those at home, means a period of dull and anxious monotony; it hangs over them like a heavy thunder cloud from which, at any moment, the lightning of grief may strike them. It is your aim to lift this cloud and to sustain the hearts of the people as it is our duty to protect them from the physical dangers which threaten them from the sky. Starve the people of news and they will feed upon gossip, a thin diet which lowers the vitality of the consumer until he or she is an easy prey to the disease of doubt and distrust.

A democracy, free to read what it chooses and to form its own opinions, well informed of the successes or reverses of its armies in the field and familiar with the hardships and trials of its soldiers, will in the darkest hour rise to those heights of courage and self sacrifice which cannot be reached by a people nurtured in ignorance and denied free will.

Never before has the machinery of information been so highly developed as it is today. The war in the air is fought as keenly by contending broadcasters as by fighting aircraft.

Relax for one moment your efforts to fill the public ear with honest facts, in this struggle between truth and designed falsehood, and the people will perish like Hamlet's father and from the same cause. The effect of the broadcast is a transitory one; the power of the newspaper is a more lasting one. It is the Press who must stimulate the public into a lively and intelligent interest in the conduct of the war. Upon the War Correspondents lies the responsibility of putting before the public a true and vivid picture of the operations of the Royal Air Force in France and of the lives of all those officers and men upon whose gallantry and skill the success of these operations depends.

Having then a common duty and a mutual interest in each others activities, we should contrive to work together in the closest harmony. We must strive to understand each others difficulties and in a sensible and practical way to overcome those difficulties. You may be sure that my staff and the Squadrons on active service will do all that they can to see that you are fully and accurately informed and to grant you every facility, within those limitations which must of necessity be imposed in a war zone, for seeing for yourselves the life of the Royal Air Force in the field and collecting your own impressions of the actions in which they are engaged. In so far as the help and co-operation which we can give you may go, our relationship, I hope, will be a personal and friendly one. Our Service Press Officers who are in touch with my staff, will do all in their power to see that you have every opportunity of getting the information which you need and of visiting the pilots who are in daily conflict with the enemy.

The limitations to which I have referred must be imposed by the Chief Field Censor. It must occasionally happen that his views are not entirely shared by the representatives of the press. In fact, as the Chief Censor during the last War, himself a famous Editor, remarked: "If the Press and the Censors do not from time to time disagree, it would be a sign that neither of them were doing their job properly". The Censor is the Guardian of the security of those who are actively engaged in the war. His rulings are given with the sole object of keeping from the enemy information which he would welcome and of preventing the publication of anything which might tend to lower the morale either of the public at home or of the Forces in the field. I need hardly say that in this respect the aims of the censor and of the representatives of the press are identical.

Although no journalist would wish to publish anything that might prejudice these aims, it is not always possible for the laymen to know how these aims can be realised without some guidance of a technical or operational nature from an expert whose duty it is to know the requirements of security. This authority is vested in the Royal Air Force Field Censor. He is your guide, philospher, and, I trust, your friend.

Owing to the close relationship between yourselves, our press officers and the censors, it is possible and in every way desirable to explain to you, in most cases, the reason for which a particular stop notice has been issued. By taking you into our confidence in this way, we can to some extent sugar a pill which may seem at the time a bitter one.

As you know, the foundations upon which the censorship is based are the defence notices issued by the Press and Censorship Bureau. These notices were drawn up by representatives of the Press, of the Services and of the Censorship and have been agreed to by all parties.

There must, however, be certain restrictions which are not included in these notices, restrictions made necessary by local conditions or by the changing nature of the operations upon which we are engaged. I would like to take this opportunity of explaining some of these restrictions and of inviting your help and co-operation in forming a policy beneficial to all concerned. Certain of these restrictions are simple to explain and easy to understand; others which more closely concern what might be styled the more domestic aspects of the Royal Air Force are evasive and less easy to confine to hard and fast rules. I will therefore classify them under two headings namely operational or practical requirements and moral requirements as regards comment on the life of personnel of the Royal Air Force in France.

The main object of Censorship is to render the enemy's Intelligence Service deaf and blind. The Intelligence Services on both sides are perpetually and diligently seeking for scraps of information which, though they seem in themselves to be of negligible importance, may complete the picture which the enemy are laboriously trying to create. Thus it is not statements of facts alone which must be closely watched. An unguarded conjecture or supposition may provide the clue which is so eagerly sought. A few examples of subjects upon

211

which it would be wise to refrain from unguarded comment might be of some help to you.

Identification of types of aircraft, descriptions of their armament or equipment may when added to other known facts complete the enemy's knowledge of our order of battle.

It is wise to assume that the enemy Intelligence Service is at least as keen and as wide awake as our own. The work of our pilots and crews is hazardous enough. The merest hint might inspire counter measures which may jeopardise the lives of our men and the success of the operation they are called upon to carry out. We must therefore guard against giving the enemy news that might betray the route or the time of our patrols or reconnaissances or the height at which they work.

By criticising favourably or adversely the enemy's defences, by commenting on the effects of his armament upon our aircraft, we give him information which, if he acts upon it, may make the tasks of our pilots harder to carry out in the future.

To betray any change in the armament of our own aircraft may defeat the very object of such armament. Surprise is a weapon in itself.

Too close a description of our tactics in the air may inspire counter measures which might dissipate any advantage which, by exercising these tactics, we may have gained.

No publicity should be given to the condition of enemy aircraft brought down behind our lines. These aircraft may prove to be valuable sources of information. Knowledge by the enemy that such information is in our hands, can often destroy its value. Early in the war an enemy reconnaissance aircraft was shot down. Details of its condition were given in the press; even photographs of it were published. That aircraft contained certain valuable codes. We were not able to enjoy the use of those codes for long. As soon as the enemy realised that their aircraft had fallen into our hands intact, the codes were changed.

Enthusiasm may lead us into making extravagant claims as to the results of certain combats. The enemy are quick to seize any chance of exploiting such errors and turning them to account for neutral propaganda. The communiqués issued by my Headquarters can be relied upon to give an accurate if conservative account of any action which has taken place. Claims to enemy aircraft which have been shot down, are only made after careful investigation. After you have been talking to pilots who have just landed, elated with victory and pardonably optimistic, they may seem disappointing; they have at least the virtue of comparative accuracy. In the stories which you write of these actions, conjecture as you will and explore the limits of probability, but do not in the interests of all concerned exaggerate the official estimate of our gains or losses.

I would ask you to bear in mind that no British newspaper is compelled to publish our communiqués. It is to retain such privileges that we are fighting against Nazism. Your own account may be the only one to reach certain sections of the public. By taking our official statement as a check and a guide, you can be certain that your public is not misinformed.

We must remember that in censorship matters, we have not only our own security to consider. It may seem, at times, that there are startling discrepancies in the administration of the censorship at home and here in France.

As you know, the French censorship is very much more rigid than ours. In order to avoid misunderstandings and friction we must be certain that our censorship conforms, in all essentials, to that practiced by the French Air Force.

We must be careful for instance, never to betray the positions of aerodromes of which we are, perhaps, only temporary tenants. On a shifting field of battle, what is today a British aerodrome, tomorrow may be a French one. It is our duty to see that our allies can take over an aerodrome from us, confident that their security interests have been well guarded.

The question of the wise use of publicity as regards life in the Royal Air Force or of personal publicity for officers and aircraftmen is a far harder problem. It is one, moreover, which requires a full measure of mutual understanding and a willingness on the part of the Service and of yourselves to appreciate the difficulties and dangers which are attendant on such publicity. It is a problem for which no simple rules can be made. If cut and dried regulations were to be drawn up, the effect of the efficacy of such publicity would be disastrous. All that is needed is a sympathetic appreciation of the issues involved and an elastic policy of give and take.

A serving officer is not in the same position as a member of the public. In the outer world a man may seek or avoid publicity as he chooses. If he welcomes and encourages your attentions, he alone is responsible for the results whether they be good or ill. Old fashioned though it may seem, it is still the tradition of the Services that, apart from recognition by His Majesty the King, an Officer will not seek to attract the limelight of publicity upon himself while his fellows remain in discreet shadow. He would prefer that any act of courage or enterprise in which he is, for a time, the leading figure, should rebound to the credit of the unit, in which he serves, as a whole. This is, as I say, an instinct; it is not an ignoble one; it is one that I would appeal to you to respect.

There are times, however, when the inspiration of hero worship may rally the spirit of the people during a long and arduous war. This is recognised by us all and it is essential that the deeds of the men who, individually and collectively, are engaged in a war far distant from their homes, should be faithfully recorded and freely publicised.

The Air Council has ruled that only on the occasion of an officer receiving a decoration from His Majesty shall he be mentioned by name in connection with the services he has performed. At first this may seem a hard rule and any attempt to suppress the heroic acts of an individual pilot may seem futile. There are however one or two very good reasons for so doing which may not have occurred to you.

It is the Fighter Pilot who captures the imagination of the public. He personifies for them the last shred of romance which war can hold, the only surviving knight who engages his enemy in hand to hand combat. His exploits are carried out with a dash and directness which in such a confused struggle as the present war, are easy to understand. But the brunt of the battle in the air, as the Fighter Pilot would be the first to admit, is borne by those who carry out the daily patrols and reconnaissances. The crews of those aircraft, which throughout a long and vigorous winter have maintained patrols over the North Sea in weather conditions which make frostbite and ice formation more dangerous than hostile fighters. The long photographic reconnaissances over enemy territory, a fixed task to be carried out unswervingly in face of heavy anti-aircraft fire and in constant danger of attack by a speedier and more heavily armed enemy. The long night flights to the widest limits of Germany and Poland, masterpieces of navigation and endurance. All these operations form the routine work of an Air Force and are often forgotten or thrown into shadow by the limelight of publicity which falls upon the Fighter Pilots. Though this is inevitable we can, with your help, see that the limelight is diffused and falls, if it must, upon all ranks and branches of the Service equally.

Tactics have changed since the last war. The individualist will, as the war in the air develops, give way to the team. It is the wish of the Royal Air Force to foster the team spirit, for which the British have a peculiar genius; by using discretion in reporting the deeds of the individual and by stressing the work of the team you can help us to develop and to maintain this spirit.

It has been the fate of the Royal Air Force, since its earliest days, that the leisure hours of its Flying Officers have received almost as much attention as their exploits in the air. Novels, plays, and films have steadily created the impression that when not occupied in destroying the enemy, they are engaged in destroying themselves through endemic alcoholism. The public appear to welcome such revelations and the fame of their alcoholic exploits has spread far and wide. Only recently the Air Ministry received a letter from the High Commissioner of one of the Dominions asking if it was a fact that excessive drinking was a feature of life in the Royal Air Force.

I need hardly say that such an accusation is entirely unfounded. It is not suggested that every Air Force Mess is a stronghold of teetotalism. The Air Force Officers consume neither more nor less alcohol than the average man. None the less the novelist and the film producer have led the public to suppose that an active Service Squadron is the victim of cracking nerves and the scene of desperate libations.

This might appear to be hardly worth mentioning to you. It has however a serious repercussion. Such a worldwide reputation, if it is not corrected, can seriously affect recruiting. Parents will not encourage their sons to join a Service which is renowned for its dissipation. We need the very best material. This material is to be found in the best homes. If you can, with honest conviction, help us to contradict this impression, which is indeed a very false one, you will be doing the Royal Air Force and the country as a whole a very great service.

While on this subject I would ask you to respect the purely domestic activities of our officers and men. It was my privilege recently to entertain some of my officers and sergeant Pilots in celebration of a remarkable day's work. Inevitably such an incident reaches your ears and the wish to make it public is a very natural one. It was, however, an entirely private affair. If such happenings are publicised, their repetition is made more difficult.

The strain of Fighter Pilots is inevitably a very great one. When interviewing them or visiting them in times of stress I would ask you to intrude as little as possible upon their privacy or to interrupt the relaxation which is essential to their health and spirit.

There is one other way in which you can help in sustaining the morale both at home and abroad. It is an old axiom of the Air Force that there is no such thing as a dangerous aircraft. Once let the idea prevail that a certain aircraft has dangerous characteristics and, as though by suggestion, casualties to those flying that particular type will increase. Similarly we should refrain from building up the reputation of a particular enemy pilot or squadron or even type of aircraft. By so doing we meet the enemy halfway in his attempt to establish a moral ascendancy over his opponent. Let no particular enemy aircraft be glorified or credited with peculiar power or performance. To plant in the mind of a young pilot that superiority or invincibility of any particular type is to prejudice his chances of success when he engages that type in combat.

If these remarks have done anything to make your task easier or to throw light on the principles upon which the censorship is exercised, our meeting has not been in vain. As I have said, if we are ready to consider sympathetically each other's problems, the cause of security and publicity will be saved.

In the heat of battle and in the hour of going to press, errors may be made on both sides and tempers may be frayed. Between us the Censor stands in the unenviable position of an umpire at a football match and he is liable to suffer accordingly. But with the knowledge that, in the last resort, we are assured of each others patience and goodwill, that each realises the difficulties of the other's job we should be able to work together for the common cause: And as to the justice of this cause there can be no two opinions.

Appendix B

24th July, 1940

MEMORANDUM

There is no doubt that the campaign in France which began on May 10th and steadily deteriorated until the Armistice, was very largely lost through the lack of direction and consequent confusion of the civil population. Indeed the tactics employed by the German High Command suggest that the intimidation and harassing of civilians was an integral part of their plan. The complete success with which large populations were stampeded into becoming herds of uncontrolled refugees, must be realised by those who are responsible for civil discipline in England. The lesson of this disaster must be quickly learned and as quickly acted upon, or our own civil defence may prove as inadequate and as vulnerable as that of the French. It would be rash to suppose that, man for man, the French civilian is less resourceful or courageous than his English equivalent; courage and resource, however, have proved to be of little avail if the futile complacency and petty rivalries of those who direct the civil defence of a nation are allowed to persist.

During the last few days we have heard much of England as an "island fortress"; those who have returned from France will, from their own experience go further and declare that each town must be organised as a fortress and each village as a strong point, ready to put up independent resistance and to help rather than to hinder military forces in their struggle against a cunning and unscrupulous enemy who, up to the present, has successfully exploited the fear of the bewildered and leaderless people.

It is necessary to review such organisations for civil defence as existed in France, and to compare them with those in England.

A.R.P., as we know it, was practically non-existent. In small towns notices were pasted up giving the direction of air raid shelters which were, as a rule, ordinary cellars. In Coulommiers, a small garrison town, there appeared to be no A.R.P. organisation or prepared shelters. Civilian gas-masks were seldom seen, and there appeared to be no auxiliary fire services. When the "alerte" was sounded troops left their barracks and found refuge among the trees in a park. Larger towns such as Tours, Blois and Nantes appeared to be similarly unprepared.

Traffic control appeared to be carried out by the military and such direction as there was for refugees seemed to be in the hands of the civil authority. In Paris there appeared to be plenty of natural shelters, and in the suburbs a few artificial ones. When the "alerte" was sounded the streets were emptied in an orderly way. There seemed to be no air raid wardens and large refuges such as underground railway stations were guarded by reservists. Police were inadequate. The evacuation of Paris was hardly controlled at all and at many key intersections there were no police to direct the traffic.

In the early stages of the campaign air raid alarms were sounded frequently. Apparently it was realised that constant sounding of sirens tended to undermine public morale for later enemy aircraft and even gunfire would be heard and no alarm would be sounded. No method seemed to have been arrived at and this haphazard sounding of alarms might well have led to disaster. There is no doubt that the method of warning the public by sirens tends to create undue alarm and to enhance the moral effect of an air raid. On the other hand, by adequate warning and good air raid discipline of the populace the number of casualties can be very considerably reduced.

Until May 10th, black-out precautions in France were completely neglected. After one or two air raids, however, drastic steps were taken, and in Paris the black-out was quite efficient. All restaurants and places of entertainment were closed at half-past-ten. This resulted in the streets being completely cleared by eleven, and this should have made the work of civil guards and watchers for parachute troops, had there been any, much easier.

It was interesting to compare the press in France and in

England, with their compulsory and voluntary censorships. The French press was rigidly controlled. Up to the very last moment very little attempt was made to prepare the public for the inevitable collapse of the Army, and the retirement from the capital. The compulsory censorship seemed to work efficiently but it failed through not being supplemented by the proper direction and instruction of the people by the Ministry of Information through the press. The people wavered between unwarranted optimism and profound pessimism, and gradually reached a state of mind which, through endless gossip and lack of reliable information, created a desire to escape at all costs from an intangible threat.

As pointed out, in the Dunkirk area it was practically impossible for the Army to operate owing to streams of refugees converging on Dunkirk, both from the east and from the south. I myself spent a week attempting to travel on the roads leading south from Paris. These roads, and those running east and west along the Loire were so completely blocked that military movements were practically impossible. Defences against mechanised troops erected outside villages and on the main bridges only added to the congestion.

In quite large towns food and petrol were rapidly exhausted. Civil authorities found their population permanently increased by those whose cars had become derelict through lack of petrol. No attempt was made to regulate this traffic.

Towns which had been selected for the setting-up of Ministries that had left Paris were found to be congested with refugees when the Ministries arrived.

The effect of uncontrolled refugees is cumulative. It was noticed that in a small town in no way immediately threatened by the enemy, the population, when the first stream of refugees began, paid little attention to them. Later as the stream increased they would stop work and stand at street corners watching them. Every refugee brought an individual story of horror and fear which spread rapidly in every village through which they passed. In a short time those who stood watching the refugees go by themselves went off, packed their belongings and joined the general migration. Few of them had any idea where they were going and no resources beyond food for one or two days. Hence they became a liability upon communities whose sole occupation should have been that of putting their town in a state of defence and in every way assisting the retreating army. In many cases through lack of proper organisation, a very small mechanised force was able to intimidate populations of comparatively large towns. The mayors of towns would refuse to allow the police or civil guards to take action for fear that the enemy would make reprisals. The evils of divided authority were apparent at every hand. Small towns and villages instead of being key points in the system of defence, fell at once into the hands of the enemy and consolidated his advance.

Nothing undermines the morale of the civil population more than rumour, almost every day and in every district, reports were spread that parachute troops had descended in the neighbourhood. Practically all of these were unfounded, they tended to create a feeling of helplessness and apprehension in the public mind. Defeatist rumours would even emanate from the Ministry of Information and, as far as I can see, no steps were taken to seize upon these rumours and to deny them publicly. During the last week there seemed to be no reliable information available at all and even movements of Embassies and Ministries would be governed by unfounded rumours. Once a general idea of disorganised retreat sets in it is very difficult to stop, and the difference between this war and the last is that where one might think twice of becoming a refugee on foot, it is a far easier matter to fall a prey to prevailing panic when all kinds of motor transport are readily available. Several times I saw military vehicles obviously given over to refugees, and many French Army and Air Force lorries had mixed cargoes of soldiers and civilians. There is no doubt that the sight of the distress, and the disorders into which the population had fallen had a most demoralising effect upon troops, who were endeavouring to move into action in the opposite direction.

Local Defence:

From these observations several lessons can be learnt and by applying them to existing conditions in England a similar disaster may be avoided. First and most important of all is the proper co-ordination of civil defence. Every small town or village should appoint a leader or Town Commandant who is responsible for the local administration of all branches of civil defence. If possible he should be a man who is thoroughly familiar with the surrounding country and one who by long residence or prominence in the business life of the town commands the respect of his neighbours. He might be the Chairman or a member of the local Council. Whether he is or not, the local Council should be subordinate to him in all matters of civil defence. He should be in close touch with the nearest Military Command and his duty would be to prepare such local defences as are needed and to hold the town in readiness in all respects for occupation by military units and to withstand for as long as possible secondary assaults by enemy units until the military can arrive. At present every town in England has several branches of civil defence working independently of each other. The heads of these units should form themselves into a Civil Defence Committee and should place themselves at the disposal of the Town Commandant. These units would include A.R.P. workers, First Aid and Medical services, Parachute Observers, L.D.V.'s and volunteer Transport and Ambulance units. All these should be trained to act together in an emergency and should be made thoroughly familiar with the forms of land and air attacks that any town or village in England may now be expected to withstand. It would be the duty of the Town Commandant to make clear to his volunteer forces the dangers and weaknesses of the parachute troops or light armoured units and by so doing to overcome the surprise and apprehension upon which the enemy rely for a great deal of their successes.

In Germany every individual is taught to believe that he has some part to play in the defence of his Country or in the running of other peoples. In England there are still thousands of competent people waiting to be told what to do. The defence of Great Britain may be too great an affair for the average man to comprehend; teach him, however, that it is essential to this defence that his town or village must be a self-contained and self reliant unit, and, under an efficient leader, he will prove to be ideal material for the purpose.

It was observed in France that local jealousies and rivalry of petty officials played straight into the hands of the enemy. In the confusion of deciding what should be done and who should do it, the enemy easily made themselves masters of the situation. One of the first duties of the local leader or Town Commandant should be to eliminate friction which exists in all small communities, and the inculcation of the team spirit for which we are supposed to be famous in the conduct of local civil defence.

The value of practicable propaganda is often lost sight of. It is far better to take men out with competent instructors to build strong posts, dig trenches, make road barriers and so forth, than to issue pamphlets on these subjects. In the same way it is often forgotten that while every preparation is made for air raid protection, little is done apart from first aid to restore the confidence and morale of the people after a raid. Voluntary workers appearing after a raid in a district which has suffered heavily, and distributing some sort of hot meal or drink to those who have undergone the strain of a bombardment, will do much to eradicate the after effects of shock and fear. If people are left to return to their homes without such attention, they will discuss interminably their recent experiences and enlarge upon the horrors of the raid and by so doing lower their nervous resistance to any attacks that may follow.

Rumour:

Rumour should be dealt with vigorously, locally and nationally. The most effective weapon against rumour is an official news service which the public have learnt to trust and can rely on. If a few examples are made of local rumour mongers, preferably by ridicule, a more dangerous type of rumour should be eliminated. Public authorities in England were taught a severe lesson during the famous poison gas balloon rumour which assumed alarming proportions, in that case the whole affair was held up to ridicule in a broadcast, and appears to have been effectively dealt with in this way. The public should be encouraged to report prevalent rumours to the Ministry of Information and adequate steps taken to see that such rumours are dispelled as quickly as possible.

Much has been heard of the Fifth Column. It is not likely that many people actively engaged in subversive activities or in preparing to help enemy invaders or parachute troops are to be found in England. There are those, however, who by defeatist talk or nagging criticism of those who are trying to do their best, can successfully undermine the enthusiasm and labour of others. This type of Fifth Columnist was frequently met with in France and did much to create the lassitude and distrust which contributed very largely to the French disaster. This type of person is difficult to compete with but can best be dealt with by individuals refusing to be drawn into dangerous gossip or argument.

Appendix C

Facsimile of 35 Wing News Sheet,
No: 31, April 1944.

35 WING NEWS SHEET No. 31.

25.4.44.

Samper Regurgitatus.

When our Group Captain Donkin,
His Mustang Cat AC,
Baled out and came down plonk in
Old Father Neptune's sea,
The latter said: "The seas can't hold
"The two of us, alack!
"Much as I like this Captain Bold
"I'll have to throw him back!"

PART I.

35 WING OPERATIONS.

On April 18th Group Captain A.F. Anderson, D.S.O.,
D.F.C., assumed command of the Wing.   Shortly before dawn
F/LT. LISSNER took off to lead a section to Exercise "SMASH",
for which it was intended to provide Arty/R.   Owing to low
cloud between here and the coast, the sortie was abandoned.
Two Tac/Rs were carried out successfully just after first
light.   As reported in our last issue, a further attempt was
made by 2 Squadron to search for G/Capt. Donkin, but the
mission was abandoned owing to bad weather.   During the
afternoon the weather cleared sufficiently to allow 4 Squadron
to carry out five tasks, four of which were completed
successfully.   One E/A made a pass at F/LT. SLACK when he
was at 28,000-ft.   He climbed away to 37,000-ft. and left
the E/A behind.

At about 0330 hours on April 19th (a day as memorable
for jubilation as the 13th had been for gloom) F/LT. CHAPMAN,
Duty Ops. Officer, loomed up alongside the Editor's bed and
announced the almost incredible news that G/CAPT. DONKIN had
been picked up and was as well as could be expected after being
at sea in his dinghy for six days and five nights.   Later it
was confirmed that the G/Capt. had been found by light naval
craft who were minesweeping off the Downs.   He was taken aboard
at about 1930 hours on the evening of April 18th and was brought
into DOVER at 0230 hours the following morning.   He was taken
to the E.M.S. Hospital.

G/Capt. Anderson and the Editor set off early in the
morning for Dover and found G/Capt. Donkin remarkably well
considering the gruelling experience which he had endured.
He was enjoying his lunch and declared himself to be fit in
all respects save for his feet, which had, of course, suffered
considerably from continuous immersion in the sea.   It is
hoped that (at a later date) a full account will be given of
this remarkable escape, which can justifiably be described as
miraculous.   The main facts are these:-

First Day.   G/Capt. Donkin is of the opinion that he was not
hit by flak.   His first intimation of trouble was
the smell of glycol and later he saw the reflection
of escaping glycol in the sea as he turned from his
run.   As previously described he climbed away and
called his No. 2 to close.   He baled out about 15
miles North West of OSTEND.   His hand and thigh
were slightly injured as he left the aircraft.   He
made a rather rough landing in the sea.   In the
course of opening his dinghy he lost the pack
containing all the dinghy equipment except the

/paddles and....

paddles and baler. Within two hours the A.S.R.
Spitfires and Walrus arrived and made a thorough
search of an area about two miles from him.
Shortly after this, four Mustangs (those led by
F/O. Normoyle) passed right over him low down; he
felt certain that they must have seen him. The
weather was calm and throughout his voyage he took
advantage of such southerly winds as there were
while trying to prevent himself drifting before
northerly winds by laying out the sea anchor.

First Night. G/Capt. Donkin reports that psychologically the
first night at sea was the worst. After that his
mental approach became purely objective - a
determination to survive buoyed up by a persistent
optimism.

Second Day. Again 12 Mustangs (probably from 39 Wing) flew from
North to South leaving him on their port beam.
They swung through East to North and, as he flashed
the inside of his cigarette case, the furthest aircraft
of the formation broke across the remaining eleven
and flew straight towards the dinghy. When within
200 yards of the dinghy, the aircraft broke away in
a steep turn towards the North and rejoined the
formation. G/Capt. Donkin had retained possession
of his escape box. He rationed himself rigorously
and when picked up still had two Horlicks tablets,
some chocolate and condensed milk. All miracles
are a combination of Providence and human
co-operation. G/Capt. Donkin owes his life to
this self-discipline as much as he does to the
moderation of the weather.

Third Day. Towards the end of the third day, when water was
becoming a problem, there was a heavy fall of rain.
G/Capt. Donkin collected a fair quantity of drinking
water and could have got more. This was the only
rainfall he experienced and he was to wish later
that he had made the most of this opportunity.

The remaining days were monotonously without
incident. On one occasion the G/Capt. fell out
of his dinghy. He managed to get back but realised
that he would have a poor chance of recovery if this
occurred again. Once when he drifted towards the
French coast he planned a landing and perhaps the
capture of a boat of some kind - unaware that by
this time the state of his feet would have made
walking impossible. Much to his annoyance seagulls
were apt to alight on the dinghy. He succeeded
in catching one but the attempt to make a meal of
it was a failure - as was the drinking of its blood
which made him sick.

At 1930 hours on the sixth day he sighted a coastal
motor boat and mustered enough strength to hail her.
At the same time he looked over his shoulder and
saw another C.M.B. almost on top of him. They soon
had him aboard. He was given six cups of naval
cocoa and laid to rest in the Captain's quarters,
but rest was hard to come by owing to the racket
of the propeller shaft which ran through the cabin.

During the afternoon of the 19th the weather favoured
high level operations and 4 Squadron took full advantage of it.
Ten sorties were flown and the greater portion of two important

/tasks was....

tasks was completed. Unsuccessful attempts were made by enemy fighters to intercept two of the sorties.

On the morning of April 20th, G/Capt. Anderson held an INDABA outside the 130 Airfield Ops. Room. All available aircrew attended. He expounded the lessons gained from G/Capt. Donkin's experience, stressing particularly the flaws in our search and the need for the very careful planning and execution of A.S.R. operations by ordinary squadrons. He insisted on the necessity for intensive dinghy drill and coated the pill of a rather bitter lesson by telling us of the high opinion of 35 Wing held by all Army formations who have had cause to use the photographs which are taken by the Wing.

During the afternoon, F/LT. CORRIGAN and F/O. HOWELLS of 2 Squadron flew a Tac/R mission in search of tanks thought to be entraining at AUBIGNY Station. They followed the line from ST. POL to DOULLENS, meeting with flak at several points. No tanks were seen at AUBIGNY.

On April 21st one section of 268 Squadron carried out a successful Arty/R for Exercise "SMASH", which was followed up by three successful Tec/Rs. This Exercise was attended by F/LT. CLAPIN and CAPT. HUGILL, who wrote an excellent report, but "SMASH-SMASH" is so Hush-Hush that it cannot be included in these pages. Later in the day 4 Squadron completed one of three missions attempted; one was abandoned owing to attempted interception by E/A, the other owing to cloud. One section of 268 Squadron covered successfully two NOBALL targets, while another section took photographs of AUBIGNY which confirmed the negative report of the previous day.

April 22nd was a perfect day for high level photography. No. 4 Squadron got to work on a large mosaic which had been demanded, putting up eight sorties for this and other tasks. On April 23rd, 4 Squadron flew five sorties, four in completion of the mosaic begun on the previous day and one on NOBALLS. These were carried out without interference or incident, except in the case of F/LT. PALMER and F/O. SNELL in a Mosquito, the latter collapsing through lack of oxygen. While over DIEPPE, F/O. Snell, in order to get down into the nose of the Mosquito to take photographs, had to shift his position from kneeling to sitting in his seat. Later the pilot, F/LT. Palmer, failing to get a reply over the inter-com, noticed that his nagivator, his hands and face turning blue, was passing out. As F/Lt. Palmer started a steep diving turn, F/O. Snell fell forward and in so doing revealed the fact that he had been sitting on the long flexible oxygen tube. F/Lt. Palmer made every effort to pull the tube out but found it impossible to do so. Although unable to use both hands (for whenever he took his hands off the control column the aircraft, being in a steep dive, started to roll) he managed to get F/O. Snell onto the floor but unfortunately the tube went with him. After some difficulty F/Lt. Palmer managed to get both hands on his oxygen tube and to pull it free, the tube parting at the bayonet union. Holding the tube to F/O. Snell's nose, he continued to dive. To his relief he saw his navigator's chest begin to move and his face to regain a more normal colour. Both returned safely to base. F/O. Snell, having been extracted from the aircraft with considerable difficulty, was taken to hospital and is now making a satisfactory recovery.

The weather deteriorated on April 24th and rendered abortive two NOBALL tasks attempted by 2 Squadron.

/Good News....

226

4

Good News.

German sources report that F/O. T.M. HARRIES, 268 Squadron, who was shot down by flak in the PAS DE CALAIS on February 28th, is now a prisoner of war.

PART II

EXERCISE "FREEDOM".

The exercises, each of 12 hours duration, began at 0800 hrs. on the 21st and 22nd April, 1944, and ended at 2000 hrs. the same days.

For the sake of the exercises the coastline ran along the London—Brighton railway line, with the sea to the East side.

The object of the escapists was to reach certain points on the coastline (Horley and Redhill Police Stations) by 1700 hrs. or as soon after as possible. They were attired in uniforms (some with modifications) and carried the following articles:-

(a) Form 1250 and a letter to the police authority in a sealed envelope. Two pennies and a compass were carried in the pocket.

(b) Ration Pack.

The following rules were observed:-

(a) Escapists were permitted to speak only broken English.

(b) No civilian property was to be stolen.

The escapists were dropped in districts of Western Surrey and immediately after this was reported to the police.

On April 21st there were 23 participants, 18 being from 2 Squadron and 5 from 4 Squadron. Of these, 10 escapists were successful in arriving safely at Horley Police Station, which was that day's destination.

On the 22nd there were 33 participants, mainly from 268 Squadron, but including 5 of 4 Squadron and also W/Cdr. Noel Smith, Lt. Col. Young (Local Defence Officer), S/Ldr. Squires (130 Airfield S.M.O.) and F/O. Laverick (130 Airfield Flying Control). 14 escapists were successful in reaching Redhill Police Station.

The exercises were undoubtedly successful and many of the escapists claim to have learned from them. In addition, considerable enjoyment was derived from those taking part.

The success of the exercise was due to the whole-hearted co-operation very willingly extended to us by the Chief Constable of the Surrey Constabulary Area; in particular we are most grateful to the Superintendent of E Dept. for his unstinted help in preliminary advice and subsequent organisation. We are also most grateful for the enthusiastic co-operation of the Police, No. 2777 Squadron R.A.F. Regiment and other wervices who took part.

All the report written by those who took part in the exercise make good reading. The following selection gives an idea of the scope of the exercise and the opportunity for individual self-expression which it offered.

/(i) F/Lt. Woodward...

(i) F/LT. WOODWARD, 268 Squadron.

I have the honour to report that I was dropped from the lorry outside the area and some 12 miles from HORSHAM in a S.W. direction.   F/O. TUELE was also dropped at the same spot, but we separated at once.   A large wood was visible on the horizon to the North, for which I made.   Several small streams proved a handicap and it was not until an hour after starting that I reached the outskirts of the wood.   Only once did I join a road and then only for about five hundred yards. However, I was observed on the road by several labourers, all of whom were obviously too curious.   If I were to continue walking opening I decided that I must lose my R.A.F. identity. Shortly after walking through an Italian labour camp without incident I found a small cultivated clearing in the wood which sported a scarecrow wearing a decrepit blue serge jacket.   This jacket I put on.   A few minutes later I found a sack into which I put the battledress blouse.   In this guise, with the sack over my shoulder, I took to the road, where I was unnoticed by police and pedestrians, though I was passed by several.

A military camp was investigated for food or transport but was deserted.   A later attempt to walk into a transport camp was foiled by efficient and suspicious guards.

At 1230 I asked a landgirl the direction of REDHILL. I used the poor English of a Free Frenchman.   The effort was successful, and believing me a Free French land worker, she walked half a mile with me, and also we shared sandwiches. At no time did I use more than a minimum of poor English - but it did quite well.

I reached Horsham at 1400 very tired and decided to obtain a vehicle.   I entered a Canadian Army H.Q., changed my jacket in a privy at the rear of the house and then attempted to get into a parked truck.   I got in from the nearside, furthest from the wheel.   Whilst trying to slide over a soldier opened the other door.   I ran for it, complete with the sack and jacket.

Outside the railway station I used a public lavatory to change back to the guise of a tramp and then lounged around the station car park.   A fifteen cwt. van drove up and I walked alongside it.   As the driver got out, I got in.   Within a minute of the driver leaving, his van had left also.

Driving only by side roads I reached the main Brighton road without incident.   Again by parallel side roads I reached the Reigate - Redhill fork on the main road.   A military policeman was visible on the Redhill road and so I turned off to Reigate, doubling back by side roads at the foot of a hill. The car I abandoned outside a church.   I found myself thirsty and changed back to uniform in the car.   As a Polish airman I enquired the way to the Police Station, and also enjoyed a soft drink in a small sweet shop.

I changed back to civvies in the car, and then slept for half an hour in an adjacent park on the side of a hill. At 1645 I walked out to the main road and then slouched through the town to the Police Station, arriving unmolested.

In our opinion, this is the most successful exploit of the exercise.   Though less spectacular than most of the reports, all the incidents approximate the circumstances of an actual escape in enemy occupied territory.

/(ii) S/Ldr. Gray & ....

(ii) S/LDR. GRAY and F/O. HASELDEN, 2 Squadron.

     In the best wild west and Keystone police tradition, this escape is a riot from start to finish. The fantasy could only be enhanced if the escapers had commandeered a funeral cortege.

     Jack and I were dropped in a side road just North of the main GUILDFORD - LONDON road.

     We got a lift from a civilian car to Esher, having in mind to wait until lunch time and pinch a car from the car park of the Bear Hotel. This we were unable to do as all Service cars were either attended or immobilised. We then managed to get the "cockpit drill" of a double-deck bus from the bus terminus outside the "Windsor Arms". Two things prevented us taking a bus.

    (i)   The chance of driving a large bus with "EAST ACTON" on the front in the DORKING direction was small.

    (ii) The bus always filled up with people as soon as it came in.

     Jack said the second reason was a wonderful chance to make a bit of money by charging the passengers 5/- to get off. However, we gave up the bus idea and walked along to the fire station where we tried to start a N.F.S. van without success. We began to walk out of the fire station when we saw a lovely big white ambulance. We jumped in and she started at once so we drove out on to the main road - much to the surprise of a type who was repairing the back of the ambulance at the time.

     We reached LEATHERHEAD without trouble and by ringing the bell managed to keep up a fair speed. However, between Leatherhead and Dorking we were picked up by one speed cop and two M.P.s on motor cycles. For the next four miles a first class chase ensued, including a good effort by the police when they blocked the road with Army lorries, leaving us just enough room to get past on the pavement. At this point the ambulance was boiling badly and we decided we must get off the road and run. We turned up a lane which, as bad luck would have it, took us into the courtyard of a large house taken over by the Army. We jumped out and Jack threw a large lamp at the police who were hard on our heels - this allowed me to get through a window and into the house - but Jack got caught by an enormous M.P. (at least 18 stone).

     I ran through the house and saw a room marked "Ante Room" and went in. I was then caught by the speed cop and a Major. I got away for a few minutes by kicking the Major on the shin and causing him to let go. We were now in the courtyard and being heavily guarded by police and M.P.s. For my part it was the end and I was taken to Police H.Q. and released.

     Jack was taken in a car to the M.P. H.Q. with four M.P.s on motor cycles as escort, and in Leatherhead High Street managed to jump out of the car at a traffic light.

     He dashed up the street and up an alley and through a door, finding himself in a Butcher's shop, where he tried to persuade a rather slow witted butcher to hide him. However the police arrived before this could be done and Jack made another dash and once again got through the police, only to be captured in a yard nearby.   /(iii) S/LDR. SQUIRE....

(iii) S/LDR. SQUIRE, 130 Airfield.

I was dropped with Lt. Col. Young about 5 miles N.
of WISBOROUGH GREEN at about 1000 hrs.   We proceeded to
RUDGWICK on ordinary roads, in the hope of getting transport.
After Rudgewick, going N.E., we picked up a lift to CRANLEIGH,
representing ourselves as Poles.   The tradesman was attending
the Polish Airfield, so this caused no suspicion.   We had
been taken a little too far North, but made across country in
the correct direction.   Owing to the fact that I was
hindering Col. Young, who wanted to go faster than I could,
we parted.   Taking my own time, with an airman's cap on my
head and rank badges removed, I strolled about 3 miles an
hour over the hills to SHERE.   I laid up for about an hour
outside an Officers' Mess, as there was a big staff car which
I coveted, but it was unconsciously continuously protected.
I did not join the main road at Shere but circled by the
churchyard, thus avoiding incidents which worried others.
Thereafter I quietly walked along through a police cordon,
which stopped all road users but not pedestrians, past several
police cars and M.P. motor-bikes.   I was obviously enjoying
a country stroll.   At DORKING my feet packed up, but I
luckily got a lift to Reigate in a staff car (Canadian).
Without further incident I walked into Redhill Police Station.

Comment.   Risks are enormously increased by haste.   If
you are inconspicuous, strolling along as if you
have every right to the road, you are less likely to be
molested.   I was older than the aircrews and therefore not
suspected.   A small touch of white make-up over the ears
puts years on people at casual glance.   Would it help to
supply this and a pair of plain glasses.

Though by no means sensational, this escape contains
many valuable lessons and its comparison with the one above
makes a fair parallel to the fable of the Hare and the Tortoise.

One pair, who shall be nameless, made an admirable
escape from an airfield in a captured Tiger Moth.   Both were
happily unaware that the pinching of aircraft was against the
rules.   Good show!

PART III.

ON AND OFF THE PERIMETER.

(i) Peculiar Penguin Dept.

Steve (late 4 Squadron) arrived at an aerodrome in
No. 9 Group.   From Flying Control he rang up a Squadron
Leader and asked for transport.

"Transport!" replied this Gallant, "Good Lord NO!
And why is it that you people who come up for interviews
always fly up?"

"I don't know" replied Steve, with strange self-
restraint, "But maybe its because we are in the Air Force!"

25.4.44.

Squadron Leader,
Intelligence Officer,
No. 35 Wing.   R.A.F.

Index